The Sweet SEASON

The Sweet SEASON

A SPORTSWRITER REDISCOVERS FOOTBALL,
FAMILY, AND A BIT OF FAITH
AT MINNESOTA'S ST. JOHN'S UNIVERSITY

AUSTIN MURPHY

HarperCollins*Publishers*

HarperCollins books may be purchased for educational, business, or sales promotional use. For information, please write; Special Markets Department, HarperCollins Publishers Inc., 10 East 53rd Street, New York, NY 10022.

FIRST EDITION

Designed by David Lane

Library of Congress Cataloging-in-Publication Data

Murphy, Austin
The sweet season / Austin Murphy.—1st ed.
p. cm.
ISBN 0-06-019547-9
1. St. John's University (Collegeville, Minn.)—Football. 2. St. John's Johnnies (Football team) 3. Gagliardi, John. I. Title.

GV958.S697 M87 2001
796.332'63'0977647—dc21 2001024217

01 02 03 04 05 ❖/RRD 10 9 8 7 6 5 4 3 2 1

To Laura
My only sunshine

ACKNOWLEDGMENTS

Biggest thanks go to two people. First, to my wife Laura Hilgers, who endured four months away from Peets coffee, organic produce, and the nominal humidity of northern California. I owe you a trip to Paris. Can I come?

John Gagliardi, I know you had some qualms about having a scribe around for four months—and rightly so, as you shall soon see. But there was never a time when I stuck my head in your office that you didn't wave me in, even after I kicked over my commuter mug, coffee-staining your carpet forever. While there may be a few words and anecdotes in these pages that you may wish I'd left out—do us both a favor and skip over the passage on the Beef Jar, for instance—none of them reflects on the operation you run, which is pure class. Thanks for the best season I've ever had. (And thanks Gary Fasching, Jimmy Gagliardi, and Jerry Haugen for never rolling your eyes or showing me the door when I pulled up a chair in your offices.)

Thanks to *Sports Illustrated* managing editor Bill Colson, who cheerfully gave me permission to take a season off, despite the havoc my prolonged absence stood to wreak on the magazine's subscription base, ad rates and overall morale. (When I returned, half the staff hadn't realized I'd gone.) Thanks to my agent, David Black, who believed I had a book in me, and who found (somehow) nice things to say about the first version of this one. Equally patient and nurturing was Megan Newman, my editor at HarperCollins, who made me stretch (a polite way of saying she made me rewrite). Thanks, boss. Let's do it again sometime.

Thanks to Peg Gagliardi, who fussed over us and mothered us in Collegeville; and to Amy Behrendt, who helped us out with baby-sitting, dressing Devin up to a half-dozen times per day. We owe an immense debt of gratitude to the Benedictines of St. John's, especially Father Tim Backous and Brother Paul Richards, who became our soul mates and tour guides, revealing the real Stearns County to us. Thank you, Patty Weishaar, for finding room for us in Emmaus Hall, and to Patrick Henry and Sister Dolores Schuh, for green-lighting our move to the Ecumenical Institute. (On our second morning there, Dolores came over and half-disappeared under the sink, fixing our DisposAll and providing my most lasting memory of this can-do nun.)

Thanks to my parents and seven siblings for providing such rich source material, and for being good sports about it. Thanks to Barb Schleck for her hospitality and generosity; and to Dr. Rod and Nancy Peterson, for a brilliant Thanksgiving. It bears mentioning that, were it not for Maisa Oliveira, my favorite Brazilian, this book would only be half-finished.

To every St. John's and St. Ben's student who went out of his or her way to make us feel welcome, we are grateful. And thanks to my friend and adventure-racing teammate Gordon Wright, who also happens to be a crack publicist. Because a book like this doesn't happen without the cerebral cortex–enhancing, synapse-inducing stores of iron, magnesium, protein and omega-3 fatty acids found, in rich quantities, in every tin of King Oscar Sardines.

He says try the kipper snacks, too.

CONTENTS

Introduction..xi

Chapter 1: The Journey..1

Chapter 2: Architects..8

Chapter 3: Wisconsin-Eau Claire......................39

Chapter 4: Macalester...................................... 49

Chapter 5: St. Thomas......................................70

Chapter 6: Augsburg..87

Chapter 7: Prairie View..................................110

Chapter 8: Bethel..130

Chapter 9: A Walk in the Woods....................140

Chapter 10: Concordia 145

Chapter 11: Hamline 166

Chapter 12: St. Olaf 182

Chapter 13: Carleton 199

Chapter 14: Gustavus Adolphus 214

Chapter 15: Wisconsin-Stevens Point 227

Chapter 16: Central 242

Chapter 17: Pacific Lutheran 259

Chapter 18: Last Call 276

Epilogue 289

INTRODUCTION

The news itself was less surprising than how my wife chose to deliver it. She had made no secret of her loneliness during my frequent and prolonged absences. Lithe, blonde, and blue-eyed, Laura Hilgers at thirty-seven looks better now than she did as an undergraduate, and she struck me dumb then. It stood to reason that her eye would wander during one of my business trips, that some young stud might take notice, and bust a move.

"He's gorgeous and I'm in love with him," she told me on that memorable night, the night everything changed. "I looked in his eyes and it was all over." So much for breaking it to me gently.

How helpless one feels, hearing it over the phone! I was in room 102 at the Valley River Inn in Eugene, Oregon. Instead of polishing my notes on the upcoming "Civil War" between Oregon and Oregon State, I was watching a show called *Dangerous Pursuits* on TLC. A deranged man had commandeered a bus, and was smashing squad cars and turfing lawns all over Beverly Hills. It was damned good television. Then Laura called and rocked my world.

She went on about his saucer eyes and curly hair, but I'd stopped listening. I was reflecting on hints she'd dropped earlier in the season, clues I had ignored at my peril. A week earlier, I was holed up at the University Inn in West Lafayette, Indiana, one of my editors having decided that America should not go another week without a story on the Purdue receiving corps. Laura and I argued that night. I sympathized with her loneliness, but disagreed with her solution for it.

"I want a dog," she said.

"A poodle is not a dog," I rejoined. Round and round like this we went. Among Laura's myriad allergies is an aversion to dog fur. If we were to get a dog, she said, it had to be a poodle. While I chronicled the 2000 college football season for *Sports Illustrated*, searching out decent anecdotes and the green Starbucks maiden in such unpromising outposts as Manhattan, Kansas, Corvallis, Oregon, and the aforementioned West Lafayette, Laura was going behind my back, poodle hunting. A month into her search she met Moon River, a three-year-old, fifty-five-pound white standard, and that was all she wrote. "I want this dog," she said.

River's trainers asked Laura, Shouldn't your husband meet him first? That's not how our marriage works, she explained. She told them how she bid on our house before I'd even seen it. I was in Europe, reporting a feature on the World League of American Football. I remember this great trick Michael Stonebraker taught me. Stonebraker was a linebacker for the Frankfurt Galaxy. To pronounce the German farewell "*auf Wiedersehen*," he told me, "Just say as fast as you can 'Our feet are the same.'"

I caved on the poodle, in keeping with my secret for maintaining, if not a consistently happy marriage, at least an intact one: The Path of Least Resistance Is Your Friend. I learned this thirteen years ago, during preparations for our wedding. Things went much more smoothly, I noticed, if I replied in response to every question—on everything from guest lists to readings to floral arrangements—"Yes, that would be lovely." (Ixnayed a cash bar at the reception, however. Didn't need my brothers boycotting my own nuptials.)

Fine, get a poodle, I said. I had neither the energy nor the right to refuse Laura, for whom football season is an annual, months-long penance. From mid-August to early January, when the season ended, I spent most of my time on the road, waking up in hotel rooms from Los Angeles to Lincoln, Nebraska, staring up at stucco ceilings and rather enjoying those predawn moments, so pregnant with possibility, when I wondered, *Where the hell am I?* Some days *(Oh yeah—the Santa Monica Loews!)* were better than others *(Oh yeah, the Oklahoma City Airport Sheraton).*

I'm on the road about half the year for this job. On autumn Saturdays I attend a football game, then stay up most or all of the night writing about it. By Halloween, the travel and all-nighters have reduced me to walking catatonia. Desperate to return home, I am narcoleptic and cranky when I get there.

Laura calls my crankiness and raises it. It's not as if she is baking bread in my absence. It's not as if she is hosting napkin-folding parties for the other Mommies in the 'hood. Laura is a writer whose curse it is to have more talent than time to utilize it. She is the semisingle mother of our daughter, Willa, and son, Devin, who are six and four, respectively, as I write this. Some parents have docile, happy children who do as they're told, gratefully eat the food they are served; who do not leave rooms looking as if a grenade has gone off in them, or feel a dark compulsion to put their fingers inside the ears of the new dog, or tug on its Johnson. We are not those parents, those are not our children.

As the 2000 football season got underway, and we descended into our familiar anarchy, Laura and I found ourselves looking back with sharp nostalgia, reflecting on where we were "this time a year ago." After fifteen years at *SI*, I had taken a six-month sabbatical. Leaving our home in northern California, we spent the '99 season at St. John's University in Collegeville, Minnesota—Lake Wobegon with a monastery, basically.

Several things would happen, we felt certain. With the kids shipping out at 11:30 each morning—Willa to kindergarten, Devin to daycare—we would catch up on our sleep. Laura would have a breakthrough on her screenplay. I would write a book on the Johnnies' season. My steady presence would complete us as a family, lightening Laura's load and leading us to uncharted levels of intimacy and happiness. Stress would take its own sabbatical!

That book, while easier to write, would have been a work of fiction. From the jaw-dropping incompetence of the U-Haul people to the sanctions levied against the Johnnies midway through the season to unseasonably mild weather awaiting us in Minnesota, our interlude on the prairie seldom stuck to the script. The idea was to decompress, chill, unpucker. You know what, though? Uprooting and moving to a strange place, leaving old friends and making new ones—it was all rather effort-intensive, rather *stressful.* Come to think of it, if I had it to do over again, I might give myself more than six months to write a book, considering that the only other one I'd ever finished was a connect-the-dots history of the Super Bowl, a work now available for the price of a New York subway token in a remainder bin near you.

Between my nights cooped up in an office in the bowels of the Alcuin Library, typing up my notes, and the occasional evening I felt compelled to spend watching the World Wrestling Federation with my Johnny buddies, Laura still spent some evenings alone. Instead of panicking over magazine stories, I panicked over the chapters that follow. Our idyll, for the first month or so, was not idyllic, as will happen when you trade one set of pressures for another.

But it is impossible to spend time at St. John's and not decompress a little. There is something about the bells in the abbey church tolling the hours; about the sight of the Benedictines walking unhurriedly to afternoon prayer, that whispers, *Yo, pal, what's the rush?* In time, we loosened up. We unpuckered. We had a sabbatical.

Epiphanies followed—just not the Hallmark Hall of Fame kind. We did not stop arguing. That will happen when one of us stops fogging a mirror. But we argued less. No longer required to stay up all night four times per month, I was less of an ogre. Laura and I went for long walks in the woods around St. John's, drinking in the foliage, startling deer. Regardless of what we did during waking hours, we slept each night together. That right there made the trip worthwhile.

This is an account of what happens when a family pulls up stakes and spends four months in a strange (and wonderful) place;

when the stresses of everyday life are, if not stripped away, significantly reduced, and two people are allowed to remember what they saw in each other in the first place.

It is also, not incidentally, the story of the most incredible football program in the country, run by a smiling wise man who has forgotten more about this game than most of his peers know. What I loved most about John Gagliardi was that he never forgot this: that is *all* he coaches, a game.

What a blast it was to get small, and fly beneath the radar of big-time sports! How bracing, to go an entire season without interviewing a felon! What a welcome exchange, trading the loons in the Meadowlands parking lot for the loons on Lake Sagatagan! How refreshing, to have as one's neighbors students, painters, theologians, and monks who cracked jokes, sneaked smokes, and taped the *South Park* Christmas special!

If you were a football writer looking to escape from the NFL for a while, the '99 season wasn't a bad one to miss. The Carolina Panthers' Rae Carruth put out a hit on his pregnant girlfriend; the Baltimore Ravens' Ray Lewis was present at (but not convicted for) a post–Super Bowl party slaughter in which two men were stabbed to death. The dueling snuffs that, in a sad way, eclipsed the season also overshadowed a cavalcade of lesser assaults, a depressing number of which involved NFL players smacking up (A) their wives, (B) their girlfriends, (C) exotic dancers.

Please put out a hit on *me*, or arrange something with Rae, if it sounds as if I am whining. As a senior writer at *Sports Illustrated*, I am not always dealing with megalomaniacal coaches and spoiled athletes. A few years ago, for instance, I was sent to a private island resort in the tropics to write a story about the bodypainting of naked supermodels for the swimsuit issue. Because I was a gentleman, because I looked the naked supermodels in the eye as I spoke to them, because I successfully feigned an interest in the process—*So you're saying the pastels tend to flake more readily than darker tones? That's fascinating!*—they got used to having me around. We got along. So it came to pass that I found myself relaxing in the resort's pool one Sunday morning, discussing the fall of the Berlin Wall with a topless Heidi Klum.

What do you do for a living?

Assignments like those aren't the best part of this job. The best part of this job is working for a company that allows its employees, after fifteen years of service, to take a six-month sabbatical at half-pay. Since 1985, I'd averaged more than thirty weeks a year on the road, earning more frequent flyer miles than I could give away to my seven freeloading siblings, and lamenting the passing of the era when your first five minutes of Spectravision were free.

I married the woman upon whom I once cast concupiscent glances in a classroom at Colgate University. Laura balances me, grounds me, edits me, and cracks me up. At Colgate, she would not give me the time of day. A few years later, when we both lived in New York City, the calculus had changed. She was no longer one of, say, two dozen attractive women in a thirty-mile radius. We met for a drink and struck sparks, most of them the good kind. A second date followed. At the time, Laura was an editorial assistant at *Cosmopolitan*. I figured we'd be experimenting with blindfolds and riding crops within the fortnight. Things didn't work out exactly that way, but we were married eighteen months later. We moved to San Francisco; Laura bore us two children. By April of 1999, the end of my fifteenth year at *SI*, I'd been on the road for half of our marriage and half our children's lives. The sabbatical beckoned.

But where to take it? We discussed Tahiti, but found it impractical, and settled on the next best thing: Collegeville, Minnesota.

In the spring of 1992 I flew into the Twin Cities, rented a car and drove the seventy-nine miles north and west to St. John's, a tiny, top-notch liberal arts university tucked off I-94 behind a massive stand of druidlike evergreens, the so-called Pine Curtain. I was covering college football for *SI*, where we had received reports of a weird but wonderful coach in the Minnesota hinterlands, a maverick who'd been winning since 1953 with an unorthodox style and a list of seventy-four "No's," including: no whistles, no playbooks, no hitting during the week, no use of the words like "hit" or "kill," no cuts—they had 159 guys out for the team in 1999—no spring football, no calisthenics.

The man behind the curtain was John Gagliardi, a grinning iconoclast whose philosophy owes more to Yoda than Lombardi, a coach unafraid to send his players inside when the gnats on the practice field get too thick. After too many interviews with the coronary-courting control freaks comprising the ranks of today's big-time coaches, meeting Gags was like a hit of pure oxygen. I was accustomed to charismatically challenged head men with hypertrophied egos; here was someone who'd won more games than any five NFL coaches, who still insisted that his quarterbacks call their own plays. "Why not?" says Gags. "These guys are a hell of a lot smarter than I am."

He is dumb as a fox. Gagliardi (pronounced Gah-LAR-dee) was sixteen when his own high school coach in Trinidad, Colorado, went off to war. Gags ran the team himself, and discovered that most of football's hidebound, militaristic traditions—the whistles, the calisthenics, the pointless, sadistic drills, the beating one another to a pulp all week—were impediments, rather than keys, to success.

In 1953 he interviewed for the head coaching position at St. John's of the Minnesota Intercollegiate Athletic Conference. The MIAC is a quaint band of small, proud, academically rigorous institutions so idyllic that if it did not exist, Garrison Keillor would have had to invent it. St. John's was chartered in 1857 by Benedictines who'd come west from Pennsylvania to minister to the German immigrants pouring into the middle of Minnesota. Without spiritual leadership, one Benedictine fretted, "many of our Catholic countrymen, as elsewhere, will succumb to the Methodist sect." By the late 1940s, St. John's was known as "the Priest Factory," so methodically was it minting men of the cloth.

But the monks had grown weary of serial gridiron thrashings at the hands of Concordia, St. Olaf's, and Gustavus Adolphus. Gagliardi was hired, and college football hasn't been the same since. All his seniors are captains—"They're all great guys, and this way they can all put 'Captain' on their resumé," he says. Their calisthenics, a parody of a typical team's cals, include such exercises as Mary Catharine Gallagher–Superstar Lunges (often performed in wavelike fashion, left to right), Ear Warmups, Deep Breath with Bruce Lee Exhale, and a Nice Day Drill, which requires them to drop to the grass, roll onto their backs and remark to one another, "Nice day, isn't it?"

If you don't know anything about St. John's, you're wondering, around now, if they ever win. Surely there is a price to be paid for this nonconformity? Surely the Johnnies are pushovers on the field?

Gagliardi has led his teams to three national titles, and to within a gnat's eyelash of a fourth. With a record of 377-109-11, he is the NCAA's winningest active coach, second on the all-time list to Grambling's Eddie Robinson, who retired in 1997 with 408 victories. When and if Gags overtakes his friend, the most unique football program in the country will have become its most successful.

I wrote an enthusiastic story, and Gags ended up with his picture on the cover of *SI*'s 1992 college football issue. Two years later Laura bore us a daughter, Willa. Our son, Devin, arrived two summers later. We had two beautiful children, a nice little house in northern California, two cars, and one weekly session with a marriage counselor.

It wasn't so bad. There was a Starbucks on the way to the shrink. I'd try to nurse a double-tall hazelnut latte through an hour of therapy.

The problem was my meal ticket. Yes, writing for *SI* is a cool job, and yes, as I have mentioned, we do meet the swimsuit models. We are also on the road half the year. While I'm out talking to genetic mutants like Tony Boselli and Warren Sapp about the battle in the trenches, Laura is home *fighting* that battle, scrubbing crayon off the wall, calling the glass repairman when Devin head-butts his bedroom window; rinsing his eyes when he climbs on top of the dryer, reaches into an off-limits cupboard and sprays himself in the face with Windex. She's making three different lunches for Willa, a finicky eater who is fairly certain that her *real* parents will arrive at the front door any day now and whisk her back to the palace.

I get home late Monday afternoon after a week in which I've wheedled and pleaded for interviews with surly athletes and humorless coaches, then stayed up most or all of Sunday night laboring over a story that will be rewritten by editors who have ascended to their slots in the Time Inc. hierarchy by virtue, largely, of their inability to write. By the time I get out of the taxi and stumble up the front steps, I feel like Bruce Willis at the end of one of the *Die Hard* movies. To Laura I look like the cavalry. To Laura I am fresh blood.

I know better than to hope for sympathy from my wife. Instead of writing, she ends up spending much of her day running the household—sending in the mortgage payment; waging war with soulless health insurance companies. Somehow, she knows when the car needs tuning and the dog needs grooming; when the kids need shots; when the vacuum-cleaner and air-purifier filters are due to be changed—all the banal, vital chores of which I had only a dim awareness, before asking her to list some of them, just a moment ago. (She wasn't amused.) Her response to my exhaustion: at least you're *writing*. She envies me and resents her own lot. I pity myself and resent her resentment.

Off to therapy we went.

Every so often, between missed connections and arguments with Laura over which of us has it worse, I would daydream of an autumn away from big-time football, a season in central Minnesota. It was an idea whose time had come even before I walked too close to some Raider fans—rookie move—and was pulled up into the Oakland Coliseum stands and worked over (they put me in a headlock and mussed my hair). The idea was ripe before a pear-shaped despot named Parcells ripped me a new orifice for eliciting off-the-record quotes from his players; before Denver Broncos linebacker Bill Romanowski started telling my colleagues that he wanted to kill me (Romo didn't care for my profile on him). I'd toyed with the idea of this book before being yanked out of a postgame prayer circle at Lambeau Field (I wanted to hear the Reverend Reggie White sling some Scripture, a Packers flak objected); before Chargers quarterback Ryan Leaf called me "bitch" (he meant it as an endearment); before Cincinnati Bengals wide receiver Carl

Pickens referred to me as a "f—— cracker." (He didn't.)

I have met wonderful people in the course of my work for *SI*: humble, considerate, intelligent individuals who have influenced the way I live my life. But then, how many times can you cover the Little League World Series? Having written about players involved in domestic disputes, paternity suits, drugs (recreational and performance enhancing); after nodding intently one week as a player explained to me that his good fortune was attributable to the Almighty, then nodding intently the next week as the same player expressed remorse for his arrest for allegedly soliciting oral sex from an undercover police officer, I wanted to step off this carousel. I wanted to spend a season with the Johnnies.

Do not think it odd that a Californian should find himself longing to kill time in rural Minnesota. I looked forward to earning fewer than 20,000 frequent flier miles in a given quarter, to going an entire season without waiting ninety minutes for a room-service meal that gave me bad gas. I wanted to familiarize my little native Californians with the concept of fall foliage. Hell, I wanted to familiarize them with the concept of *their father.* I wanted them to know what it's like to miss a day of school on account of snow. I wanted to sleep with their mother 100 nights in a row. I wanted to be governed, however briefly, by Jesse (the Body) Ventura. I wanted to fall in love with football again.

I wanted to hang with the brothers (an activity, which, at St. John's, carried an altogether different connotation than it does on the NFL beat). In addition to being a fine university with its unique football program, St. John's is an internationally renowned liturgical center, boasting the world's largest collection of medieval manuscripts outside of the Vatican. There are a lot of smart people thinking and talking about God at St. John's, and that worked for me. As one of the eight children of Patricia and John Austin Murphy Jr., I grew up in a household in which football and God were reverenced equally; in which longsnapping was practiced but birth control was not. My hope was that, in addition to shoring up my marriage, a season in Collegeville might improve my attitude toward these twin monoliths, with which I found myself, at the age of thirty-eight, on uneasy terms.

At the very least I looked forward to limbering up with the Johnnies, to gazing at an autumn sky and asking no one in particular, "Nice day, isn't it?"

Be careful what you wish for. I wrote a proposal, got a publisher, took a sabbatical. Next thing I knew we were barreling east on I-94, Fargo in the rearview mirror.

Collegeville, while wonderful, was not utopia. How uninteresting if it had been! Laura, she of the gluten intolerance and *Gourmet* subscription, was both underwhelmed and, I think, a bit frightened by the culinary offerings of Stearns County, where we were greeted by a billboard advertisement for a ribs restaurant which proclaimed: SMALL PORTIONS ARE FOR CALIFORNIANS. Gagliardi, as sage and funny as I remembered, had lost a bit of stamina since I'd seen him last—the man turned seventy-three midway through the season—and every so often flashed a temper that was to be both feared and admired. To my astonishment (and secret, vast amusement), the cleanest team in the country managed to get itself put on MIAC probation. The violation was a trifle, an accident; the punishment widely construed as a joke. But it embarrassed Gagliardi and delighted his critics, many of whose backsides he has been kicking for half a century.

The boys will forgive me, I trust, for having preconceived notions of the caliber of athletes I would find in Division III. I didn't think they'd suck, but I didn't know they'd be this quick, talented, or tough. Don't let the Roman numeral throw you—there's damned good football in D-III.

While most of the Johnnies are too small to have gotten a serious look from, say, a Big 10 school, half a dozen were invited to walk on with the Minnesota Gophers. Most of the Johnny starters, it seems, knocked back scholarship offers from D-II schools—your St. Cloud States, Mankato States, Winona States—to have a chance to play for a national title in Collegeville. Some guys go the D-II route, then change their minds. After a month at South Dakota State, Todd Fultz phoned a friend in Minnesota with the grim news: "The women here chew tobacco." After seeing nine of his teammates blow out their knees in spring football, Fultz transferred to St. John's and started three years at wide receiver.

The Johnnies have cast a cold eye on their professional prospects, found them nonexistent, and opted to emphasize education. Says Beau LaBore, one of the two best linebackers I saw all season—the other one played next to him—"I wanted to go to school to go to school, know what I mean?"

I think so, Beau. Just because you want to spend more time going to college than you do practicing football—and watching films and pumping iron and rotting in meetings—doesn't mean you couldn't *play*. My boys could play.

Laura and I were stunned and humbled by the generosity of the St. John's community, from the gifts bestowed on our children by Peg Gagliardi, John's wife, to the ski cap that cornerback Grady McGovern left at my door when the weather turned, to the hospitality of the monks. The fountainhead of this beneficence is, of course, the monastery. In following their 1,500-year-old tradition of *ora et labora*, worship and work, the Benedictines set the tone and the pace at this place. It is prayerful, reflective, purposeful, unhurried. I don't know exactly when it happened, but it happened: Laura and I slowed down and fell into its rhythms.

Just as quickly, we fell out of them. We were living near the monastery, after all, not in it. Driving across three time zones had not altered the fact that we were, and are, the parents of young children. Two weeks after arriving in Collegeville, we moved out of one apartment into another. We had day-care problems. The car broke down. Devin contracted something called hand-foot-and-mouth disease. Delightful. As surely as the monks gathered in prayer three times a day, our crises passed, and were followed by intervals of tranquillity, even bliss, that we have yet to duplicate, postsabbatical.

Harried and frazzled before leaving for Minnesota, we have been frazzled and harried since our return. When the kids are fighting and the toilet is clogged and I have bounced a check to American Express; when the new dog has vomited on the newer carpet and the editor is on the phone asking why the story is not on his desk, we draw comfort from our most important Collegeville discovery:

When life slowed down, Laura and I saw that the bonds between us remain sound and strong. We still see sparks.

1

THE JOURNEY

Minnesota was a go! All that remained—after tying up a mere two or three hundred logistical details—was to have a trailer hitch affixed to the family station wagon, rent a U-Haul, and hit the trail!

If you need a trailer and long for a taste of good, old-fashioned Soviet Union-style customer service, I would recommend the U-Haul Moving Center in San Rafael, California. These people could screw up a cup of coffee, and how they stay in business is a mystery to me.

I'd phoned a fortnight ahead of time to set up a date to come and have a trailer hitch attached to the station wagon. When I showed up, they looked at me as if I were an idiot and pathological liar. There was no hitch. The eczema-afflicted U-Haul guy behind the counter asked, Did you call to confirm that it was here? Actually, I replied, the way that works is when an appointment is set up weeks in advance, *you* call *me* if the part is not in. That's when he began to get flustered, asking the person in line behind me, "Can I help you, sir?" which is when I began to feel sorry for him, because the individual he was addressing happened to be a very buff, very butch woman who was not amused by his confusion over her gender, and looked as if she might tear off his head and defecate down his neck. About ten minutes later a UPS person walked in and leaned my hitch against the counter.

Two days later I was back in the Soviet Union, so to speak, to pick up the five-by-eight trailer I'd reserved. Naturally, it was not available. I was sent to a U-Haul outlet three towns away, where things went more smoothly. But then, really, how could they have gone less smoothly?

August 11: Hard to believe, but we got a *late start.* But that's okay. A short day is scheduled—it only takes four hours to cross the Central Valley, skirt Sacramento, and commence climbing the Sierra Nevada mountains. Our first night will be spent at the Resort at Squaw Creek, near Lake Tahoe. The Resort has several pools, one with a bitching waterslide. I have been selling this waterslide to the kids for a good three months. We check in, change into bathing suits, and get down to the pool by 5:15. The waterslide is closed. "We close at five everyday," an off-duty lifeguard tells me on his way to the parking lot. We are the Griswolds, standing before a shuttered WallyWorld. I stand before my children exposed as an impotent bungler.

Go ahead and use the waterslide, I tell the kids once the lifeguard is safely out of sight. I'll guard your lives myself.

They do, and I do.

August 12: It is beginning to dawn on me that the concept of additional time in the bosom of family, virtuous and swell in the abstract, takes on an altogether different meaning when one is called upon to actually *pass that time.* As we cruise past Reno this morning, Willa and Devin, the lights of our lives, are attempting to stab one another with the plastic legs of the Wild Wild West mechanized tarantula facsimiles dispensed by a fast-food chain.

This is but a sampler of the hostilities that will erupt between them over the next 1,800 miles. Projectiles will be thrown, pinches and gougings meted out, hair pulled, epithets cast. The warfare is not always conventional. Checking the rearview mirror one afternoon in the middle of Montana, I saw my son thrust his fingers under his sister's nose.

"Hey, Willa," he said, sounding quite sinister, "smell this part of my body."

"Devin, God *damn* it!" I said. "It's *disgusting* to put your fingers in your crack." (He is, alas, a recidivist crack-scratcher.)

Without skipping a beat he asked, "Does Jar Jar Binks have a crack?"

That threw me, I will admit. Flustered, defeated, resigned, amused, I asked him, *"Why?"*

After a pause, he came back with this: "Because I don't know."

Jar Jar Binks, the grating, bug-eyed amphibian from *Star Wars: Episode 1—The Phantom Menace*, is among the *dramatis personae* in one of the half-dozen cassettes I purchased for the trip. The tape is called the *Jedi Training Manual*, and the kids will insist on hearing it six times a day, on average, throughout the trip. I don't know if Jar Jar has a crack. I don't where our kids come up with this stuff, just as I don't remember what Laura and I did before we had them. We share dim memories of carefree dinners in Manhattan; lengthy workouts, fortnight-long vacations abroad.

It all came to an end in the small hours of March 28, 1996, twenty-five days before Laura was due to deliver our first child. When she shook me awake to report that her water had broken, I assured her she had merely experienced incontinence, and went back to sleep. Fifteen minutes later she curled into a comma and began regular contractions, between which she said things like, "We still don't have a pediatrician!" and "I never got sheets for the bassinet!"

Nine hours later, without benefit of anesthetic, she delivered seven-pound, eight-ounce Willa Madigan Murphy, who has been in a hurry to get places ever since. Willa's early arrival was both an augury of her impatience, and a kind of cosmic rebuke for our hubris—our smug, yuppie expectations of a tidy, micromanaged birth. No, we hadn't set up her nursery or found a doctor for her because, well, the kid wasn't due for another month! We had time!

We did not have time. We have not had time since. We had less than an hour to bond with Willa before she was whisked to another room, where a doctor checked her heartbeat and subjected her to a whole-body prodding, to ensure that all her organs were present. "Man," said the doc as Willa squalled at him, "she is *pissed*!"

He got that right. Willa has never been inclined to suffer fools. She is a sweet, bright, and intense child whose name is a near homonym for her signature personality trait: willfullness. She is forever jonesing for art supplies, and is happiest when drawing or painting, scissoring or gluing, *creating*.

Her little brother, the towhead with blue eyes and a linebacker's build, floats more easily on the surface of things. I have no doubt that Devin will, someday, evince an interest in letters and numbers; will eventually learn to hold writing implements between his thumb and forefinger, rather than in the palm of his hand, as Neanderthal Man held a spear. For now, his interests lie in diesel-powered machines: your big rigs, your car-carriers, your graders, and excavators; your cement mixers, cranes, backhoes, bulldozers, fork lifts. It was a transcendent moment for Devin, as we crossed the dirtscape of Nevada, when he spied a vehicle he recognized from one of his many, many truck books. "Look!" he shouted, "An articulated dump truck!"

The boy may yet gravitate toward engineering or medicine. For now, I see a hardhat and steel-toed boots in his future.

No offense to our friends in the Silver State, but Nevada strikes me as grim and barren, a David Lynch movie waiting to happen. We amuse ourselves by suggesting chamber-of-commerce-type slogans for towns we pass. "Mill City," says Laura. "The Abandoned Car Capital of the World!"

Mayhem is narrowly averted at the McDonald's in Lovelock, where Devin tries not only to touch but also to *mount* the Harley-Davidsons of a band of bikers who have also sought sustenance beneath the golden arches. "No, no, no," I say, pulling him away from the hogs, by which I mean the vehicles, rather than their owners. "Daddy needs all his teeth."

★ ★ ★

August 14: Brief, beautiful drive to the Flying W Ranch in the toe of the boot that is Idaho. Cruising north out of Ashton we ascend a long grade up the side of an ancient, imploded volcano. To the east the Grand Teton mountain juts like a massive canine.

The ranch is a perfect layover: horses for Willa, a backhoe for heavy-equipment aficionado Devin. We enjoy good company—Laura's stepbrother, Eric Noyes, and his fiancée, Juliette Shaw—and good wine for dinner. Both kids are thrilled to meet Rick, a local who works on the ranch, a rough-hewn, burly man with callused hands and actual spurs on his boots. He is a real cowboy.

Late afternoon finds me sitting on the porch, listening as Rick discusses his testosterone-drenched day: he roped a calf, dug a culvert with the backhoe, then changed the machine's oil. While I am listening, Laura approaches with a basket of laundry. "Murph," she says. "Could you fold this?"

Of course I can. When we are alone, however, I must ask Laura to refrain, in the future, from asking me to fold laundry in front of a real cowboy.

August 16: Windfall nature buzz! After crossing into North Dakota, we go through the canyons of the Theodore Roosevelt National Park. Jagged and spectacular, they would make ideal hideouts for antagonists in the novels of Louis L'Amour, who was born, incidentally, in Jamestown, where we will flop this evening.

We pull over at the Painted Canyon rest stop. Devin has to tinkle. This trip has given our son his first prolonged exposure to the exciting new world of public urinals. We spend quite a bit of time on the road discussing upcoming urinals. Will the urinal flush itself, as the fancier ones do? Will it be low enough for Devin to use without Dad having to lift him up? Will there be an aromatic white disk inside? Devin pronounces urinal "journal," leading Laura and me to suspect that he has been reading ours.

Back in the parking lot, Laura takes the wheel. As we're pulling out, a minivan in front of us is pulling back. Although a slight tap on the horn would have sufficed, Laura leans on it for five seconds. Every head at the rest area snaps around. There is a group of senior citizens at the railing twenty feet away: it is likely that Laura induced cardiac arrest in one or more of them.

She becomes angry with me when I slide down in my seat. I remind her of the difference between the light tap and the angry blast. "Sometimes the light tap doesn't get it done," she says, tight-lipped.

But really, how would she know? The only thing she's ever done to a car horn is lean on it. And now she's mad at me.

August 17: Eighty miles to the Minnesota border! We're anxious to hit the road this morning, but how can you leave Jamestown without visiting the Jamestown Buffalo Museum? We couldn't. After the kids played on an old Wells Fargo stagecoach, we paid homage to the museum's main attraction, the world's largest buffalo. Sculpted in 1959 by Elmer Paul Peterson, it is twenty-six feet high, forty-four feet long, and weighs sixty tons. As we pass underneath it, the children cannot help but be transfixed by the beast's realistically executed, five-ton scrotum.

As we enter Minnesota and bear down on our destination—MOORHEAD . . . FERGUS FALLS . . . POMME DE TERRE LAKE—Laura congratulates the kids on their terrific behavior, causing me to wonder what hallucinogens she scored in that gas station restroom outside Bismarck. Rather than bust her for concocting a revisionist history, I keep my mouth shut.

SINCLAIR LEWIS BOYHOOD HOME MUSEUM . . . SAUK CENTRE . . . MELROSE.

I mean, sure there were times when they sought to injure one another, and us; when they assaulted our eardrums with their high-pitched screams and raged against their restraints. How else are healthy kids supposed to respond to incarceration? What's amazing is the amount of time they spent singing, sightseeing, and playing harmoniously.

NEW MUNICH . . . ALBANY . . . AVON.

In four months Laura and the kids will fly home. I'll drive the car back alone. I will make the trip in two and a half days, stopping when I please, listening to the music of my choice, longing for the company of the savages and their mother.

EXIT 156, ST. JOHN'S UNIVERSITY, 1 MILE.

2

ARCHITECTS

You feel its tug before you leave the freeway. The vast, concrete bell tower of the St. John's abbey church lords over the landscape, announcing on behalf of the Benedictines: We are in this for the long run.

In the intervening days and weeks it looked like different things at different times: now a menorah, now a piece of plywood squeezed upright in a vise, now a zany edifice designed to be easily recognized by the Mothership. As we bedraggled pilgrims peeled off I-94 and glided the last of our 2,000 or so miles, that bell banner loomed before us like Mecca, the Holy Land, the skyline of Oz. It meant that we had made it.

Which was good, because if I saw another Chicken McNugget or had to listen to another minute of Radio Disney, I was going to get out of the car with the engine still running and toke on the tailpipe until blessed oblivion came for me.

That iconic bell banner, which is to this place what the Golden Dome is to Notre Dame, was built because the university hosted a handful of visionary visitors in the spring of 1953. Having decided to follow through on some overdue capital improvements—a bigger church, an expanded monastery, a new library—the monks contacted a dozen world-renowned architects. Ten applied for the job, five were invited to Collegeville.

That explains why a good-looking young man, a fellow whose modish wire rims lent him a certain bookishness, was approached as he wandered the campus. Said a monk to the curly-haired stranger: "Are you an architect?"

The twenty-six-year-old John Gagliardi politely explained that he was a football coach, in town to interview for the school's vacant head-coaching position. St. John's had been mired in mediocrity under the previous head coach, a likeable raconteur named John McNally, who in between playing for the Johnnies in the early twenties and coaching them in the fifties gained renown for his exploits in the uniform of the Green Bay Packers, under the *nom de grid* Johnny Blood.

"Why are you leaving?" Gagliardi recalls asking the future NFL Hall of Famer. "These Benedictines," replied McNally. "They want to win, but they won't give you a nickel."

Gagliardi found them relatively generous. He was coming from Carroll College in Helena, Montana, where he coached the Fighting Saints to three Frontier Conference titles in three seasons, made $2,400 a year, and thought himself the luckiest man on earth. His assistant coach at the time was Father Raymond (Dutch) Hunthausen, who could punt the ball a mile, and who later became the archbishop of Seattle. When the Benedictines offered to nearly double his salary, to $4,400 a year, Gagliardi jumped.

Having secured a football coach, the school still needed an architect. "The Benedictine tradition at its best challenges us to think boldly," Abbot Baldwin Dworschak had written. Boldness then, would be required of whichever architect was chosen to transform the university. The abbot could not have known, as he shook the hand of this son of an immigrant blacksmith, how completely Gagliardi would fulfill those requirements in his own line of work.

Boldness? In an era of screaming troglodytes who routinely abused their charges, verbally and physically; at a time when denying players water during practice and having them beat each other into steak tartare five times a week was seen not as sadism or idiocy but as *instilling toughness*, Gagliardi had the intelligence and courage to go in the other direction. You've heard of the uncola. Here was the uncoach, eschewing whistles, playbooks, blocking sleds, and agility drills. We've got limited time to work, Gags reasoned, so *let's practice the plays*. Let the other guys knock themselves out perfecting their pregame calisthenics. Let them do quarter eagles, monkey rolls, bull-in-the-ring, and a hundred other drills as ridiculous as they are extraneous. Gagliardi's focus has always been on preparation, execution, and fun. This philosophy has translated into a lifetime winning percentage of .758, not bad for a coach whose players have trouble executing a single synchronized jumping jack.

Speaking of boldness, the architect the monks settled on was the Hungarian-born Marcel Breuer, an ex-Bauhaus professor whose design for the abbey church, with its corrugated concrete and pierced-concrete bell banner, made jaws drop and eyebrows arch throughout the Catholic world. After sneaking in on our second night in Minnesota, Laura returned enraptured, speaking of a "truly sacred space." The building tends to provoke strong reactions, pro and con. Another friend, a *Star Wars* buff, likened it to the Death Star.

While Breuer's design didn't make everyone happy, it pleased the most important critics: his Benedictine bosses. In addition to appreciating his work, we are told in *Worship and Work*, a history of St. John's written by the late Colman Barry, O.S.B. (Order of Saint Benedict), the monks liked him because he was, according to Abbot Baldwin, "a simple, straightforward, sincere and rather humble person."

He might have said the same of his new football coach, save for the straightforwardness. If Gagliardi in conversation back then was anything like Gagliardi in conversation today, he arrived at his point only after diving into it from a scaffolding of digressions that were often hilarious and sometimes relevant.

Obviously he interviewed well. After accepting the job, Gagliardi was billeted in a spartan room in St. Mary Hall. Even though the new coach had not taken a vow of simplicity, as had the

Benedictines, the monks were reluctant to indulge his request for a television. None of the students, after all, were permitted so modern and potentially decadent a luxury. In that first season, Gagliardi won six of his seven conference games—including a 21–7 thumping of the Lutherans at Gustavus Adolphus—and the cochampionship of the MIAC, the first time St. John's had tasted the title in fifteen years. Not long after, a television appeared in his room. Lurking within many of the Benedictines, he discovered, was a repressed couch potato. On Saturday nights, Gagliardi would find his cell crowded with monks watching Jackie Gleason on the tube and filling the air with cigar smoke.

The Johnnies have been the scourge of the conference ever since, winning the title twenty-three times, advancing to the national playoffs on sixteen occasions, four times advancing to the title game, three times winning it. Quietly, modestly, honestly, Gagliardi has built one of the nation's most remarkable programs. Hindsight shows that he answered incorrectly on that spring day a half-century ago when an unknowing monk asked him, Are you an architect?

The pierced concrete of Breuer's banner relieves the heaviness of the façade, allowing sunlight to stream through. The banner houses a ninety-ton cross that is hewn from native white oak; and five bells, each dedicated to a specific saint or Christian mystery, and cast to the notes of A, B, D, E, and F-sharp. In addition to summoning the monks to prayer thrice daily, the bells chime on the quarter hour.

Though I will come to love those bells, I curse softly upon hearing them toll six o'clock. I mutter the curse because (1) I am walking past the monastery, and (2) I am still a quarter mile from Alcuin Library, where the first meeting of the season I have driven 2,000 miles to chronicle is now underway without me.

I slink soundlessly into the amphitheater in Alcuin's basement and behold a prairie of crewcuts. This was me half my life ago. The freshmen are on stage in a semicircle. Gagliardi has them state their names, hometowns and positions. Being Minnesotans, schooled on the importance of modesty, most of them speak too softly and too fast. *BlakeElliottfromMelrosewidereceiver.*

When they are finished, Gagliardi turns to the rest of the team and delivers an admonition echoing the Second Commandment. "Treat these guys the way you were treated, or the way you want to be treated. You never know," he says, flashing his vulpine grin, "you might walk into a job interview some day and one of 'em might be sitting at the desk in front of you."

I look at these eighteen-year-olds, wide-eyed, acne prone, smiling through their butterflies. I wonder if they know how lucky they are. Not only does Gagliardi not belittle freshmen, he goes out of his way to make them feel welcome, encourages the older guys to help them, academically and socially. The baffling premise so prevalent elsewhere is that freshmen and rookies are to be abused.

A study released later in the season will report that 80 percent of college athletes are hazed. The National Survey of Initiation Rites and Athletics, conducted by Alfred University, found widespread hazing from Divisions I to III, in a wide variety of sports. Why is it so prevalent? No one can give a better reason than: Well, that's the way we've always done it around here. It's tradition.

It's also asinine. Hazing simply isn't tolerated by the NFL's more enlightened coaches, who see it for what it is, a moronic vestige of the league's Dark Ages. They recognize the stupidity of a tradition that purports to build cohesion by degrading and occasionally injuring players.

Although he seldom plays a freshman, Gagliardi's message to first-year guys is: We're delighted you're here. You are welcome, you are valued. "When freshmen show up," he tells his upperclassmen, "I want you to act toward them the way you'd act toward new acquaintances in the professional world. People are *nice* to each other. I want you to be nice to each other."

"Enough sermonizing," he concludes. "Most of all, I want guys that don't need sermons."

There is an hour of sunlight left, so we follow a beaten path a quarter mile to Lake Sagatagan, a spring-fed jewel several miles long and wide. Lake Sag, as it is known, has been a source of recreation and picturesque beauty for monk and student alike since the mid-1800s, when a Benedictine missionary named Bruno Riess arrived on its shores. Father Bruno was surveying the north basin of the Watab River, west of St. Cloud, staking the claims that would provide the land for the monastery and university. The area was known as "Indianbush," we learn in *Worship and Work*, because it had until recently been hunting grounds of Chippewa and Sioux, "who still made occasional forays through it."

Bruno's lust for the lake—"I was bound to acquire this sheet of water"—shouts to us from between the lines of Colman Barry's book. But Bruno had already claimed as much land as was legal. There was the additional problem of paying for it: "We had no money on hand . . . and could expect nothing of the grasshopper-stricken congregations."

His solution was ingenious, if slightly unscrupulous. After asking a Washington friend to petition Congress for the land, the shrewd cleric posted twenty signs all around the lake. APPLICATION FOR THIS LAND IS MADE TO CONGRESS FOR SAINT JOHN'S COLLEGE, they said. The petition was denied, but the signs had the desired effect of discouraging "intruders"—Bruno's word—until such time as the monks could come up with the cash. Those signs, he exulted, kept the "land-sharks" away. (Father Bruno's eagerness to tar others with that brush might have amused the Chippewa and Sioux.)

This beautiful body of water, the source of so much happiness, has seen its share of tragedy down through the decades. In the fine print in the back of Barry's book can be found the sad story of Sylvester Sheire, a student from St. Paul who in 1869 unwisely taunted Murro, a domesticated black bear the monks kept as a pet. When the beast lunged at him, Sylvester fled to the lakeside, jumped into a boat, and began rowing. Murro, mightily pissed off, swam after him, climbed into the boat, "threw his forelegs around the boy and bit him in the neck. Father Wolfgang arrived on the scene too late to save the boy's life."

Think about it. If Sylvester's parents had had access to a good personal-injury lawyer, there would be no St. John's. This whole place would be known as the Sheire Estate.

In the summer of 1872, the monks began construction of the Stella Maris Chapel, dedicated to the Virgin Mary, on the south shore of the lake. "The chapel had no bell," one monk told me, repeating his version of one of the lake's dark legends, "and one fervent young monk felt it should. He took it upon himself—some say against the wishes of the abbot!—to raise the money and buy the bell." Upon purchasing the bell, the monk loaded it onto a boat and set off proudly (sin!) for the chapel. The boat never made it. "No one knows what happened," says the monk. "A sudden wind? A huge fish? A vision from the underworld because of his pride? At any rate, neither bell nor body were ever recovered. Every fall, on the anniversary of the tragedy, one can hear the mournful pealing of a bell in the vicinity of the chapel . . . that has no bell."

While the kids lie supine on the dock, staring down at a school of unfazed sunfish and blissfully unaware of the Legend of the Prideful Monk, Laura and I strike up conversation with a serene, good-looking woman who, until we showed up, had been enjoying the solitude on a bench. She is Judy Steingraeber; her son Joe is a sophomore wide receiver and one of several Steingraeber brothers to attend St. John's. Whenever the opportunity arises, Judy tells us, she volunteers to drive her boys to Collegeville, then stays an extra day or two. It restores her. "There is something special, something magical, about this place," she says.

I agree. During our walk home, an eerie ululation echoes across the water. The moon is rising, the loons are in full throat. Wide-eyed, each of my children reaches for a hand.

Emmaus Hall used to be the seminary, back in the days when St. John's was known as "the Priest Factory," when every fall brought a bumper crop of candidates for the priesthood. Nowadays, as Gagliardi says, "the old ones are dying faster than the new ones are coming in." The seminary is now in a smaller building. Emmaus provides housing for graduate students in the School of Theology, solemn, contemplative seekers of truth who are fine people, I have no doubt, but who look askance at my boisterous children and avoid eye contact with Laura and me when we walk past in the lounge. Little wonder, after a week or so of this, that Laura says, "These people need to drink some wine, have a few laughs, and get laid. It's like they think if they crack a smile they won't be taking their degrees seriously."

To reach our apartment, we walk through the lounge, with its stained-glass windows, and past the large crucifix in the foyer. Devin and Willa spend much time before this crucifix, transfixed. They want to know who did this to Jesus, and why. The more you evade them, the more they bore in, like Perry Mason on cross-examination.

Everywhere you look—in Emmaus in particular and at St. John's in general—there are crosses, crucifixes, reminders that we Catholics are lowdown sinners for whom God sacrificed his only son. Standing in front of this crucifix, I am reminded of my nine years in Catholic schools, and of a greeting card drawn by a warped cartoonist named Callahan. In it, an immense nun in full habit and wimple stands over a distressed student who is writing over and over on a blackboard:

I am personally responsible for the agony of Christ.

The prevalence of crucifixes on campus should at least clear up some confusion for Willa, who recently returned from Sunday school and confidently announced, "Jesus died on the crust."

It is not raining, but it has *been* raining, and might soon rain again. That is reason enough for Gagliardi to move this morning's practice, the first of the season, into the McNeeley Spectrum, the school's enormous new fieldhouse. I thought that was a scream, then one of the guys told me Gags has been known to move practice inside if the gnats are too thick or there is *too much dew* on the practice field.

A few years ago, an offensive lineman suffered a hundred or so gnat bites on the exposed flesh of his legs—these Stearns County gnats draw blood, apparently—and had to be hospitalized. Went into some kind of gnat-shock, or so the story goes. Around the same time, a gnat burrowed into one of Gagliardi's ears, driving the coach to distraction. As the team looked on—curious, bemused, and finally convulsed with laughter—their legendary leader walked to his car, turned on the headlights, then pressed his ear to one of them, hoping the pest would be drawn to the light.

So please, don't tell Gagliardi that gnats are harmless. Nor should you underestimate the danger of dew. Slippery conditions might lead to a loss of footing, which could result in an injury. And Gagliardi loathes injuries more than he loathes telemarketers and incompetent officials. He empathizes with the suffering, feels their pain. And he abhors waste, which is what has transpired, in his opinion, when he loses a player in practice. On three different afternoons last season, a Johnny succumbed to injury during the final thirty minutes of a practice. This year, Gagliardi has devised a brilliant solution to eradicate all such injuries.

He has cancelled the last half-hour of practice. Starting with this season, two-a-day sessions have been shaved from two hours to ninety minutes, which means that most football-playing ninth-graders will spend more time practicing than will St. John's, a perennial contender for the D-III national championship. No team hits less. Most coaches put their quarterbacks off-limits; everyone else is fair game.

"What about those other guys?" says Gags. "Hell, they've got mothers, too." So the Johnnies do not tackle or cut-block one another in practice. Not in the preseason, not during the regular season. Never. "Visualize yourself doing it," the coach tells his players. "Fantasies don't always have to be about the opposite sex."

"Guys from more traditional high school programs actually have trouble adjusting," senior center Andy Gregory tells me. "They think, 'If I'm not suffering, can this be football?'" Considering all the things the Johnnies don't do, I find myself wondering how they win a game, let alone the conference title every season.

Things make more sense at the first practice. Despite being built like a bank safe, the left guard, Chris Salvato, runs like a fullback. Number 3, a Smurf-sized wideout named Ben Sieben, can flat-out fly. Halfback Chris Moore is smooth as single malt Scotch.

The starting quarterback is a smart-assed senior named Tom Linnemann, a natural leader who runs the huddle the way Paul Newman would run a diamond heist. He has a quick release and a quicker wit. Noticing that I'd arrived fifteen minutes into practice on that first morning, for instance, Linnemann said, "Hey, glad you could join us today. Should I talk to John? Do you need us to start practicing a little later?"

Been here not quite a day and I'm already getting static from the starting quarterback. I find this a very encouraging development.

The sun having come out and the grass having dried, the boys will practice outdoors this afternoon. But first they must limber up with some calisthenics, right? At the stroke of four comes the call from a score of voices: "Cal up!"

Some background is in order.

In the summer of 1943, Gagliardi was going into his senior year at Trinidad (Colorado) Catholic High. When the football coach went off to war, the principal, Father Sebastiani, decided to cancel the season. Gagliardi sought him out. "Father," he said, "a lot of the guys are thinking of transferring to the public school." This news, which Gagliardi had made up on the spot, distressed the priest. "How about if we run practice ourselves," Gagliardi suggested. "Just give us a week. If it's not working, you can always call it off."

Father Sebastiani gave his tentative approval, and the grand experiment was underway. Playing halfback in Trinidad's triple-threat offense and acting as coach, Gagliardi learned that many of football's hoariest traditions were superfluous—even downright stupid. The team stopped hitting five days a week. When the players got thirsty—here was a radical departure—they *drank water.* "Hell, we figured they let horses drink water," he says.

The one thing that this newly minted player-coach most enjoyed about that season was that it included no calisthenics. Recalling Dutch Clark, the coach he succeeded, Gagliardi says, "He was a traditional, military-type coach, fierce on the calisthenics, which I hated with a passion." So much for calisthenics. The

Trinidad Tigers stopped doing them, and their season, predictably, collapsed.

Actually, Trinidad won the first league championship in school history, proving what the adolescent Gagliardi had suspected: that jumping jacks, leg lifts, duckwalks and their idiotic ilk had as much to do with football as torture has to do with religion. Before a game against Wisconsin-LaCrosse in the seventies, Gags recalls, "They came out and executed the most breathlessly flawless calisthenics. We stumbled around for a few minutes and that was it. I told our guys, 'We got 'em. They can't win. They've spent way too much time on their pregame calisthenics.'" He was right.

The Johnny huddle is a study in slovenliness. The boys only achieve precision running the play. The team's warm-ups have evolved, over the years, into a parody of a normal team's cals, a *Monty Python* skit on turf.

They *line up* as if to participate in normal calisthenics. But then the laughter begins, and you remember that you are in Collegeville. A few seniors, and maybe a birthday boy, face the team, which fans out in a vast semicircle in front of them. There are 159 guys out for the squad. Have I mentioned that everyone who comes out for the team makes it? Gags lacks the heart to cut anyone.

This afternoon's cals begin with arm circles—"One front, one back, one clap." They are followed by "ear warm-ups," in which the lobe is taken between thumb and forefinger and stretched up, back, and to the side. Next are "around the tummies," in which the athlete rubs his stomach in a clockwise fashion (or, if left-handed, counterclockwise). These exercises, it is explained to me, aid in the digestion of "Reefer food"—the sometimes-heavy fare served at the refectory.

I hear the words "Beautiful Day Drill" and drop to the grass with the boys. This drill does for me what a sharp handclap does for a Buddhist, bringing me into the moment. Cirrus wisps float across a blue sky framed by the treetops. To actually remark to a nearby Johnny, "It's a beautiful day," as the drill requires, would be to belabor the obvious. I soak it up in silence.

★ ★ ★

What would I be doing if I weren't doing this? Maybe it would be my good fortune to visit the Cincinnati Bengals, where wideout Carl Pickens would fix me with his notorious "death stare," as members of the club's front office refer to it. When he was a senior at Tennessee I did a feature on Pickens entitled, "The Dude with the 'Tude." It was an accurate, if not completely flattering piece. Years later, Pickens saw me in the Bengals dressing room and jumped all over me. He was complaining about the story, and me, to a teammate, when the teammate said, "Who?"

Said Pickens, gesturing at me—I was ten feet away—"This f—— cracker." To this day my pals on the Bengals beat call me Cracker.

Maybe I'd be bound for Indianapolis, where Robert Irsay Jr., son of the Colts owner, once had me ejected from the team's facilities. The Irsays were still upset about a profile *SI* had run on Robert Irsay Sr., who had not appreciated the magazine's quoting his mother describing him as "the devil on earth."

Maybe Jacksonville, where I once saw Tom Coughlin, the most uptight white man in the profession of uptight white men, scream at a player for stopping in the corridor to say hello to a reporter. Coughlin has designated specific times and places in which players are permitted to speak to reporters. This was not one of those times.

Maybe UCLA, where a petulant, whining Terry Donahue, then the Bruins head coach, refused to talk to me about why his talented team stank so badly at the beginning of the '93 season. Maybe Foxboro, where Bill Parcells once turned on me in a stairwell, shouting, "I know what you're doing here! You're trying to get guys to go off the record!" I told him not to worry—his players were all so scared of him they had nothing interesting to say.

Maybe Philly, where I spent a Halloween holed up in the cavelike office of Eagles offensive coordinator Jon Gruden. While Gru talked about how he intended to attack the Cowboys, I thought about my two-year-old daughter, who was trick-or-treating for the first time. Years earlier, I had walked out of the nearby Spectrum after an NHL playoff game, past a clutch of autograph-seeking Flyers fans. The expectant hush—was I a player, and if so, which one?—was broken by a genuinely disappointed kid of about ten who said, "Aww, he's nobody."

There is no place this nobody would rather be right now than on his back, watching clouds drift across the Minnesota sky.

It is the afternoon of our fourth day of practice. Calisthenics include a fraction of a jumping jack—"no jump, just a clap," instructs senior wide receiver Joel Torborg, to appreciative murmurs. Gregory, the keg-shaped center to whom I have taken a shine, orders his mates to "Roll out your ankles!" After seven or so seconds, he commands, "Switch!"

After cals, John calls the players together and introduces Father Wilfred Theisen, a professor of physics and avid astronomer. (During dinner in our apartment later in the season, Wilfred will mention offhandedly that, as a hobby, he translates alchemy texts from Latin. Laura and I will marvel, at the end of our trip, at how few of these seemingly staid Midwesterners are what they seem.)

"Jupiter is very bright right now," he tells the players. "The planets are aligned for an excellent season."

Over on the defensive field, Grady McGovern has Majik Markered above his knees a message to the scout team wide receivers he will cover. When they line up across from him, just before the ball is snapped, he hikes his shorts a few inches. On his right quadriceps is printed YOU; on his left, SUCK. A half-hour or so into practice, defensive coordinator Jerry Haugen loses interest in the ball-hawking drills, and decides to share a joke with the defensive backs, who sit cross-legged in the grass around him. Haugen was a ponytailed terror for the Johnnies in the midseventies, one of the best baseball players ever to come out of St. John's and a four-year football starter who still holds the school record for interceptions. The impromptu session comes to a halt when Grady tells an off-color gag involving amputee sex, and is hooted and booed.

Over on the offensive field, wideout John Treptau has made a friend. The butterfly that landed on his jersey yesterday is hovering around him again today. He calls his practice pet "Petey."

The hulking Blugolds of Wisconsin-Eau Claire will bus to the

Natural Bowl in three weeks. Here on the Johnnies practice field, you can cut the tension with a knife.

John, in fact, is deeply concerned about Eau Claire.

John, I will discover, is deeply concerned every time his film study reveals that an upcoming opponent can walk and chew gum at the same time. He will sit in his office, shoes off, brow furrowed, poring over video of, say, Macalester. Thanks to a peculiar, selective memory he has developed over the decades, Gags is able to focus on the two plays out of ten the other team executes well. By Friday, he will warn anyone who cares to listen of the unrealized potential of this underappreciated, 2-6 team. "They've got some good athletes down there," he will tell the team. "The coaches don't just pull these guys out of the corridor, you know."

And, more often than not, the Johnnies will play 150 guys in a forty-point rout. Afterward, you can't tell Gags he overestimated the team he just thumped, because he's already begun overestimating the team he is destined to thump the following week.

On this humid, gnat-rich day, however, his anxiety is well founded. These same Blugolds snuffed the Johnnies' season last November, coming into Collegeville and eking out a 10–7 upset win in the second round of the playoffs. It was a galling defeat: that Johnny squad, the most talented in years, had been projected to go deep into the postseason. But the Johnnies fumbled on the Blugolds' four-yard line, then had a seventy-yard punt return called back on a phantom clip. The next thing you knew the season was over and Jimmy Gagliardi, John's son and the offensive coordinator, was chasing the officials into the parking lot.

Driving back to his office after the morning practice, John says of the Blugolds, "They'll already have played a game, they'll have mostly five-year guys, they'll be a hell of a lot bigger than we are."

I have interviewed enough coaches to recognize blatant poor-mouthing, an activity that was elevated to an art form by the lisping genius and former Notre Dame head coach Lou Holtz, who is known by some of his former players as Loucifer. *We have the utmost regard for Navy. They've got some excellent athletes. Yes, they are winless in seven games, but they've caught some tough breaks.*

While not in Holtz's league, Gags can blow some serious smoke, although in this case he has a legitimate point. It is remarkable, really, that St. John's should even be able to hang with the teams in the Wisconsin Intercollegiate Athletic Conference, let alone dominate them, as the Johnnies have down through the years. If you are a good prep player in Minnesota, but not big or talented enough to rate a full ride from the Gophers, there are still plenty of in-state scholarships available from Division II schools: Winona State, Mankato State, Bemidji State, and, just down the road from St. John's, St. Cloud State—if you don't mind struggling to reach .500 every season, and playing in one of the world's homeliest and most depressing facilities. Those D-II scholarships shrink the pool of good football players willing to pay full freight at a pricey ($22,500 per year) private school such as St. John's.

If you're a high school stud in Wisconsin but Barry Alvarez and the Badgers don't come calling, D-III is your only other option if you want to play in your native state. Of course, a lot of those D-III schools have a D-II flavor. They average around 9,000 students, redshirt most of their players, and are relatively cheap to attend—less than half of what it costs to go to St. John's.

While Eau Claire will have a game under its belt, the Johnnies will not have so much as executed a single chop block or tackle. Not to worry, Gagliardi is telling his guys after the afternoon practice. "It's like riding a bike or kissing a girl," he says. "It all comes right back to you."

"But, John," rejoins an anonymous wiseacre, "I've never kissed a girl."

Linnemann stands up, a dandelion protruding from one of his helmet earholes. The Namath of the MIAC invites everyone to a barbecue at his house on Saturday afternoon. Like virtually every other Johnny who lives off-campus, Tom resides a few miles away in the town of St. Joseph, the site of the College of St. Benedict, the Johnnies' sister school, whose students share classes with the

Johnnies and are affectionately known as Bennies. While St. John's is technically an all-male school, there are Bennies in its classrooms, on its campus, everywhere (in theory) but in its dormitories. There is hope for the Johnny who's never been kissed. "We've invited the St. Ben's soccer team," says Linnemann.

He is a good-looking kid from just up the road in Melrose, where Charles Lindbergh's father built a sod house in 1859. Preceding the Lindberghs by a decade or so in Stearns County was Tom's great-great-grandfather, John H. Linnemann, who ran a general store in St. Joseph. There is John H., in fact, nobly rising to the occasion on page 135 of *Worship and Work*, coming across with a loan to the cash-poor abbey in the 1870s. It has long been speculated by the Linnemanns that John H.'s hasty departure from his native Deutschland had something to do with his desire to avoid involvement in a revolution percolating in northern Germany around the time he left. "There might be a bit of draft-dodging in the family tree," says Tom's father, John, who teaches German and manages the baseball team at Melrose High. Thus, perhaps, the flower in Tom's earhole.

Throwing touchdown passes to Sieben, the quicksilver wideout I noticed on the first day of practice, Linnemann led the Melrose Dutchmen to a league title his senior year. Four ex-Melrose players dot the Johnnies roster; whenever any of them does something good in practice, Linnemann cannot resist shouting, "Go Dutchmen!"

Tom got a sniff from the University of Minnesota—known statewide as the "U." He was invited to make the drive down to Minneapolis, and throw a few passes under the watchful eyes of the Gophers staff. Amiable Jim Wacker, Minnesota's coach at the time, tousled his hair and said "How ya doin', Tommy?"

"I felt like telling him, 'Don't ever touch my hair again,'" says Linnemann, who can read a defense like the side of a cereal box, but lacks the howitzer arm that causes D-I recruiting coordinators to experience stiffness in their boxers. "Tommy is a playmaker," says Daryl Oja, who coached Linnemann in high school. "That's his biggest thing. He makes plays. But all the big schools are into computer recruiting. A guy like Tom doesn't fit the profile. So they bring in some great big kid who can throw the ball a mile but who can't move, and they can't protect him."

Linnemann, meanwhile, turned down a bunch of D-II offers in order to "come to St. John's, play for a legend, and win championships."

I head over to Linnemann's barbecue when the kids go down for naps on Saturday. Most of the off-campus apartments have their own names—the Alamo, the Creamery, the Jungle, the Maze—that are handed down from student to student, year in, year out. The often sad and ramshackle exteriors of these homes belie the amount of fun, the quantity of high-quality carousing, taking place inside. Linnemann lives in a particularly creaking and moldy abode named the Power House. As he gives me a tour of the place, irregular stairways, frightening bathrooms, and dimly lit basement bedrooms, I realize how soft I have become since college. I wonder how these guys retain girlfriends.

Linnemann shares the Power House with four other students, including the mysterious right tackle Chad O'Hara, whom I will come to look upon as a kind of Boo Radley in cleats. O'Hara is a rawboned six-six 250 pounds, with a pallor of one whose main source of income is donating blood. Lethargy seems to be his natural state. Everything about him seems anemic, right up until the moment he comes out of his stance. Chad is probably the most talented offensive lineman in the conference. Unfortunately, he has the work ethic of a three-toed sloth.

"I guess I could be really good if I worked at it," he speculates. The problem is, you can't get him in the weight room without tranquilizer darts and a fork lift—or unless you tell him representatives of Brunswick are in there holding a half-price sale on bowling equipment. (Every Friday night, Chad bowls in a league for his team, Summit Excavation; he is far more passionate for that sport than for the one that got him into St. John's.) Chad has not found it within himself to make it to practice yet, citing "family problems." Most of the guys refer to his absence as "Chad's holdout."

In a lounge area bracketed by distressed sofas redolent of wet dog, the Power People have piggybacked one large color TV atop another. This way, they explain, they can simultaneously watch *SportsCenter and* compete at PlayStation. Whatever debauchery takes place in this space occurs with the benediction of *Hustler* publisher Larry Flynt, who stares out from a framed eight-by-twelve-inch photo mounted on what Linnemann calls his Celebrity Wall. The wall features airbrushed publicity stills of demiluminaries to whom Linnemann has written obsequious letters. In addition to Flynt, there is Hulk Hogan, Bill Gates, and someone called the Menard's Guy—"the boisterous fuehrer of Menard's commercials," Linnemann explains. Cindy Crawford is cheek-by-jowl with Dave Thomas, whose annoying television commercials are ameliorated, as far as Linnemann is concerned, by the sheaf of coupons for free Frosties he enclosed with his picture. Wall neighbors Jimmy Carter and Gerald Ford are bereft of the dignity of their former office, slumming with the likes of Judge Wapner and Richard Simmons, who sent a picture of himself chained to an enormous fork.

"I didn't know whether to laugh or cry," says Tom.

Al Pacino sends his best wishes, as does Fred Rogers, to whom Linnemann sent a moving letter: "I told him how much I used to love his show," says Tom. "Even the mean kids at day care would cool down when we took the Trolley to the Land of Make Believe." Mr. Rogers's cardiganed presence provides a countervailing measure of rectitude and neighborliness to the darkness and depravity of *Hustler*'s Flynt, who gazes out like Nero, holding a finger to pursed lips as if in contemplation of his next sick act.

I miss the hell out of college.

None of the seniors are drinking beer at the barbecue, which means that no one is drinking beer. Incoming Johnny ballplayers sign a form stating that they will not ingest alcohol during the season. For the most part, they keep their promise. Some might slake their thirst with a malt beverage on Saturday evening after a game. Some, in the interest of making up for lost socializing opportunities on Friday night, might tilt a glass on Sunday night as well, the better to fortify their roundtable discussion of that morning's

Gospel and homily. Come to think of it, Monday nights usually find a Johnny or two taking in the football game and a brew or two at the Ultimate Sports Bar on Division Street in Waite Park. As it happened, I was standing with Linnemann after the season when he opened a Christmas card addressed to THE POWER HOUSE. It was from the Ultimate, thanking the guys "For all you do."

"Jesus," said Tom. "Maybe that's a sign that things are getting a little out of control."

He never drinks and drives. If slightly impaired, Linnemann says, it is his custom to simply walk from the bar to a nearby pizzeria, where he has himself—and a large pie with pepperoni and pineapples—delivered to his room.

During the season, the boys are models of temperance. That discipline comes from the top. The night before the barbecue, for instance, Linnemann and cornerback Mike Mikkelson took a few freshmen players to a St. Ben's party. Mikk brought a bottle of PowerAde, Linnemann a Coke, "just to show the younger guys that you don't need to drink to have a good time," said Tom. He also brought a small, electric fan. "Stick with me," he told the frosh. "When it gets hot, I'll plug this baby in. Next thing you know, we'll have women hanging all over us."

While he is an accomplished flirt, Linnemann is true to his girlfriend of a year, Becky Karnes, who lives in the Twin Cities. I once heard Tom introduce himself to a female reporter as "Linnemann—rhymes with cinnamon, 'cause I got flavor." Such a line would, of course, be sick-making if Linnemann did not deliver it with a self-knowing wink. He is deliberately over the top, looking to entertain, not score.

Two weeks after I returned from Collegeville in 1992, Laura and I flew to Australia, where we spent four months living in Sydney and helping to put out the short-lived *Sports Illustrated-Australia*. It was there that we first heard of the Tall Poppy syndrome. To enjoy a surfeit of success, to stand out *too* much, is to become a "tall poppy." Modesty-loving Minnesotans, we found, are as disapproving of Tall Poppies as anyone Down Under.

Tom has some Tall Poppy in him. He has game, he has brains, and he knows it. There are those who chafe at his superabundance of self-assurance. I applaud it, and come to rely on Linnemann throughout the season for laughs, gossip, and friendship. He is not without flaws. He is a mild hypochondriac, a high-maintenance quarterback and a competitor so intense that, while lining up a putt a few years back, he turned and shouted at a group of unruly boys on an adjacent hole.

"Mind you, this was minigolf we were playing—friggin' putt-putt," says O'Hara. "The kids all looked at Tom like they were about to start crying."

It is a source of resentment among some of the Bennies that Linnemann has gone off-campus for companionship, further evidence that he is—I love it that kids in school still use this word—"conceited." After exchanging testy e-mails, Becky and Carla Staffa, a St. Ben's senior who is a friend of mine, nearly came to blows one night in the LaPlayette Bar and Restaurant. Cooler heads prevailed, however . . . up until the moment Carla walked across the bar and slapped the face of a *different* woman, whom Carla was all but certain had stolen her purse.

Upon leaving another tavern that night, I would watch a St. Joe cop shouting "Stop, police!" sprint down an alley chasing a Johnny (not a ballplayer) who'd decided to climb onto the roof of the bar. At an after-party, which some of the Johnnies *insisted* I attend, a strange but well-intentioned undergrad would walk up behind me and put me in a full nelson, leaving me no choice but to snake my right foot behind his, then fall backward on him, momentarily stunning him, enabling me to flip around and pin him to the carpet, after which I counted him out, then stood over him, hands clasped over my head in victory, as I posed the question to my friends: "Who is this Jabroni?"

Aficionados of the World Wrestling Federation will recognize "Jabroni" as a pejorative favored by the Rock, a glowering, ripped mainstay of that circuit whose physical assaults on his victims are often preceded by verbal abuse, such as the promise of "a complimentary dinner at the Candy Ass Café." My semester was not without its disappointments. I made it to fewer prayer services than I'd hoped to; wasn't able to carve out enough time to audit the advanced theology class that had caught my eye; and spent far less time than I'd originally envisioned poring over microfilm in the university's world-renowned Hill Monastic Manuscript Library. On the bright side, some of my Johnny buddies turned me on to the WWF.

Every evening, following dinner, we descend into the cool of the library basement to watch "the Classics"—Johnny-speak for highlights of last season's games. Before the lights are dimmed, the head coach says a few (hundred) words. As he makes his slow, steady septuagenarian's way to the middle of the stage, casting an Alfred Hitchcock-like silhouette on the screen, 158 voices fall silent. (We started the season with 159 players, but a kicker quit just two days into practice.) The John Gagliardi Show is about to begin. This is John's time to make announcements, crack jokes, and give rein to his Columbo-like meanders, the broken field runs of his mind. Amidst the levity, so subtly that you hardly notice it is happening, he imparts his philosophy.

"We don't go into the archives very often," says Gags on the evening of the second Tuesday in camp, "but this is the way you've got to do it if you're going against a great guy." That was Jimmy's cue to roll the tape.

The lights are dimmed. Onto the screen leaps Brian Kohorst, an ex-Johnny defensive tackle who weighed *maybe* 210 pounds. In the film he is up against a 270-pound monster from Bethel. Kohorst feints one way, goes another. The Bethel ogre falls on his face.

In the second clip, we see a Johnny halfback coming out of the backfield and puncturing a Concordia defensive lineman, bending him into a sideways *V*—the symbol for "greater than"—then depositing him on his Cobbers' can. The back is five-foot-seven-inch, 160-pound Bernie Beckman, who played for the Johnnies in the sixties. The Concordia defender is 250-pound Gary Larsen, a future Viking and member of the Purple People Eaters. (Minnesota pigskin trivia: Before Larsen, Jim Marshal, Alan Page, and Carl Eller earned that sobriquet, they were known to Vikings fans as the Four Norsemen—"something of a misnomer," *Time* pointed out in 1969, "since three of the men are Negroes.")

Larsen is still looking up at the sky and wondering how the midget pancaked him when the lights go on and John starts talking. "These guys, Kohorst, Beckman—neither of 'em had a big *S* on their chest," he says. "They weren't from Krypton. They were just guys like you. They were ordinary people doing ordinary things extraordinarily well."

Ordinary people doing ordinary things extraordinarily well. If he hears it once, the Johnny who plays four years for Gagliardi will hear that mantra 500 times.

"Deep Breath with Cheerleader Exhale!" commands senior cornerback Dustin Schultz. After inhaling deeply, 158 Johnnies cheer, jump, and gesticulate hysterically—*like cheerleaders.* Amusing, but I prefer its martially artistic cousin, the Deep Breath with Bruce Lee Exhale. You'd think with all the stinking brutes out here, the gnats would cut me some slack. But no, they're in my nose, they're in my hair, they're in my nosehair. I'm a little cranky.

As is the head coach. The opener is less than two weeks away, and this team has problems. On the defensive side of the field, Haugen is still trying to figure out who will play strong safety and who'll be his left cornerback. Even with the recent addition of O'Hara, who graced us with his presence a week into camp, the offensive line appears to have protection problems. It's hard to say, since they never go "live." But when the team goes "first on first"—first team offense against first team defense—Linnemann hardly has time to set up before Phil Trier or Brian Zirbes or Tim Pahula or some other defensive lineman is pile-driving a fist into his shoulder pad, the maximum punishment they are allowed to inflict on him.

When Pahula lays out a receiver coming over the middle—a major no-no—Gags jumps him: "Are we hitting now? Is that it? We're hitting now? How long have you been here, Pahula?" John, it seems, is on the verge of an eruption, which comes when Krych fumbles a handoff. "Don't fumble that damn ball," he yells. "You fumble, we're in trouble. But you're in *worse* trouble."

"He's turning up the heat," says LaBore, the linebacker, smiling grimly. "He'll keep turning it up until about a week before the game, then he'll back off."

Following the afternoon practice it is a concerned Gagliardi who gathers his players around him and attempts to speak to them. Twice he gets rolling, twice he is interrupted by the war whoops of soldiers stalking through nearby underbrush. They are members of the university's Reserve Officer Training Corps. "What in God's name are they doing in there," says John, mildly irritated.

"Their Challenge Course," someone answers.

"The challenge right now," says Gags, "is to resist the temptation to go up there and beat the hell out of them." The nervous laughter subsides quickly, and he continues. "I hope you're having fun. But at the end of the day, you've gotta ask yourselves, 'Am I getting better? Did I do a better job helping us carry on the tradition here?' My job is to find guys who can do that. All I can do is go by what I see on the practice field. Because whatever the hell you did in high school, I didn't see it."

The solemn silence is broken only by the bloodcurdling cries of the ROTC boys. Gagliardi cannot conclude on such a stern note, doesn't have it in him. The pass-blocking of the offensive line having put him in mind of blindness, he tells the story of the poor old football coach who watched so many miles of film he lost his sight. To make ends meet, he raised seeing-eye dogs. One day, a confused canine walked against the light, leading the coach into traffic. Only the alertness of passing motorists prevented a tragedy. At the far intersection, the old coach gave the dog a biscuit.

Why are you rewarding that dog, asked an onlooker.

"Actually," says Gags, his grin telegraphing the punchline, "I just wanna know where his face is so I can kick him in the ass."

And there is John in a nutshell, expressing his displeasure with a joke rather than a kick in the ass.

* * *

All is not quiet on the home front. Laura has been a trouper for a fortnight, gamely enduring the cross-country drive, and our first week in Emmaus Hall. The apartment where we will spend the semester, in the Ecumenical Institute on the other side of campus, will not be ready for another week. Laura isn't sure if she can take it. The ancient bedding, the thick, wall-to-wall carpets, the heavy air—all combined to make our little apartment a breeding ground for molds and allergens. Laura is red-eyed, sneezing and miserable. While I attend two practices a day, then cut out for the evening's Classics, she attends to the children. Pat Robertson or Jerry Falwell might ask, "So what's the problem?" The problem is, Laura is a talented, ambitious writer who isn't getting a hell of a lot of writing done, these days. "The highlight of our day," she reports, "is going to check the mail."

Naptime is her daily surcease from the shrill demands of the savages. They will not nap, however, in a room together. But the apartment has only two rooms. I returned from practice one gloomy afternoon during which a daylong, steady rain had driven the Johnnies back indoors. Devin was passed out in the master—in fact, the *only*—bedroom; Willa on the sofa. Laura had escaped to Paris: she was crowded up against the window reading *Everybody Was So Young*, a biography of Gerald and Sara Murphy, a couple who befriended and supported the main players of the Lost Generation of Paris: Hemingway, Fitzgerald, Picasso, Léger. Probably not the ideal book for Laura to be immersed in, just now. The passages about the writers and artists remind her that she is not exactly following her creative muse; the descriptions of Paris remind her that she is a long way from the City of Lights.

"St. Cloud is actually named after a Parisian suburb," I pointed out, inanely.

She thought about that for a moment, then said, "There's a Rome, Georgia, too, but I'll bet no one decides to uproot their family and live there for four months." I won't lie to you: we had our low moments in Minnesota.

She read another page or two, look out at the rain and said, "The next time we decide to step off the treadmill, let's do it in the south of France."

This was a woman counting the hours until Date Night.

When Laura decreed, by the power vested in her by, well, *her,* that Tuesday night was henceforth and in perpetuity to be our Date Night, I was not on board.

I opposed Date Night in general because it is my job to reflexively oppose any and all fiats handed down by Laura, lest she become overly comfortable exercising absolute power. I opposed Date Night in particular because when I return from a road trip, I've often got two nights at home, three max, before I pack the bag and hit the road again. The last thing I want to do on one of those nights is shower, groom myself, find nice, clean clothes, and leave the children with a babysitter.

"I miss them and they miss me," I told Laura.

"Tough shit," she replied. "They'll live. We're going on a date."

She was right. You go too long without having an intimate conversation with your wife, things in your marriage can get strained and strange. Even when I am home, I noticed that, in the course of a given day, we interact like the CEO and CFO of a corporation. Our exchanges are business transactions.

Can you walk the dog today? I'm taking Willa to CCD.

Yeah, no problem. When does Devin get picked up from his play date?

Five o'clock. And could you pick up soy milk on the way home?

We continued in this bloodless vein for the first half-hour or so of our dates. Then the wine kicks in, we stop talking business, and are reminded why we began dating in the first place. As Laura put it, "It's like meeting each other all over again."

Men, if you're not already, get on board with Date Night.

But where to take one's date in St. Cloud?

Laura puts down her Paris book and begins combing the local Yellow Pages for restaurant options. This is a prescription for the catty remark that follows:

"What we need is the Zagat's for St. Cloud."

Get it? Zagat publishes guides for popular vacation destinations.

Laura has backhandedly made the point that, unless you have a friend or relative marking time in the state prison—which is not far from where St. Cloud State plays its home football games—you probably wouldn't go out of your way to kill time in this city of sixty-plus thousand.

Like many people from large families, I have gone through life more concerned about the quantity, rather than the quality, of the food I eat. For her part, Laura is a food snob. She is fanatically neat; I am . . . less so. She is a self-described "schedule sort of person"; I tend to lose day planners and watches. She is meticulous about finances; when I checked my balance on the ATM this morning, it said "-$74.46," then asked me (rhetorically, I assume) if I wanted to "continue this transaction."

We have plenty in common—as writers, we love to read and love the language; we love the outdoors—but it is our differences that lend piquancy to the marriage, and that, I think, attracted us to each other in the first place. We publicly plumbed these differences later in the semester when Father Timothy Backous, the university chaplain and a theology professor, asked us to address his class, called "The Theology of Sexuality and Marriage." (The first year it was offered, the course was entitled "Sex without Love." Some 1,000 students attempted to enroll, nearly blowing up the computer system and prompting Father Tim to come up with a tamer name for it.) The questions were restrained and chaste, almost disappointingly so. Several years earlier, Timo had told us, a Benny posed an open-ended query to the class: "Why is it that after my boyfriend and I make love, and I want to make love again, right away, he can't?"

Up shot the hand of a young man who said, "Could I get your phone number?"

Someone asked how we met. That's a cautionary tale, I answered. We met in a college class. Any one of you could be sitting within a few feet of your future spouse.

That she hailed from New Mexico made Laura exotic at Colgate, where everyone is from New England or New York. She favored an ensemble—denim miniskirt with cowboy boots—that I remember to this day. The class we shared, "Values and Institutions in a Changing World," was taught by Professor Robert Kraynak, a stern and pallid genius who took special pleasure in eviscerating the blarney with which I was accustomed to filling my papers. *Late. Disappointing. C-plus,* he wrote on one. We were also graded on class participation. Laura raised her hand often. I would look at her during her disquisitions, nodding and feigning interest in her answer as I ravished her with my eyes. If I could just get her to talk to me, I thought, I know we could be friends.

She never would talk to me. When the semester ended, I had not engaged her in a conversation longer than thirty seconds. She had been deliberately freezing me out, I later learned. As she told my father the first time they met, "Frankly, Mr. Murphy, I thought he was a jerk." Those two got along from minute one.

Two and a half years after I graduated, I literally bumped into Laura in the stairwell at the Sixty-third Street YMCA. I blurted out her name as if I'd never stopped thinking about her. After taking several steps backward—onlookers would have assumed she was trying to keep me at a safe distance—she allowed as how she vaguely remembered me. A few days later I got a note at work. It was from Laura. She misspelled my name (deliberately, I suspect). She suggested getting together for a drink, to talk about magazine publishing.

When the evening was over—she later told me I'd been worse than useless as a career counselor—we walked up Columbus Avenue toward her apartment. As we approached her street, she said an abrupt goodbye and jaywalked across the avenue. She later confessed that she was concerned that, if we got to her apartment building, I might try to kiss her at the door. After a business meeting! What did she take me for?

We went out again. If our marriage is based on commitment, trust, and true love, it is also grounded on the sublime slush dispensed by the frozen margarita machine at Juanita's, the Upper East Side Mexican restaurant where we had our first real date. We talked about family. So formidably intelligent, so firmly *in control* was Laura that it surprised me to learn that she was still rocked by the divorce of her parents, who split up when she was in high school. The more vulnerability she showed me, the harder and farther I fell for her.

Before her parents divorced, Laura and her three siblings appeared in an advertisement for an Albuquerque photo salon. While picture perfect, her family was fractured. Mine was the inverse, a chocolate mess built on bedrock. Beneath the riotous portrait I painted of my clan—the fistfights and arrests; the smashed cars and microscopic grade-point averages—she discerned something stable and permanent, and was drawn to it. While my sibs and I are perhaps a bit too eager to obey our thirst; while we all want for couth and more clearly defined career paths, "I'll give you this much," Laura has said. "At least you Murphy men stick around."

Over the years she came up with a corollary to that observation, and trots it out when I am on the road and the children are missing me: "Daddy leaves," she says, "but he always comes back."

Three weekends into our Collegeville adventure, it seems like old times. Daddy is leaving. I am off to the Bahamas for the wedding of my sister, Gibby. In my absence, Laura will supervise our move from Emmaus Hall to an apartment in the Ecumenical Institute, on the other side of campus.

Gibby was the last of my seven siblings to enter into holy matrimony, which explained, in part, why the license and bloodshed at her wedding did not approach levels they have at previous Murphy nuptials. Unlike my sister Lorin's first wedding, for instance, the priest did not come pubcrawling with us after the rehearsal dinner, then puke his guts up the morning of the ceremony. Unlike that wedding, none of my brothers ended up with poison oak all over his buttocks after being lured into the woods by a randy bridesmaid. In contrast to the wedding of my brother Mark, the police were not summoned to quell riotous partying at the Holiday Inn in Portland, Maine. "If we have to come to this room again," warned an officer, "someone's getting arrested." (This prompted one of Mark's friends—the ex-New York Jet and Minnesota Viking Blake Galvin—to ask, "What if you have to come to the room *next door*? Would someone still get arrested?")

Unlike my wedding, Laura's brother RJ did not wipe out while taking a corner too fast in a hotel corridor, having been rousted from the pool after midnight by hotel security. RJ, who had been skinny-dipping, rolled to a stop on the slippery tiles at the feet of the imperturbable Pat Murphy, my mother, who bid him good night while stepping over his nude body. No one drank beer from Pat's blue leather pumps, as happened at my brother Matt's wedding, where a seriously inebriated reception attendee leapt onto the hood of a departing rental car. He had mistaken the car for a similar one, owned by his father.

The car was being driven not by a thief, but rather by my stegosaurian brother Chris, who goes six-six, 300. After extricating himself from the car, Chris lifted the poor fellow nine or so feet in the air—devotees of professional wrestling recognized the move as an Ultra Suplex—and spiked him onto the macadam, from which the victim bounced a foot or so in the air, then lay still.

As pro wrestlers cast from the ring before the bloodlust of the paying public has been sated are often stuffed back under the bottom rope, Chris's tormentor was revived and forced to endure further punishment. He found himself being cuffed about the head and shoulders and slammed into the wall of a nearby structure by none other than the bridegroom, a bouncer now availing himself of a busman's holiday.

The violence at Gibby's wedding—most of it, anyway—was meteorological. Questioned about the wisdom of a late-August wedding in the Caribbean, Gibby assured us, "The people at the resort told me that hurricane season comes along much later. Plus, we got a really good rate."

Long story short, we all arrived about twenty-four hours ahead of Hurricane Dennis, which struck the island a glancing blow on the night of the rehearsal dinner. Not that we noticed. We were too busy watching Matt stand on the bar and use his tongue to stop a ceiling fan; too busy feigning deep concern when the wedding photographer, having had a cocktail too many, lost his footing by the pool and cut and bruised his face in a fall.

"Who finally punched that guy?" asked my twelve-year-old nephew Hank Goff the next morning, before we set him straight.

To venture behind the Pine Curtain is to shrink the world: Father Simeon, who performed the ceremony, was a Benedictine who'd actually spent a couple years at St. John's. So strong does his faith burn within him, alas, that it appears to have consumed his sense of humor. Father Simeon was a pill. After the rehearsal, when Gibby invited him over to the hotel for cocktails, he scolded, "On the altar, she speaks of cocktails!"

So the padre was definitely not amused when, early in the ceremony, Gibby and her fiancé, John Ries, knelt before the altar. In kneeling, you see, Gibby inadvertently pulled down the front of her dress, granting amnesty to her considerable bosom. As she made frantic adjustments, John leaned over and whispered, to his everlasting credit, "Them're some big titties."

I related these and other highlights upon returning to Collegeville, where Laura had almost finished unpacking.

The Ecumenical Institute was founded in 1967 on land formerly used by the monks to pasture their dairy cows, and by the Gagliardi kids to ride ponies and minibikes. (John and Peg live less than a quarter mile from our apartment; I cut through their backyard to get to the campus.) It consists of ten sleek, streamlined, deceptively spacious apartments, also designed by Breuer. Here, scholars of various religious backgrounds immerse themselves in research and writing for a semester, or a year. Through "study, prayer, reflection and dialogue," Institute literature informs us, they seek to "re-weave the torn fabric of Christian tradition and community."

It is a holy place, a cutting-edge place, a place where, if you need to do laundry on Saturday, you'd better have your clothes in the machine, lid down and quarters in the slots, by sunrise. Or earlier. Because these Ph.D.'s are cutthroat. They think nothing of tying up both machines all morning. They'll leave a dry load in the machine just to dibs it, then drive to St. Joe for quarters. I've seen it happen.

We don't let this stand in the way of befriending them. We don't allow their inability (advanced degrees notwithstanding) to grasp the meaning of the phrase "please empty lint filter" to erode our goodwill toward them. We're bigger people than that. Besides, we're lucky to be here. They are doctorate-holding, fabric-mending scholars doing serious academic work, crumbling barriers so that people of all faiths may someday be united, like in that song by John Lennon. I'm going to football practice every day, holding one nostril shut so I can blow a gnat out the other.

"Gnats are pretty tough this morning," Gagliardi notes during cals three days before the opener. "Everybody swallow three or four—that'll put a dent in 'em." I look around, because there are freshmen gullible enough to take him at his word. Today's cals: One perfect jumping jack, followed by "finger exercises," followed by something requiring the Johnnies to lie on their stomachs and make barking, seal-like noises.

As Beau had predicted, Gags's tone has changed in the week before the game. He is encouraging, upbeat. Most of the guys have now seen and drawn comfort from a tape of Eau Claire's opener. While St. John's was idle, the Blugolds played dismally, losing to Tiffin, a Division II team from Ohio. As with virtually every squad the Johnnies will face this season, Eau Claire will substantially outweigh them. Jeff Bretherton, one of four Johnny assistants who made the drive to Eau Claire to scout the game, isn't worried. "Big but slow," is his description of the Blugold defensive line. "They don't do much stunting, twisting, or blitzing, just come at you. Moore should be able to run around them pretty easily."

In private, John refuses to share Bretherton's, or anyone's, optimism. Sure, the Blugolds played like Keystone Kops last week. "What worries me," he says, "is that they used up all their mistakes in the first game."

The winningest coach in the country says this with a straight face, as if it would be just his luck. It really does worry him. That, I realize, is why he is the winningest coach in the country.

3

WISCONSIN-EAU CLAIRE

Game day! This is the culmination of our first three weeks in Collegeville, yet my brow is unfurrowed, my pucker factor low. It helps that the stadium is a five-minute walk from my door; that after the game I will not be scrambling like a meth addict from the winners' locker room to the losers', fighting for position with mannerless and hygiene-deficient cameramen, shagging quotes from cyborg coaches and players intent on going their entire careers without sharing an interesting or original observation.

It is comforting to know that I will not be up till 4:30 A.M. slapping together some dogshit game story that even my parents will be hard-pressed to finish; will not then have to speed to the nearest airport in order to be home as soon as possible to alleviate the suffering of Laura, who has had the kids by herself for six days. It soothes me to know that I will not have to phone Mark Godich, my senior editor and a great guy, and hear him say:

"Sorry, pal, but the Niners lost to Tampa Bay, so we've gotta cut you from four pages to two paragraphs" or:

"Hey, pal, hope you're not calling from the airport, 'cause this baby needs some work."

Before the game we drive out to a nearby apple orchard, where we pick up a peck. (Who knew "peck" was a real unit of measurement? I'd thought it was a kind of kiss, or a nonsense word in a tongue twister.) It is such a gorgeous Saturday morning that I can't even muster much outrage upon returning to discover that I've been leapfrogged in the laundry room by a cunning, coldblooded Ph.D.

I arrive at the game later than I had planned, my underwear still damp around the edges. Before venturing out on the field, I pop into the training room. For every other team I've ever covered, the training room has been strictly off-limits, a postgame refuge where goats and screw-ups hide out until we, the media, despair and retreat from the dressing room. Here, head trainer Scott Berscheid and his staff seem offended if you *don't* visit often. Today assistant trainer Amy Behrendt waves me in and insists that I have a bagel.

Linnemann is sitting with his throwing elbow in a cooler of ice, watching the Pitt-Penn State game. "I figure I got about forty-five minutes till I throw up," he says. He's serious. He ralphs before every game. He and Amy are discussing the merits of "party pants"—the black stretch pants in vogue right now. "If they make girls feel sexy," Tom is saying, "if they make them feel good about themselves, if they make them feel comfortable wearing thong underwear, well, *good for* party pants."

Attitudes like those, Behrendt informs him, contribute to warped body images, which lead to low self-esteem and eating disorders among young women. "You," she concludes, "are a sexist pig."

Most of the guys are loosening up in the fieldhouse, stretching, tossing the football. A few stand at the doorway, watching the Blugolds take the field. Like all WIAC teams, these guys are colossal, but a lot of their bulk seems to come from enthusiastic consumption of those Badger State staples, cheese and beer. John brings the team together and delivers a few encouraging words. The squad launches into the Our Father. Uncertain of what to do, I finally kneel and mouth a few syllables, hoping my atrophied faith will not hurt the Johnnies.

We file out of the fieldhouse into bright sunshine—and into a kind of pigskin paradise, a picnic with a football game thrown in. John Updike famously described Fenway Park as "a lyrical little bandbox of a ballpark" in which everything "seems in curiously sharp focus, like the inside of an old-fashioned peeping-type Easter egg." The Natural Bowl on this golden Saturday is, if possible, more idyllic, more intimate. Beneath the emerald wall of Swayed Pines—our own Green Monster—the bleachers are packed with sweat-shirted alums, Bennies in tight shirts, black-robed monks. The tang of grilled bratwurst is in the air. At the stadium entrance, a student sits peddling loaves of Johnny Bread baked by the monks this morning. On the hill overlooking the south end zone, the rim of the bowl, as it were, resourceful (or tightfisted) onlookers have parked lawn chairs. One guy has strung a hammock between oaks. Kids with no clue whom the Johnnies are playing are sliding on their rumps down the grassy bank to the track. It is all like a drug to me.

Adults have paid six dollars for their tickets. Children get in free. While the game is hugely important to the players and coaches, there is, at the same time, an absence of urgency in the air. I have covered games in Ann Arbor, Columbus, South Bend, and Tallahassee. I have seen the ugliness born of high hopes dashed. I have smiled at the sight of Alabama fans holding a roll of toilet paper and a box of Tide detergent—Roll Tide, get it? I have seen Florida State fans cheer the sight of Miami mascot Sebastian the Ibis being roughed up by Tallahassee police. (In truth, it was rather gratifying.) I have talked to an Arkansas couple who vacationed in Fayetteville every August in order to watch Razorbacks two-a-days. I have thought, but lacked the courage to suggest to these super-fans: *Get a Life!*

After the Penn State Nittany Lions got their leonine asses kicked by Nebraska in the '83 Kickoff Classic, I was suckerpunched in the parking lot by a frustrated (and shitfaced) Nittany Lions fan. I remember the double-barreled humiliation of not getting a good shot back at my assailant, then having to crawl under a tour bus to retrieve my glasses.

A loss today will not result in someone getting slugged in the parking lot. It will not result in a team missing out on a bowl payday, thus wreaking havoc on the athletic department's budget. No one's draft position will suffer. No one will drive away in a SkyLab-sized recreational vehicle that has provided him with lodging for the previous five nights. Are there Division III fans who second-guess the coach and curse lousy officiating? Of *course* there are. A lot of them live in the monastery, in fact. Fans at this level do not lack for passion. And yet, from what I will observe over the course of a season, their identity, their sense of self-worth, is not hitched to the outcome of a game.

One must pay a price to reclaim perspective. The Division III game is slower, the players smaller. Pacing the Johnny sideline this afternoon, this season, in the shadow of the bell banner, I am thrilled to pay it. Small college, major college, NFL, Texas high school—a good game is a good game. As Stonebraker said, our feet are the same.

Directed by Dr. Axel Theimer, who in his youth sang for the Vienna Boys' Choir, the St. John's Men's Choir knocks out a tight, harmonious national anthem. I get windfall goosebumps from its unexpected encore:

Fight, you Johnnies! Fight, you Johnnies
Stand and fight like men for old St. John's

This is, of course, the nonsensical, indispensable "Johnny Fight Song," which concludes thusly:

Rah! Rah! Rah! Rah! Rah! U-Rah! St. John's
Rah! Rah! Rah! Rah! Rah! U-Rah! St. John's

It is a kick to hear these phrases, archaic as a raccoon coat, emanating from the throats of a bunch of boys born during the Reagan administration; guys with goatees, soul patches, bandannas, and earrings.

I watch the kickoff transfixed, half-expecting Eau Claire's returner to go all the way. I mean, I've been with the Johnnies damned near a month and haven't seen them make a tackle. Who's to say they can do it? The guys on defense say the no-hitting-in-practice policy actually makes them hungrier to light somebody up on Saturday. We shall see. Joe Linhoff's boot carries to the 10, and backup safety Marc Jerzak knifes in for hard, low takedown. Okay. The Johnnies can tackle.

On the Johnnies' second offensive play of the season, Linnemann calls "Sieben Iso," a long pass to his best friend. Tom's bomb appears to be overthrown, but Sieben somehow accelerates while the ball is in the air, snagging it in stride, racing for a ninety-one-yard touchdown. The Natural Bowl, suddenly, isn't such a mellow place. Who knew seven thousand people could make this much noise?

It's easier to be on the same wavelength with your go-to receiver when he's been catching your passes since preschool. That's when these two met. "I didn't know what I was supposed to do with the football until Benny told me, 'Pick it up and throw it to me,'" Linnemann says. "I did, and I've been doing it ever since." Before they became battery mates at Melrose High, they spent many a happy afternoon playing pickup games in a field next to Lance Stueve's house. Lance was their buddy. His dad owned a shoe store in town. "It was a nice field," Sieben recalls, "but you had to watch out for old lady Weber's rhubarb patch."

At halftime, the Johnnies lead 26–15. Sheepish campus police make a sweep of the field, ostensibly to disperse Nerf-ball-tossing kids. The perpetrators simply loiter on the sidelines for a moment then fill in behind the cops as soon as they have passed.

Linnemann is picked off at the start of the second half. Eau Claire scores, cutting the Johnnies' lead to 26–21. Unhappy on the sideline in the best of circumstances, Gagliardi is now acutely miserable, no doubt recalling a playoff game his team squandered to another Wisconsin squad three years ago. Having led UW-LaCrosse 30-8 in the third quarter, the Johnnies lost, 38–37.

All seems lost on an ensuing third-and-long. Linnemann drops back into a collapsing pocket and is dead meat as two Blugolds close in. In the nanosecond before he is hit, however, he makes a blind, desperate heave toward the far right corner of the end zone and I'll be damned if Sieben, having broken off his route to freelance, isn't there to complete the afternoon's most improbable touchdown.

Linnemann comes off the field with an arm draped around his buddy, who along with the rest of the team suspects that Tom was simply trying to throw the ball away, but lacked the arm strength. "No, no," says Linnemann, "I knew where you were gonna be. Just like Stueve's field."

Forgive me: my notes for the fourth quarter are somewhat sketchy. I know this much—the Johnnies won, 40–28. Throughout the season, whenever pacing the sidelines got old, I would walk the short distance to where Laura and the children were perched on the hillside just south of the bleachers. I would stash the notebook and park my butt on the grass.

Normally I am several time zones removed from my family on game day. In Collegeville, I am several strides away. Everytime I joined them, Laura would pose a question betraying a comprehensive ignorance of what was happening on the field—*Who are we playing? How much time is left in the game?*—and who could blame her? She was usually digging through her backpack for a snack for one or both of her needy children, or trying to prevent them from rolling down the hill into innocent spectators.

The job I left, the job I will return to, is a damned-near–perfect job, but for this one, crushing downer: for half the weekends in a given year, I am a widower, Laura a widow. The proximity of my family at these Johnny games is more than a convenience. It is the sweetest aspect of this sweet, stolen season, a sublime union of personal and professional lives, one that grants Instant Perspective. Yes, Linnemann needs to do a better job throwing the short and intermediate passes, and the Johnny safeties need to be more mindful of play-action . . . but if Willa and Devin don't stop rolling down the hill, they're going to barf up their bratwursts.

★ ★ ★

No prayer circles afterward, just plenty of handshakes, "Nice game" and "Good luck the rest of the season." I ask Grady the cornerback if any of the Blugolds had any smack to talk on the field. "Nahh," he says, "they're good guys."

He does mention one defender who, after making a tackle, turned to the Johnny sideline and motioned, as if to say, Anyone want a piece of me? The fellow must have been too adrenaline-addled to see the humor in his challenge, coming from someone who was busy helping his team give up forty points and 499 yards of offense in a losing cause. "We laughed at him," says Grady.

The Johnnies aren't afraid to fight. They simply know that if they succumb to the urge, they may never get on the field again. Fighting, to Gagliardi, is idiotic and inexcusable. "We don't think it shows how tough you are," he says. "We think it shows you're dumb as hell, and you don't know the rules. If we wanted to show the other team how tough we were, we'd sucker-punch 'em coming out of the dressing room. We'd slug 'em while the coin is in the air."

The Blugolds kneel around their first-year head coach, Todd Hoffner, who grimly informs them that the two nonconference losses they've racked up are meaningless, that they can still win the WIAC, make the playoffs, go all the way. The Blugolds disperse with long faces, recognizing, perhaps, that they are a deeply flawed team—they will win two games this season—and obeying the unwritten football rule that states that those who are not authentically crestfallen in defeat must *act* crestfallen, or risk censure for not harboring a sufficient hatred of losing.

Small reunions spring up all over the field. Parents stand with their uniformed sons, praising them for their play or, if the young man's uniform is immaculate, tactfully finding something else to talk about: classes, perhaps, or the upcoming duck opener. There is much hugging and posing for pictures. It is a sweet time for everyone involved with Johnny football, with the possible exception of Brother Mark, the gruff but lovable Benedictine in charge of the grounds crew. Mark has devised a sure-fire method of dispersing those who linger too long on his field, bruising and crushing blades of his precious bluegrass. He activates the sprinklers, which gets people to the sideline in a hurry.

Instead of repelling Devin, the sprinklers awaken in him a deep biological imperative to strip. Devin, who turned three in July, is going through a phase in which he finds garments of any kind unbearably oppressive. He's doing a lot of streaking. At the beginning of our stay this was a slight concern. One of the people running the Ecumenical Institute is Sister Dolores Schuh. To our relief, Sister Dolores is unfazed by the sight of Devin roaming the grounds in his altogether. "Devin," she says, passing him on the way to her office, "you're a funny little boy."

Once the offending garments are on the turf, he heads for the water. He will repeat this performance for the next two home games. His streaking routine will become my most enduring memory of Devin in Collegeville: jets of water thwacking his chunky buns while he runs pell-mell through the spray, laughing as hard as I have heard him laugh, his excitement heightened, no doubt, by the tingle of an occasional cold-water enema.

Here come the men in black.

On this ultrafine Sunday morning, Laura and I decided to walk the half-mile to the abbey church. The children complain about the uphill trek. We ignore, and ultimately carry them. Just before 10:30, the black-cowled monks process two-by-two, as an ark is boarded, up the center aisle and into the choir stalls that form a semicircle behind the altar. A portly, older Benedictine fixes Willa with a Grinch-like glare: she is perusing a *Sesame Street* magazine. I glare back at him. That's right, Bro, I want to say, we bribe them for their silence. She gets a magazine, he gets matchbox cars, they both get peanut butter crackers and milk in sippy cups. If we thought it would work, we'd pay them cold, hard cash to sit still and be quiet for the duration of mass.

If the churlish monk will forgive Willa, I will forgive him. The first reading, from the Book of Sirach, assures us that "the vengeful will suffer the Lord's vengeance," and calls for forgiveness in all things. It occurs to me that one of the reasons we are in Minnesota this morning is because I have yet to let go of an old grudge.

Of the sixty-nine freshmen in the picture, three of us are smiling. I am not one of them. I am fourteen and riddled with doubts about my masculinity. I am a late-blooming, 135-pound defensive end for the Shamrocks of Trinity High School in Louisville, Kentucky. So desperately am I trying to look the hard-ass that my sneer is a caricature of a sneer. Who has time for this team-photo foolishness, my expression is saying, when I could be putting a snot bubble on some pantywaist running back?

Putting "a snot bubble" on one's opponent was something the Trinity coaches were forever screaming at us to do. I'd learned what one of those was a year before, playing my first season of organized football. I'd taken a handoff and gone through the line upright as the Nutcracker. A linebacker obligingly drove his helmet into my solar plexus, knocking the wind out of me and forcing from one of my nostrils a balloon of mucilage that adhered, quivering, to the inside of my facemask, then burst. My first snot bubble.

In mid-August of 1975, well over a hundred Trinity freshmen—they called us "Greenies"—reported for our first practice. I'd met one of our coaches over the summer and been polite and respectful. He looked me up and down and said, "Boy, I'm gon' run your dick off."

He tried. That first afternoon was three hours of isometrics, sprints, and grass drills, performed in Sumatran humidity. The session was designed to cull the herd, and did. At least thirty guys quit after the first day. After a week, we practiced in full pads. To the extent that fourteen-year-olds can, we beat the hell out of each other. For calisthenics, boys who'd been designated "starters" formed a circle. Behind each starter stood the second-stringer; behind him the third-stringer, and so on. At the end of calisthenics, you fought for your position.

This was how the Trinity coaches built team unity: mandatory fistfights. While other teams worked on execution, we became adept at throwing haymakers without breaking our hands on one another's helmets. We excelled at other things, too. No team's pregame calisthenics were as smart or synchronized. It is doubtful any of our opponents could outperform us in such football-irrelevant exercises as box drill, bull-in-the-ring, and belly-bombers—which we performed for two hours on the Monday after a midseason loss to Bishop David High. We had dishonored the Shamrock, and needed to be punished. The next day, several of my teammates' mothers phoned the school to complain that their boys had come home with concussions.

Halfway through the school year, my family moved from Louisville to Philadelphia. I played another five years of organized football, three in high school, two in college, and have spent ten of the last fifteen years covering college and pro football. I have played for and met some genuine boobs but have never encountered the Neanderthal coaching I got as a ninth grader.

We Greenies had more talent than anyone we played, and still lost four of our nine games. I know because I recorded each score in my scrapbook. I attribute those losses to the coaches, who stand frowning two rows behind me in that photograph, and whom I would love to run into today. I would tell them that, by some cosmic quirk, I have spent much of my adult life picking the finest football brains in the nation. I would tell them about the time Bill Walsh stopped a practice at Stanford University and chastised his assistants. "Stop screaming," he said, "and start teaching." I would tell them about Gagliardi. Since they are not around, however—having moved on to careers, presumably, as prison guards and attack-dog trainers—I am telling you.

4

MACALESTER

It feels most like a sabbatical in the morning. Mornings are great. Mornings are everything we hoped mornings in Minnesota would be. We don't set an alarm. We're on sabbatical! The first words we hear each day are usually shouted by Devin from the bathroom down the hall: "What number did I make?"

While caught up in the excitement of one of his early, successful tinkles into an actual toilet—"Such a big boy!"—Laura or I pointed out how the bubbles had formed a circle, or zero. Now, every time the kid takes a leak, he wants to know what number he has created. For the first couple weeks we would actually peer into the bowl, making good-faith efforts to discern numerals. *Two circles, one on top of the other. Looks like an eight to me!*

Now we just call out any number that pops into our heads—"Twenty-three!"—and he's fine with that, flushing the toilet while bidding his handiwork adieu: "Bye-bye twenty-three!"

I make their breakfast. Lately it has been omelets. Cheese omelets, or, as Devin says, "omlins." Some mornings I leave around 9 A.M. for the office. The Ecumenical Institute has been kind enough to rent me a room in the basement of Alcuin Library. It is a seven-minute walk from home, the best commute I will ever have. I cut through the Gagliardis' backyard, over the bridge spanning Stumpf Lake—actually a dammed section of the Watab—then head up a slight eminence toward the bell banner. I do not remember ever making this walk without seeing Gagliardi's car in its accustomed parking spot. For a guy who works so hard to give the impression that he is hardly working, he works pretty damned hard. Proceeding past the Palaestra, I walk beneath the Swayed Pines, glimpsing the field, and, on several occasions, deer nibbling the bluegrass on it. At the top of the hill, Alcuin Library is on my left. What do I do in my office? I conduct interviews with coaches of upcoming Johnny opponents. I type up the scores of pages of notes I am taking. I drink coffee and read three newspapers.

Other mornings, Laura retreats to her office, leaving me on kid duty until shortly before noon, when we ship them out: Willa to kindergarten, Devin to day care. There is a little playground a hundred yards from the apartment: a swing set, seesaw, and wooden carousel that appear to have been there since the days when the monks kept bears as pets. There is an isthmus of woods separating the Ecumenical Institute from Fruitfarm Road. We spend many happy hours exploring these woods, throwing rocks in bogs, keeping an eye peeled for deer—we see at least thirty throughout the summer and fall—and talking about the Indian children who played here before the Benedictines arrived. Devin does not like to begin bushwacking until he has selected for himself a bitching walking stick. Once in the forest, he uses the stick to bludgeon logs and boulders, as if he is Moses, expecting to draw water.

In the adjoining apartment are our friends, the Immelmans. Aubrey is a highly regarded psychology professor at the university. His wife, Pam, is also dauntingly bright: she has a master's in education, but is devoting her energies these days to raising and chasing their three children: Timmy, Matthew, and Elizabeth. A half-hour after making one anothers' acquaintances, Willa, Devin, and the Immelman fry are friends for life. An open-door policy soon exists between families. Devin feels at home walking over and playing with Timmy's trucks; Timmy knows that if he is ever jonesing to bust out Willa and Devin's Brio train set, he couldn't be more welcome.

They create games, lining up boxes left over from our move, climbing in them and pretending to be passengers on a train. They "camp out" in a tent I erect in the backyard, pestering any available adult to be the "bear." They drag the patio furniture down the gentle slope to the lawn near the offices of the Ecumenical Institute, then serve one another imaginary tea. Devin's nudist leanings influence his young peers: there are nude train rides, camp-outs, and at least one all-nude tea party. The kids play together outside almost every day, which Laura and I find at once delightful and slightly disconcerting.

It is lamentable but a fact that such spontaneous, unstructured play—*real* play—has become foreign to us. Both of us grew up roaming our respective neighborhoods, beholden only to the cowbells our mothers rang to signal that dinner was about to be served. By the time we had our own kids, the concept of such a happy-go-lucky, free-range childhood was obsolete. The odds that an unsupervised child would end up on a milk carton had become unacceptably high.

The cowbell has given way to the play date. We are used to driving our children to friends' houses for recreational assignations; to walking them to the playground, where we stand, keeping an eye on them, all the while scanning the periphery of the park for suspicious characters. For our kids to be able to simply walk out the door, hook up with their friends and roam the grounds around the apartment is novel and liberating for all parties involved.

No place, of course, is completely safe, and Stearns County is no exception. As the Johnnies prepare for Macalester, a crew from NBC's *Dateline* news program is in St. Joe, taping a segment to be broadcast on the tenth anniversary of the most notorious kidnapping in the history of Minnesota. On October 22, 1989, eleven-year-old Jacob Wetterling set out on his bike, with his brother and a friend, for a convenience store in St. Joe. On their way home, around 9:15 P.M., a masked man pulled a gun on them, forced them into a ditch, and ordered Jacob's brother and friend to go away. Neither Jacob nor his abductor has been seen since.

Jacob's mother, Patty, has since become a nationally recognized expert and speaker on child abduction. The Jacob Wetterling Foundation opened in 1990: it is a resource for the families of other abducted children, and for law-enforcement officials. A year ago, nine years after her son was snatched, Patty wrote an open letter to the kidnapper. "I often wonder does October 22 mean anything to you?" she wrote. "Do you remember the young boy you took from us?"

She went on to tell the man that she had "found some comfort picturing you not as a mean old ugly bad guy, but [as] an 11-year-old boy. Someone's son . . . possibly someone's brother needing and hopefully sharing the love an 11-year-old boy deserves. If this love wasn't shared in your family, I'm sorry."

Her idea, she told a local news station, was "to touch that little kid inside of this man and see if he would talk to me. I need to know what happened. And, perhaps, this person needs to tell."

Ten years after it happened, the kidnapping still casts a pall over the community. Before I'd even heard of Jacob Wetterling, I'd felt his disappearance in the looks people cast my way: as a strange, adult male, I was a suspicious character. I remember walking into Willa's school, and having it gently explained to me that parents were to wait outside.

On the tenth anniversary of his disappearance, Jacob would have been twenty-one, old enough to buy beer at that convenience store. The case remains open. The kid might still be alive. The lack of resolution seduces and torments Patty Wetterling, who recently told a local journalist that she still drives by the ditch where her son was taken, and cries out, "Jacob! Where are you?"

It stops feeling like a sabbatical around 11:45 A.M. That's when the station wagon leaves for St. Joe. Willa is in the afternoon kindergarten session at Kennedy Elementary School. She has to be there by noon. She is fine with kindergarten. She is not the problem.

After dropping Willa at Kennedy, I drive several blocks to Swanson's Day Care, where Devin will spend the next five hours

(Willa joins him at three o'clock). It is during this short drive that Devin falls silent. He waddles from the driveway to the front door of Swanson's like a convict walking the Green Mile.

It's not like Devin is a day-care rookie. He's got half a year of a California preschool under his belt. He's not even that shy. But, like every kid, he's got a finely tuned sense of what is and isn't fair. Being forced to abandon his favorite toys, to endure the overland passage to this foreign land of mosquitoes and heavy, wet air—those were violations of his rights to begin with. To be shipped out, on top of that, four days a week to this low-security prison—all this strikes Devin as profoundly unfair. It is this strangeness heaped *upon* strangeness that causes him to sink his talons in my leg the instant we step inside the door at Swanson's. Our routine goes something like this: I start to tell him everything's going to be fine, that he's sure to have plenty of fun with his new friends. That's when his lower lip commences quivering and the spigot is twisted on, his eyes fill with tears that roll down his cherub's cheeks.

I will endure bitter cold later this season, frustration over the slow pace of my writing, chronic Achilles tendinitis, strep throat, and one epic hangover. Nowhere will I suffer as acutely as I do in the foyer of this building, trying to get my sobbing son to release his Death Grip on my leg, soothingly saying, over and over, "It's okay, buddy. It's okay. Everything is going to be okay."

Our checkered history with day care precedes the birth of Devin. One fine Monday morning in 1997, I flew into San Francisco from Pittsburgh, where I'd seen the Steelers edge the Jacksonville Jaguars in overtime. I could not help noticing, as the taxi pulled up to our house, that my front door was wide open, and that two police cars were parked out front. I remember how difficult it was to sit there while the cabby made change.

I walked in the house and found a cop in my kitchen, using my telephone. Upon seeing me, he hung up. "Your daughter is fine," he told me. It was the babysitter who was in a world of shit. While Laura was on a Costco run three towns away, our babysitter had taken Willa to a nearby shopping center. While pushing our daughter's stroller through the aisles of Long's Drugs, the sitter had shoplifted a few things—some cosmetics and fake jewelry—stashing them in the stroller. She was observed by an undercover detective and busted after leaving the store. Willa got a ride home in a squad car. (For a year or so thereafter, the sight of a police car would induce her to shout, "*I* got a ride in a police car!")

The officer had been on the phone with the county's department of social services. Had I not arrived when I did, they were prepared to take Willa into custody. This made Laura and me feel like splendid parents, as did the lecture that same officer felt entitled to give us. He would never hire a babysitter he did not know. (Laura had interviewed the sitter at length, and spoken to her references.) He worked two jobs so that his wife could stay home with their children.

This lecture has become a mainstay of Laura's riff on the mixed message mothers get from society: "If you're a working mom, well, why aren't you spending more time with your children? And if you're a full-time mom, why aren't you using your brain? Well, which is it?"

I was inclined to give the sitter another chance. Laura fired her that very day.

The offense watches video in a room I call the Cavern, a vast, unused space in the Palaestra above the basketball court. The Johnnies have dragged into this room an assortment of tortured sofas and creaking La-Z-Boys. The furniture faces the white wall onto which the video is projected. When I duck in, the guys are talking about the Vikings' recent win over the Atlanta Falcons.

Jimmy asks me, "Do you miss it?"

Before the NFL season is out, there is plenty I will miss about it. I will miss checking in with Steelers running back Jerome Bettis. If you're coming to Pittsburgh and don't call the Bus ahead of time, so he can make dinner plans, he gets offended. I miss chewing the fat with San Diego Chargers quarterback Jim Harbaugh, the best-natured and most accommodating athlete I know. I was once a passenger in Harbaugh's car when he was pulled over for speeding.

Spying the flashing lights in his rearview mirror, Captain Comeback said, "This'll be good for your story."

Do I miss it? I miss Sunday afternoons, when the NFL guys put a matchless, breathless product on the field. The rest of their act, I can take or leave. Earlier this summer, NFL offensive linemen Jumbo Elliott, Matt O'Dwyer, and Jason Fabini got a little out of hand at a Long Island bar. It took thirty-one police officers to subdue them. The brawl was reportedly triggered when one of the Three Musketeers entered the ladies' room and relieved himself in the sink. Later this season, Miami Dolphins running back Cecil Collins will be arrested and charged with breaking into the apartment of a neighboring couple. The woman will tell police that she was being stalked by Collins, who, as it happened, was drafted by the Dolphins despite two previous arrests for breaking into women's apartments and fondling them against their wishes. Indianapolis Colts defensive back Steve Muhammad will be charged with misdemeanor battery for beating his pregnant wife, who will die ten days later. A coroner will rule that her death was caused by injuries sustained in a car accident, not by the beating. So Steve has that thought to console himself with before he drifts off each night.

Two days before the Super Bowl—after Rae but before Ray—commissioner Paul Tagliabue will argue that the rate of felonious behavior among its players is lower than that of society at large. My selfish problem with that is, I don't work closely with society at large, I work with NFL players, and it blows me away how many of them can't keep themselves out of jail.

Malfeasance has reared its ugly head in the college ranks as well. A pair of Michigan Wolverines stand charged with embezzling merchandise from a Kmart; they are not to be confused with the dozen or so Michigan *State* athletes to be fingerprinted and photographed of late from the front and the side. The all-time Spartan arrest king was football player Robert Newkirk, who according to the *Detroit News* was collared eight times on ten charges with four convictions without ever missing a game! As then-Spartan head man Nick Saban demonstrated, Division I coaches can find within themselves extraordinary depths of compassion, especially when the lawbreaker is a game-breaker.

I don't miss it yet, I tell Jimmy. But give me time.

Not that the Johnnies are lily-white.

Let me rephrase that, since, racewise, they *are* lily-white. The most exotic minority on the roster is defensive tackle Pete Corkrean, a redheaded Iowan. Gagliardi likes to say that he can field national championship teams from within a seventy-five-mile radius of Collegeville. That is one monochromatic circle, racially speaking—the world's largest picnic paper plate. There is a reason St. Cloud is also known as the White Cloud. Dropping Willa off at kindergarten and Devin at day care, we have noticed that our fair-haired little angels look like everyone else's fair-haired little angels, towheaded descendants of the Norse and Rhinelanders who settled here in the previous century. Should Laura or I ever be required to testify against the Mob, we know where the Witness Protection Program might safely plunk us down.

While the Johnnies are without diversity, they are not without sin. On a recent Friday night, two were caught *in flagrante delicto* by campus security while attempting to remove two large potted plants from the foyer area of the Warner Palaestra. "We thought they'd look good in our living room," one of the perps confessed to me. Security let them off with a warning.

A few days before the Great Houseplant Caper, reserve linebacker Mike Omann injured his foot during an unauthorized, barefoot run through the sprinklers on the stadium grass. He inadvertently kicked a sprinkler head, splitting the webbing between two toes, earning more ire than sympathy from his head coach, who grumbled, "If we wanted to tear up the game field, we'd practice on it." Gags is notoriously protective of his field, and can be a bit dictatorial about keeping people off it. Scolded by the coach years ago, one young monk took revenge. After fortifying himself with strong drink on the night before a home game, the fellow stumbled into his monastery room with what appeared to be a dense, rolled-up shag carpet. It was, in fact, the "5" from the fifty-yard-line, which the drunk monk had carved out, rolled up, and taken home as a souvenir. Clearer heads prevailed; the turf was replaced and tamped down before dawn, and Gags was never the wiser.

The guys on defense check out video in the spartan office of defensive-line coach Gary Fasching, who looks as if he could suit up right now and make all-conference. Many was the morning I'd drop in at the McGlynn Fitness Center and see Gary knocking out reps of 350 pounds on the bench press. I'd remind myself to stay on his good side.

Gary started for Gags for two years at linebacker, then went into coaching. In 1986 he took over a down program at St. Cloud's Cathedral High. Using Gagliardi's philosophy, he led the Crusaders to two state championships. Four years ago he came back to Collegeville. His office is a cramped, windowless cell containing a desk, a TV and VCR, and a small couch. Wedged into the sofa on this Tuesday afternoon, as if it were a tub in a nursery rhyme, are Beau LaBore, Phil Trier, and Phil Barry. Beau you've met—he starts at linebacker. Trier starts at defensive tackle, Barry starts at free safety, and happens to be the best punter in the D-III. They are watching tape of this Saturday's opponent, Macalester.

I have a question. What's Macalester's nickname?

"The Fighting Scots," Fasching tells me. "One of the more interesting MIAC traditions is that their coach wears a kilt during the game."

He is poker-faced studying video; I can't tell if he is serious. LaBore, cracking up, gives it away.

The Scots are in orange, playing a team called Crown. The first three plays I see feature (1) a ball thrown well behind a Mac receiver, (2) a Mac tailback dropping a short flare pass that hits him in the tummy, (3) the Mac longsnapper getting the ball back to his punter on the third bounce.

"They play better as the game goes on," says Gary. How couldn't they, I say.

No matter how bad they are, you don't waste pity on the Scots. These guys are all going to end up in law school or med school or making a pile of dot-com dough. It's a prestigious academic institution with more money than it knows what to do with. The school's biggest benefactors are the Wallaces—the family that owns *Reader's Digest.* Down through the years, the Wallaces have dropped a ton of cash on Macalester. We may suck, the Scots can say, but we're destined to succeed in business and marry beautiful women with expensive highlight jobs. And we could buy your school with the interest on our endowment.

The bells have gone mad, they have broken out in euphonious riot at 3:45 on this Wednesday afternoon. A novice in the monastery named Gerard will profess "simple vows" in a four o'clock ceremony at the abbey church. He has been in the monastery for a year, and is now signing on for at least three more. The rite will transform him from a novice to a "junior monk." I crash the proceedings and am welcomed by a Benedictine who points me to a seat in the choir stalls horseshoeing the altar. If the pews facing the altar are general admission, these choir stalls are luxury boxes. In the pews, the presence of the balcony overhead forces your eyes to the front of the church, to the altar. From the choir stalls, one sees the huge, honeycombed stained-glass window of the façade, the bell banner beyond the glass, the sky beyond the bells.

Monks file in, swinging censers, the smoke lending this rite the feel of a Kiss concert. Unlike Gagliardi, Abbot Timothy Kelly cannot tape the names of his monks above their facemasks. The abbot stumbles briefly in welcoming the professee:

"Gerald. Gerry? Gerard!"

He recovers with aplomb, pointing out that at least *Gerard* knows who he is, and what he wants. The ceremony proceeds smoothly thereafter, Gerard kneeling before the abbot and accepting the Rule of St. Benedict, as Timothy says, "as the law of your life."

While we kneel—I have fallen out of kneeling shape—Father Tim Backous and Brother Paul Richards sing the Litany of St. Benedict, an ancient text of twenty-or-so petitions, or high hopes, for the junior monk. Among them:

May he live by faith.
May he take up his cross daily.
May he show forgiveness when wronged.
May he be filled with wisdom and understanding.

A smart-ass monk whispers amendments to the litany:

May he brush his teeth before prayer.
May he not chew his food with his mouth open.
May he abstain from looking at dirty pictures on the Internet.

He is trying to get me to laugh, but I am too strong.

Walking from church to football practice, I reflect on the momentousness of Gerard's decision. I recall my father's vague disappointment over the failure of any of his four sons to enter the priesthood. Several summers in a row, in the heart of Little League season, we were sent on a parish-sponsored retreat, the inauspiciously named "Project Probe." Its purpose was to give boys a chance to "explore" with members of the clergy the possibility of our having a priestly vocation.

Had any of the Murphy brothers heard such a call—believe me, we didn't—it would almost surely have been muted by the abominable assistant pastor at our parish outside Philadelphia in the seventies. The priest would maneuver me into his bedroom, ostensibly to take my confession. So I would fend off the advances of this goat, then sit in church while he stood at the rostrum, presuming to tell the parishioners how to live their lives. Since my earliest days in parochial school I had been dimly aware of a disconnect between the teachings of Christ and some of the lieutenants he chose to impart them here on earth. Around the time this creep came along, I stopped listening to priests altogether.

Shortly after I graduated from college, I began keeping a "Catholicism" file. Perusing it now, I find clippings with headlines such as: POPE STANDS FIRM AGAINST DIVORCE; GERMAN BISHOPS CITE CATHOLIC "DENIAL AND GUILT" AT HOLOCAUST; VATICAN TAKES

ON POPULATION PLANNERS; CATHOLIC FEMINISTS ASK, CAN WE REMAIN CATHOLIC?; ARCHBISHOP ADMITS RELATIONSHIPS; ABUSE CASE THREATENS TO BANKRUPT ARCHDIOCESE—a torrent of reasons supporting my decision to bail on the Church, a sheath of evidence of its wrong-headedness and hypocrisy (in my opinion) on so many issues, a reminder of why I've spent more than half my life pissed off at it.

My displeasure with the Church was part of the dense ball of cynicism I carried around for a long time. Benedict of Nursia would have recognized it as "an evil zeal of bitterness which separates from God and leads to hell." While it proved useful during my eight years in New York City—pushing one's way onto already-jammed subways, outracing octogenarians and pregnant women for taxis, that sort of thing—this hardheartedness turned out to be one of the things that landed me in marriage counseling. These days I'm trying to be less angry, to dissolve the ball. Hanging out with Benedictines, laughing with them, enjoying their friendship, learning about the genuinely good and far-reaching works they do in the name of God, makes it more difficult, less necessary to stay pissed off.

Speaking of pissed off, here come the Fighting Scots . . . all forty of them. As the Macalester players come sprinting and screaming out of the fieldhouse in a blaze of burnt orange and blue, their shouts strike me as a bit forced, a trifle self-conscious, as if they have seen *Braveheart* one too many times. I suspect they are trying to drown out their own fear.

If you have any choice at all, why play in a program that is cannon fodder for the league's stronger teams? There is at least one good reason, I discover.

Dennis Czech graduated from Macalester in 1983 and went into business in the Twin Cities. Even as his career flourished, he knew in his heart he wanted to be doing something else.

The call that changed his life came late in the '97 football season. The Scots were down on their luck, an assistant coach had quit, the team was in dire need of a replacement. The Scots knew that Czech had put in a couple seasons coaching after his graduation. Could he make it out to a few practices to give his alma mater a hand?

After talking it over with his wife, Sheila, Czech jumped in with both feet. He went full bore, throwing himself into recruiting in the offseason. When Tom Bell was fired, Macalester turned to Czech. Despite the fact that it would mean a "significant" pay cut, he took the job. "Sheila and I wanted to move our lives in a different direction," says Czech, who gamely undertook one of the most formidable rebuilding jobs in the country.

While the MIAC is the preserve of the student-athlete, some of its student-athletes are more studious than others. With their laudably lofty admissions standards, Macalester and Carleton will always have a harder time competing. "Our average ACT score here is a 29," says Czech. "I can't even look at a kid with anything lower than a 24, 25 ACT"—that's about the average at St. John's—"and those guys have maybe a fifty-fifty chance of getting accepted."

Salt in the wound: where a guy with a 29 or 30 ACT is eligible for academic scholarship money at other MIAC schools, "here, that's average, so he gets nothing."

He does not want to sound self-pitying. "There are kids out there for us," he says. He sells 'em on the Twin Cities, on the school's formidable reputation, on the fact that they'll play immediately. He's getting results, just not the kind you dazzle recruits with. *We're losing much closer games.*

I find myself admiring Czech, who cast off the yoke of a lucrative but unfulfilling career to follow his bliss. Like him, I have taken leave of a comfortable professional situation and ventured into the unknown. Unlike him, I'll be hauling my butt back to California—and my safe, old job—as soon as the weather turns.

You can almost hear the clown music on the Scots' first possession. Not only do they go three-and-out, but the longsnapper hikes the ball over the head of the punter, who kicks the ball out of the back of the end zone for a safety. I knew Macalester had a great soccer tradition. I just didn't expect to see evidence of it on their first possession.

For the second straight week, the Johnnies are poor closers, disinclined to go for the jugular. The offense fails to score points on its first three possessions, and St. John's sits on its absurd, 2–0 lead for the rest of the first quarter. Legions of second-, third-, fourth-, and fifth-stringers watch with mounting impatience. They've been practicing for a month, they want to get in a game and *hit* someone. But as long as the first team keeps farting around, they can't get on the field.

Now it is early in the second quarter. The Johnny offense hasn't done bubkes for four series and the Scots are starting to think, Maybe we can play with these guys. On first down at the St. John's 27, Linnemann calls a draw to Moore. O'Hara blocks down on the defensive tackle, who stands up, making Chad's job easy. Right guard Josh Pantzke pulls, gets a piece of the end—nothing textbook, but enough. Tight end Stanger drives the linebacker down into a morass of limbs in the middle, and for the first time today, Moore finds himself alone on the interstate. Fifty yards later he is tackled. Four plays later he is in the end zone. The Chris Moore show has begun, and Macalester is finished.

Moore has been a revelation to me. Father Wilfred spent three weeks in training camp poking me enthusiastically in the ribs, saying, "See that guy, 41? He's gonna have a great season." But Moore doesn't squander his moves on scout-teamers during the week, so I had to take Wilfred at his word. I assumed he was exaggerating.

He wasn't. I first saw it in the Eau Claire game, at the end of his fifty-five-yard punt return for a touchdown. With one Blugold to beat, Moore hip-faked the poor boy halfway back to Wisconsin, sold him a parcel of swampland, a used, '74 AMC Pacer with a cracked engine block. Moore is *sweet*, and could be playing a lot of places other than St. John's.

He is the best back in this little conference. Although he lacks remarkable straight-ahead speed, Moore is never run down from behind. He covers up for two dozen missed blocks every Saturday, hurling himself into fleeting creases, turning minus-twos into four-yard gains. A master of the cutback, he's got a bit of Terrell Davis in him: hard-nosed, elusive but economical, won't waste a full-fledged shimmy where a feint will do.

Moore finishes the day against Macalester with 278 yards on twenty-seven carries, breaking the twenty-three-year-old Johnny record for yards rushing in a game. The previous mark was held by Tim Schmitz. "Ironically," the next day's *St. Cloud Times* reports, Schmitz "also had [his] record-setting day against Macalester." (An inability to distinguish irony from coincidence, I will discover, is the least of the paper's problems.)

While Czech, God bless him, is refusing to claim a moral victory—"there are no moral victories at Macalester," he tells the *Times*—his players are busy finding solace in their hard-fought, moral victory. "We've got forty guys on our team and we go into the half trailing the number five team in the nation 15–0," quarterback Aaron Quitmeyer tells me. "We can build on that." Adds Mac wideout David Schumacher, "We may not get a lot of respect, but the fact is, we're a much better team than we were last season."

In response to questions about what it's like to play at Macalester, both Quitmeyer and Schumacher speak of a kind of jock apartheid, a real-life Revenge of the Nerds. "Here's Macalester," says Quitmeyer, holding his hands a yard apart, "and here's the football team." Adds Schumacher, "A lot of people aren't in the athletic crowd. We feel sort of apart."

Shunned at home, routed on the road. I feel for the Scots. I will be pulling for them. They will win one game the rest of the way.

"Let all guests who arrive be received like Christ." So it says in the 1,500-year-old volume by which the St. John's monks live their lives, *St. Benedict's Rule for Monasteries*. Hospitality is the signature virtue of the Benedictines, none of whom is more hospitable than Father Tim Backous—Timo to his friends, which would include virtually every student on campus. Timo is a big, big-hearted man who is smiling bravely when we arrive, despite his depression over the fact that his beloved Vikings were upset by the Raiders. Timo realizes that last season's sixteen wins were a cruel, illusory fluke; that the Vikes are once again destined for mediocrity. (Timo will be in Italy during Minnesota's season-ending playoff loss to the St. Louis Rams. He will send me an e-mail detailing the charms of

Orvieto and Florence, concluding it with this quintessentially Minnesotan sentiment, dour yet hopeful: "P.S. The Vikings suck . . . but I think they'll be good next year.")

One of seven Backous children from Aberdeen, South Dakota, Timo entered St. John's as an undergraduate in 1979 and has never left. In keeping with the Benedictine tradition of versatility, he wears several hats here. He is the university chaplain, presiding over the campus ministry; he is a professor of theology, teaching one of the most popular courses on campus, the Theology of Sexuality and Marriage. He celebrates the student mass at 9 P.M. each Sunday, regularly packing in six or seven hundred Johnnies and Bennies as eager to be enlightened by his homilies as they are to side-eye one another and whisper plans for after church.

Timo is also the public-address announcer at Johnny football games, a voice of warm welcome to friends and family of opposing teams. While he is no homer, he has mastered the use of subtle pauses and nuanced inflections, enabling him to insult opponents without their realizing they've been dissed.

Listen to this: "Linhoff's extra point is good, making the score St. John's 14, Wisconsin-Eau Claire . . . zero."

Note the pause. Do you think that is an accident? And when "zero" finally crosses his lips, it is weighted with tiny measures of disdain, pity, lack of surprise, and a hint of weariness. Listen again:

"Linhoff's extra point is good, making the score St. John's 14, Eau Claire"—*it is a waste of my breath and time to further belabor what is obvious to all present: that our overmatched friends from the Badger State don't belong on the same field with us; that despite being the best the Wisconsin Intercollegiate Athletic Conference has to offer, they have been playing for fifteen minutes and the number of points we have allowed them is*—"zero."

Later in the semester, to ensure that I experience the real Stearns County, Timo will take me to the Buckhorn, a taxidermy-intensive tavern in Avon, just up the road from Collegeville. Our entrance will turn the heads of the locals. The tension melts when Timo is recognized by a man on a barstool. It turns out he is a former maintenance worker at St. John's. He wants to buy Timo a drink. (Timo accepted a ginger ale.) He was marrying a wonderful woman he had known for two weeks. Would Timo do the service?

While my ecclesiastic friend tap dances around that one, I case the place. Highly suspect pickled foods—turkey gizzards, for instance—float malevolently in jars behind the bar. The walls are crowded with antique shotguns; a stuffed fox encased in Plexiglas; the heads of numerous bucks . . . a moosehead. A sign says, I GOT A GUN FOR MY WIFE . . . GOOD TRADE, HUH?

Back in the car, I betray my fear and small-mindedness by poking fun at the locals. "Actually," says Timo, "they're really nice, and they work really hard. They're good people."

I feel myself shrinking until I fall like a muffin crumb into a crease in the upholstery. When I finish resenting Timo for making me feel small, I admire him for his Benedictine charity and kindness. He is as comfortable among the dirt farmers of Stearns County as he is among cardinals and popes.

That's right, Timo has met the pope. A couple times. While studying for his doctorate in Rome, he received as guests some friends from Stearns County: Rick Theis and his parents, Gert and Ray. By calling in a favor, Timo was able to get the family "papal audience tickets" for a mass in St. Peter's Square. When the mass ended, His Holy Father Pope John Paul II descended from the altar. While Gert clutched the hand of the pontiff, tearfully informing him of how she had raised thirteen children in the church, no one noticed her husband reach beneath the pew and retrieve a brown grocery sack, then pull from it a gift for His Holiness, a cheap, red baseball cap bearing the legend:

BESTE'S CORNER BAR
SAUK CENTRE, MN

Against all odds—miraculously, really—the pontiff took the proffered cap, then raised his hands in benediction, declaiming in his heavy Polish accent, "God bless Beste's Corner Bar." Ray died some years ago, but his legend in Sauk Centre is secure.

I had always looked upon this pope as a retrograde, inflexible scold. If Timo's story is true—and if it passed Timo's lips, you know it is—maybe I need to rethink this Karol Wojtyla, this JP II.

Some devout Christians wear WHAT WOULD JESUS DO? bracelets. Timo's asks WHAT WOULD SCOOBY DO? As the season unfolds we will discover within our friend a subtle, rebellious streak. The framed illustration of *South Park*'s Eric Cartman hanging on the wall in Timo's campus ministry office is another indication that this man is not your average chaplain. While studying at San Anselmo, the Benedictines' mother abbey in Rome, Timo found himself exasperated with the dolorousness that came over the community on Good Friday. To lighten things up, he allowed a piece of spinach to dangle from the corner of his mouth at dinner, making animated conversation while pretending not to know it was there. Soon the entire refectory was in stitches, with the exception of the abbot primate—the world's highest ranking Benedictine, who glared daggers at this impertinent American, and properly so. Such "coarse jests," writes Benedict in his *Rule for Monasteries*, "we condemn everywhere with a perpetual ban."

Timo serves us pizza. After learning of Laura's gluten intolerance, he purchased wheat-free crust. She is touched. God knows I've never done any such thing for her. My attitude toward her food allergies has always been more along the lines of: Well, honey, maybe you need to just suck it up. Timo's consideration gives me pause. For the duration of our visit, he keeps what he calls "Laura's cabinet" stocked with the weird foods she is able to eat. It is incredibly thoughtful.

Brother Paul Richards, the abbey's musical director, has joined us for dinner. He is the monk I'd noticed at Brother Gerard's profession of vows. Paul was conducting the Abbey Schola, or choir, wielding his baton like Arturo Toscanini. Paul also directs the regionally renowned St. John's Boys' Choir. (When I asked him, after the season, how things were going with the choir he informed me, "We kicked some choral butt at Midnight Mass.")

Paul is a good-looking man who devotes perhaps a bit more time to his appearance than some of his brethren. (Unbeknownst to him, another monk has arranged for a woman who works at the university to remark, whenever she sees Paul, "Nice ass.") One is as likely to see him in the fitness center as one is to see him elsewhere on campus, covertly drawing on a Marlboro Light. He has a wonderful, ever so slightly wicked sense of humor and a teensy chip on his shoulder. The Benedictine order is comprised of priests, who have been ordained and can celebrate mass; and brothers, who haven't and can't. For centuries a caste system existed within the order, with brothers relegated to second-class citizenship. Only in recent decades have they closed the gap. Paul is the Al Sharpton of the St. John's brotherhood, vigilant for any slight or hint of disrespect. It is a pet peeve of his that so few people know the difference between a priest and a brother.

He fears he may someday find himself on a doomed airliner. "The crash I can handle," he says. "But in the moments *before* the crash, people will come to me for absolution, and I'll have to tell them, 'I'm sorry, I'm a monk, not a priest.' And they'll say, 'But, you're wearing black.' And I'll spend my last minutes on earth explaining the difference."

He is one of fifteen Richards kids from Virginia, Minnesota, at the base of the Mesabi Iron Range. Paul went to high school with Jack and Stevie Carlson, the real-life inspirations for the brawling, bespectacled Hanson brothers from *Slapshot*. This is, to my way of thinking, a virtually untrumpable claim to fame, *Slapshot* being the best sports movie of all time. With his long experience placating rambunctious nieces and nephews, Paul springs into action when my children make the inevitable leap from annoying to insufferable. Plucking them from Timo's apartment, we drive to the abbey church and descend into the crypt.

There are forty side chapels ringing the basement of the church. The heavy wooden doors leading to the side chapels are locked, but Paul has a key. We visit the one dedicated to the Frenchman, Saint Cloud—San KLOO, is the correct pronunciation—after whom the neighboring megalopolis is named. ("That would make him what," says Laura, later, "The patron saint of strip malls?")

We see Saint Thomas Aquinas. Rather, we see a woodcarving of that brilliant and corpulent theologian, his arms upraised, his vast bulk somehow not a burden. So fat was Thomas, says Paul, with a tour-guide's timing, that a semicircle had to be cut out of his dinner table, just so he could get close enough to eat. With the knowing grin of a man about to reveal his *pièce de résistance*, Paul ushers us into the chapel of Saint Lawrence. "Always a crowd-pleaser," he says.

In the dark, subterranean stillness, the story of Saint Lawrence takes on added awfulness. As one of the seven deacons of Rome in the mid-third century, it was Lawrence's misfortune to fall into disfavor with the city's prefect, a pagan who commanded that he be grilled over hot coals. Rather than give the prefect the satisfaction of seeing him suffer, Lawrence merely remarked, shortly before his death, "Turn me over, I'm done on this side."

There on the wall is a sculpture depicting the grisly demise: the martyr, the gridiron, the angry flames at work on him. The children are horrified, yet mesmerized.

"Why are they burning him?" asks Willa.

"Well," says Paul. He looks at me.

"Go nuts," I say. "We're all believers here."

"He believed that Jesus was God's son," says Paul. "They believed something else, and they were scared of him." This satisfies her.

I had fibbed to Paul. My faith, while not dead, is in Intensive Care. I was slapped, spanked, and otherwise corporally punished by nuns in elementary school, but then, who wasn't? While it seldom hurt, the physical discipline meted out by these crones did not exactly help me think of them as the earthly agents of Christ. Then there was the assistant pastor whose advances I literally had to fend off.

I stopped attending mass when I stopped living under my parents' roof, my faith having suffered grievous wounds long before then. When Willa got old enough to start asking questions about God, Laura and I had some decisions to make. I was inclined to boycott organized religion altogether. Bad idea, said Laura. She pointed to some of our Jewish friends, who, while not attending temple every week, nonetheless stayed under the umbrella of their faith, celebrating holidays and making sure they passed on a culture to their children.

"Religion is like baseball," says outfielder Steve Hovley in Jim Bouton's timeless *Ball Four.* "Great game, bad owners." Indeed, why let the close-mindedness of a few bad owners, a handful of reactionaries in funny hats, ruin the faith for us? Laura and I decided to pass on the Catholic culture to our children. We would become cafeteria Catholics, using those aspects of the Church we found useful, and leaving the rest of it—the intolerance of gays and birth control; the second-class citizenship that the Vatican insists is a woman's lot—on the shelf. We attend mass frequently. The children have been baptized; will take their First Holy Communion, and be confirmed. As they grow older, we will assure them that it's okay to ignore the medieval dogma emanating from the Holy See. I don't doubt that the Catholic traits that did so much to shape my personality—the consuming shame, the overriding guilt—will enter my children by osmosis. And that's okay. Many is the morning shame and guilt have gotten me out of bed.

On the way out, we peer into the locked reliquary, which holds a glass-encased tomb containing the skeleton of the boy-martyr Peregrin. It is an anticlimax. The bones are shrouded, out of sight. Plus, we don't know how Peregrin died. Some alleged skeleton, a rumor of old bones, is no match for the story of Larry on the barbie.

5

ST. THOMAS

There are book smarts and there is common sense. Aaron Krych, the name rhymes with itch, was blessed with a wealth of the former. One August evening the junior chemistry major was walking down Fruitfarm Road, past the Gagliardis' driveway, when whom did he encounter but the head coach, who was taking out the garbage. That player and coach proceeded to engage in pleasant conversation is no surprise, Gagliardi being a gregarious sort. The angry, scolding tone he'd adopted at a meeting several nights earlier was the decided exception, rather than the rule.

John's mood had darkened when he recalled the Tee-Shirt Scandal of '98. During the week preceding the St. Thomas game, some Johnny entrepreneur printed up 500 or so tee shirts. The front posed the question: WHAT DO MONICA LEWINSKY AND ST. THOMAS HAVE IN COMMON? The back provided the marginally clever reply: THEY BOTH SUCK.

The shirts sold out. Students loved them. The insult to the Johnnies' MIAC archrival was pointed; the play on words—to members of the Beavis and Butthead generation, at any rate—harmless. Gagliardi took a different view. Where others saw an almost innocuous joke, he saw a blight on a program known for its wholesomeness and integrity, a reputation he'd been five decades in the making. "How the hell can you wear a tee shirt that just tells the world how little class you have?" he thundered in the meeting room that night. "That was pretty vulgar stuff. I don't know who's more stupid, the guy who prints them up, or the guy who wears it." This occasioned uncomfortable squirming: more than a few players own the shirts, and one of them, it is said, designed and sold them.

Gagliardi was a few minutes into his chat with Krych when he noticed that the block print on his fullback's shirt posed a question . . . whose twin subjects were St. Thomas and a certain sore-kneed Clintern.

There followed the white-hot farrago of word and sentence fragments that is one's clue that Gagliardi is beyond pissed off; one's signal to get out of his way:

"Is that? Jesus Chr . . . I can't believe it! Aaron, how many times . . . Christ, get it off! Just, take it off right now!"

"I've never seen him so mad," says Krych, who obeyed wordlessly. Gagliardi took the shirt and—following some characteristic confusion about whether it belonged in the trash or one of the recycling bins—cast it in the garbage. Krych walked home half-naked.

The 2–0 Johnnies travel to O'Shaughnessy Stadium this Saturday to take on 1–1 St. Thomas. It's Tommy week, which means you will see around campus plenty of the Monica Lewinsky tees, which abound despite Gagliardi's best efforts to eradicate them. You just won't see them on any of the football players.

Jimmy is in Linnemann's face the moment the quarterback steps onto the practice field Tuesday. "Where were you today?"

Linnemann knows what he means. Despite watching a ton of St. Thomas tape yesterday, he did no video work today. "I was researching my senior thesis," he says, "and then I had to get treatment" for his sore throwing elbow. "You know I watched about four hours yesterday."

Jimmy is not placated. "I'm serious," he says. "You've *got* to watch film. This cannot be like the Eau Claire game last year, where you didn't watch enough film."

Jimmy played for his father from 1985 to 1988 and is in his eighth season as one of his assistant coaches. More so than anyone else on staff, Jimmy is willing to deliver harsh criticisms. The players see him as his father's pit bull. Linnemann has already stalked out of a film session after calling Jimmy an "asshole"; they made up over lunch a couple days later. Even by Jimmy's standards of asperity, this latest knock on Linnemann is tough. He is laying the blame for the '98-season-ending loss at the quarterback's feet. While the special teams guys practice kickoffs, I approach Tom. He is hurt and angry—precisely what Jimmy wanted.

"I think he thinks that he's challenging me, and waiting to see how I'll respond," says Tom.

Jimmy tells me the next day that he doesn't think Linnemann took the Macalester game seriously. "I know it's not that easy to get up for some opponents," he says, "but Tom has to understand, the young guys on this team are counting on him to get in the games. Plus, you let a team like that hang around long enough, all of a sudden they think they can play with you. That's how you lose games."

It's not easy being Tom during Tommy Week. Football is just *part* of his life, which is kind of the point of playing at St. John's. His morning starts at seven, when he stops by the local coffee house, the Meeting Grounds, for a cup of joe, then heads for Rocking 101.7 in St. Cloud.

Disgusted by the chronic errors and mispronunciations perpetrated every morning by the guy who read the sports news at WHMH, his favorite FM station in St. Cloud—"This guy would pronounce the *l*'s in Vinny Castilla," says Linnemann—he called to complain. "I could do a better job than the guy you got doing it now," he said.

Well, came the reply, why don't you come down here and give it a try?

Since then, "Touchdown Tommy" has been a fixture on morning drive time, bantering with DJ Justin Hannine between songs by Kiss and Guns N' Roses. A rival station has a contest they call the Secret Sound. To poke fun at it, Linnemann and Hannine came up with their own contest, the Secret Smell. Listeners who guess the correct odor—"for instance," says Linnemann, "the sweat-absorbing band of cloth lining the inside of a baseball cap"—win jackpots that sometimes approach five dollars.

On the Monday of Tommy Week, Linnemann had to bail from the radio station at 8:30 to make it to his nine o'clock: Latin-American Politics, taught by a terrific prof named Gary Prevost, who on this morning has the class divide into discussion groups. Linnemann's group agrees that until the end of World War II, the U.S. had been willing to support pro-democracy, reformist parties in Central America. "Afterward," says Tom, who has done the reading, "anyone who was a staunch anti-Communist would do. Pinochet, Batista—those were some bad dudes."

The discussion turns to the Reagan-supported contras in Nicaragua. "Oliver North's Freedom Fighters," says a guy wearing an earring. "What a joke. They ran drugs."

"We were too busy seeing if trickle-down economics really worked, to pay any attention," says Linnemann.

Tom and the anti-Ollie discuss the CIA's many bungled attempts to kill Castro. "That's why I respect him," says the anti-Ollie. "The man's a survivor."

"Good ballplayer, too," says Tom, who spent the previous January in Cuba, and whose senior thesis is on Cuban baseball players. "Couldn't hit a curve, though. Had to settle for being a dictator."

Odd that the Tommies should play in a stadium named for one Ignatius Aloysius O'Shaugnessy, considering that an Ignatius O'Shaughnessy is credited with scoring a touchdown *for St. John's* in a 16–0 triumph over St. Thomas on Thanksgiving Day, 1901.

That contest, played in St. Paul's Lexington Park, marked the Johnnies' first-ever intercollegiate football game, according to *Scoreboard: A History of Athletics at St. John's University.* "In defeating

St. Thomas," the St. John's *Record* crowed soon after, the Johnnies "hold the ball over all Minneapolis and St. Paul teams."

It turns out that Ignatius was enrolled at St. John's until he and his posse blew off Vespers one evening to attend a party, and were summarily expelled. Rather than face his parents, according to a story in the 1999 fall edition of the St. Thomas alumni magazine, O'Shaughnessy caught a bus to St. Thomas, where he threw himself on the mercy of the priest in charge of admissions.

At St. Thomas, founded by Archbishop John Ireland and built on land donated by an Irishman, O'Shaughnessy's surname could not have hurt his cause. The admissions officer's inclination toward compassion proved, for St. Thomas, a very profitable inkling indeed. After starring for the Tommies as a member of the football team *and* Philomatic Debating Society, the ex-Johnny went to Oklahoma as an oilfield wildcatter. By 1934, according to the university's I.A. O'Shaughnessy Papers, he was the head of the largest individually owned oil refineries in the world.

Which is why you will find on the St. Thomas campus, in addition to O'Shaughnessy Stadium, an O'Shaughnessy Hall, an O'Shaughnessy Library, and the O'Shaughnessy Educational Center. All told, this philanthropist donated nearly $5 million to the school. He wrote big checks, likewise, to the University of Notre Dame and the College of St. Catherine, and was widely known as the largest single benefactor to Catholic education. He was granted audiences with popes, and in 1967 was made a papal count.

When the Tommies lose to the Johnnies, as has happened five of the last six times the football teams have met, the citysiders can still draw comfort from the knowledge that O'Shaughnessy's munificence was matched, apparently, by his determination that St. John's never get a nickel of his money.

The life and times of I.A. O'Shaughnessy lend spice to one of the country's most delightfully intense little rivalries. St. John's received its charter in 1857, St. Thomas twenty-eight years later. If you want to play quality football at a private, Catholic university in Minnesota, you go to one or the other. So even though the schools have more than they care to admit in common, even though students at one often seriously considered going to the other, and have numerous friends at the other, they choose—this week in particular—to dwell on the differences.

"They have John Gagliardi, we had Vince Lombardi Jr.," wrote Gene McGivern, the Tommy sports information director. (Indeed, the son of the Hall of Fame coach was a hard-nosed Tommy fullback who scored two touchdowns in the 1962 Homecoming win over Gustavus Adolphus.) "They have the beauty of the country, we have the buzz of the cities. They have convenient parking, we have women."

So I am told. St. Thomas enjoys a reputation, enhanced by a recent mention in *Playboy*, for having exceptionally attractive women. It is this topic, more than the Tommies' offensive or defensive tendencies, to which the Johnnies most faithfully return during the week. Many of the players who make the trip, in fact, will stay in St. Paul Saturday night, crashing in the rooms of their Tommy buddies and hoping to make the acquaintance of some of their distaff classmates.

"But these young women are Catholic," I point out to a half-dozen Johnnies during a Wednesday afternoon video session. "They're chaste and pure. They're saving themselves."

"Don't kid yourself," says Linnemann. "They're filthy." He briefly dated the current girlfriend of one of the Tommies' starting defenders—something he hopes to remind the fellow of on Saturday, on the field. "Plus they're all from Wayzata, so they're loaded."

To me it is a classic example of the grass-is-always-greener syndrome. There is no shortage of pulchritude in Collegeville; I seldom cross campus without forcing myself to stifle a double take at some striking Benny. (It helps me to remind myself that my five-year-old daughter is closer in age to these students than I am.) Still, anecdotal evidence suggests that the Tommies are, in this important area, richly blessed. As the season goes on, I become friendly with Anthony LaPanta and Steve Varley, who do the Johnnies' radio broadcasts. Varley is an ex-Johnny quarterback whose first-ever start for St. John's came against the Tommies in '89. The coin was tossed by Gretchen Carlson, a native of Anoka, Minnesota, who also happened to be the reigning Miss America. The Johnny captains did not follow the flight of the coin that afternoon, Varley recalls, and could be heard making complimentary but unprintable observations about Ms. Carlson as they returned from midfield.

"St. Thomas was the preppy school," says an ex-Tommy who has been much in the news of late. "During the height of student activism in the seventies, people used to say the only reason a bunch of Tommies would take over a building would be to hold a kegger. The St. John's guys were yokels who'd stumble in from some Stearns County bar in time for class.

"Stereotypes aside, by the time they're twenty-six, they're great buddies. They realize they have more in common than they ever cared to admit."

The speaker is University of Minnesota athletic director Mark Dienhart, a former all-America offensive lineman for the Tommies who served as head coach at his alma mater from 1981 to 1986.

Is he ever nostalgic for his days in D-III? "Virtually every day for the last several months," he says, and we both have a good laugh. As everyone in this state surely knows, the U's men's athletic program has spent the last six months reeling from revelations of academic fraud and administrators' handling of sexual assault cases involving athletes. A former tutor, Jan Ganglehoff, told the *St. Paul Pioneer Press* of having written hundreds of papers for as many as twenty basketball players. University officials are reported to have intervened in assault and criminal sexual-conduct investigations involving athletes. Head basketball coach Clem Haskins, who stood accused of making cash payments to players, bailed out in June with a $1.5 million buyout under his arm.

Although Dienhart's most serious offense will turn out to be that he took people at their word when they lied to his face, the scandal will bring him down, too. In less than two months, he will resign.

This afternoon, he is happy to reminisce about his days coaching against Gagliardi, whom he beat twice in six attempts. When Dienhart was named Minnesota's AD in 1995, he took a congratulatory call from Gagliardi, who said, "Mark, the best day of my life was the day you got out of coaching."

"Come to think of it," says Dienhart, "I may be the only coach in the history of St. Thomas that's gotten along with John." Indeed, the day before, current Tommy coach Don Roney called the football office to ask why a touchdown was missing from the game tape the Johnnies had sent. The explanation—that the videographer, a fifteen-year-old son of one of the Johnny assistants, had screwed up—was met with skepticism. Suspicions run deep during Johnny-Tommy Week. When I phoned Roney to talk about his team and the upcoming game, he was guarded and curt.

In Dienhart's opinion, one of the reasons the Tommies have had such limited success is that they get too tight for this game. "We told our guys it was just another game," he says. In 1986, the Tommies arrived in a ghostly, quiet Collegeville. The previous night, two St. John's students had fallen asleep on some seldom-used railroad tracks outside of town. A train had come along and cut them to pieces. The campus was in shock. Late in the fourth quarter, St. Thomas was up 56–21, and had the ball deep in Johnny territory. Rather than score again, Dienhart called off the dogs.

His defensive coordinator that day was Jerry Miller, who passed away in the spring of 1998. Shortly before he died, Miller was visited by a group of well-wishers, including his old head coach. As the group took leave of Miller, he grabbed Dienhart by the arm and pulled him close. The last words Miller ever said to him, Dienhart recalls, were these: "I'll never forgive you for not scoring 60 on Gagliardi."

Stretched out in the last seat on the bus to St. Thomas, Linnemann announces that he's back on schedule. He failed to vomit before the Macalester game, but has just fertilized some shrubs between the church and the computer center.

The first quarter-hour of the ride is quiet. Some of the guys are checking out the foliage—the oaks are beginning to go light orange and yellow—others are reading newspapers. Linnemann recalls being inspired by seeing Patrick Reusse, the fine and funny *Minneapolis Star Tribune* columnist, before the '98 season. "St. John's isn't going anywhere," Reusse had predicted on a local sports TV show. "They don't have a quarterback."

"I remember hearing that and thinking, 'Really?'" says Linnemann. Having gone 13–1 for the Johnnies since then, he feels a bit of subdued gloating is in order. "I guess we have a quarterback now," he says.

"Yeah," says O'Hara from three rows up, "but he's playing tight end."

Everyone in the back of the bus breaks up, especially Corey Stanger, the starting tight end and backup quarterback. You wouldn't guess it from his pulling-guard's build—Stanger goes six-three, 235—but he was an all-State quarterback at Becker High, just forty minutes down the road from Collegeville. He is a quiet guy with a ready smile, which he flashes every time I give him grief about his socks. (He wears these little anklets that barely peek out over his high-tops. It is not a look that shouts *speed to burn.*)

I see Corey every afternoon in the Cavern. Whenever I arrive, he is already there, poured into an easy chair, keeping his head in the game. After losing that quarterback battle with Linnemann—there were coaches who thought the job should have been Stanger's—it would have been understandable for him to cruise through his senior year, cheat a little on his video work.

Instead, he prepares like an Eagle Scout. I detect, behind Stanger's smiling serenity, a determination to be ready when and if Tom goes down.

Tom, meanwhile, is rehearsing a few indelicate remarks he might make—should he find himself in a pileup with the Tommy whose girlfriend they have in common. He talks to Sieben about what plays to run on the first series. This is the last in a series of exchanges that began Monday in "The Age of Goethe," the German class these two share. As he does every Monday, Linnemann passes Sieben a note with the name of a possible play, then awaits the scribbled feedback of his pet receiver.

"Open with Trips Right, Spread Dark," says Sieben. "Come back with Tackles-Over, then go up top with Cold"—the latter a pass play designed to leave dejected defensive backs saying, "Man, that was *cold*."

The chitchat subsides as the bus exits the freeway and rolls down tony Cretin Avenue and the parapets of O'Shaughnessy Stadium, designed to resemble a castle, come into view. A thousand or so spectators, an eighth of today's turnout, are waiting for the gates to open. As we disembark I hear Linnemann ask Sieben the question he has posed to him for the last seven seasons: "Ready to catch some balls today, Frog?"

The home team holds a slight edge over the visitors in that always fascinating game-within-a-game, the battle of the tee shirts. The uninspired perennial TOMMIES SUCK has been effectively neutralized with JOHNNIES SWALLOW. Another shirt, worn almost exclusively by Tommy girls, says SEX KILLS, GO TO ST. JOHN'S AND LIVE FOREVER. Talk about cold.

Johnnies still speak with grudging respect of the year enterprising Tommy students stashed a keg in the woods behind the Natural Bowl, filing out of the stands for refills as the need arose. While the Tommies have no monopoly on overindulging in alcohol in this rivalry, they seem to be less ashamed of it. YOU MAY WIN, BUT WE'LL BE DRUNKER, promises one shirt; GAME SHMAME—I'M BOOZING, says another.

The atmosphere is correspondingly festive—too much so for a woman who ascends the steps to the pantry-sized pressbox to complain about the rock music being played over the loudspeakers. "As a Catholic," she huffs, "I can't believe you would have this kind of music."

She directs her gripe at St. John's sports information director Michael Hemmesch, who says, "I'm sorry if the music offends you, but I didn't select it. I don't work here. See on my shirt here where it says 'St. John's'?"

She exits in a huff, declaring, "AC/DC should *not* be played at a Catholic institute. Jesus would not be proud."

The Church Lady, as we come to refer to her, raises an interesting theological point: If one cannot crank "Back in Black" every once in a while in heaven, does one really want to go there? If the Church Lady was that exercised over a few raunchy lyrics in

"Givin' the Dog a Bone," how did she respond to the halftime streaker who broke a policeman's tackle and sprinted the length of the field before he was finally subdued? My guess is that she could not bring herself to look . . . away.

Linnemann is going up top, going for the throat. It is the second play of the second series and the offense hasn't done a thing, and what's up with that? Time to throw the bomb. Trips right, Stanger split wide to the left. Linnemann takes a five-step drop and looks . . . and looks—Stanger is open in the left flat, but really, where is the glory in such a piddling completion?—then pulls the ball down and runs.

Left tackle Spencer Sokoly does his job on the play, keeping Tommy defensive end Mike Leiss off Linnemann for at least three seconds. As Linnemann runs up the middle, Leiss sheds Spencer and lassoes Linnemann around the waist. Leiss somehow swings around and ends up behind Tom, underneath him, anchoring his left leg to the turf as middle linebacker Frank Streit flies in for his free shot.

Streit played with Linnemann in the '96 Minnesota High School all-Star game. Tom wore Sieben's No. 3 in that game to protest Frog's exclusion from it. That night, Linnemann became the only quarterback in the history of the Minnesota High School all-Star game to be flagged for unsportsmanlike conduct. "I got blatantly facemasked, the official wouldn't call it," he recalls, "so I called him a 'f_____ puke.'"

On that helmet, now gathering dust in Tom's basement, is a sticker from Streit, who is not thinking about the '96 all-Star game as he comes in high and hard and bends his rooted quarry over backward, snapping Linnemann's left fibula with an audible pop. It is a vertical fracture, spiraling halfway up his shin, and will require a titanium plate and eight screws.

"When I got high-lowed, it was the weirdest thing," Tom would later recall. "I could hear my own bone crack. I'm lying there thinking, 'Wow, I can't believe I'm done.' At least it took away all the suspense."

No one on the sideline knows what Tom knows. When he goes

fetal and stays down, we mill around, hoping it's a strain or a sprain. A trainer comes off the field to fetch a splint. Not good. A few Tommy students, obviously under the influence, take up the cry, "Let's go, Linnemann."

"Now there's some class," says Grady McGovern, on the sideline. Tom's Aunt Beth is in the stands shouting, "Those sons of bitches!" To the medical personnel, she yells, "Get him on a cart!"

"Get up and walk it off," says Beau to no one. But Linnemann isn't going anywhere but to St. Paul's United Hospital. He will be driven by his father, John, the baseball coach and German teacher who will lose his cool in the car, shouting at innocent motorists who impair his swift passage to the emergency room, "Get out of the way! My son's got a broken leg!" Tom, in agony, will go slack the instant the morphine hits his bloodstream and start telling jokes to the nurses.

"Screwdriver walks into a bar, bartender says, 'Hey, we got a drink named after you.' Screwdriver says, 'You got a drink named Steve?'"

One of the nurses is a black guy named Sedrick. By keeping the Linnemanns laughing, he keeps them from crying. Sedrick played high school football, but he played safety. "Quarterback," he huffs, feigning disgust when he learns Tom's position. "Now, if you were a *safety*, you wouldn't have this whole *entourage* with you."

Suddenly, Linnemann feels cold, which reminds him of a joke:

"Baby polar asks his father, Dad, are we 100 percent polar bear? The dad says, As far as I know, we are. Ask your mother.

"Mom, are we 100 percent polar bear? Are you sure we don't have some brown bear, maybe some Kodiak mixed in?

"As far as I know we're pure polar bear, son. Why do you ask?

"'Cause I'm f______ *cold*."

On a bitter February weekend in 1997, Linnemann borrowed Aunt Beth's Buick Park Avenue, picked up his buddy Frog and drove two hundred-plus miles through a snowstorm to Northern State University in Aberdeen, South Dakota. Northern's coaches wanted them to become a part of the Wolves' rich Division II football tradition. Sieben and Linnemann arrived late, but were not as tardy as another bad-attitude recruit, a gangly and lethargic tackle with no apparent pigment in his skin. This was Chad O'Hara, from St. Cloud Tech High. The Minnesotans banded together. While the other recruits sat politely at a welcome meeting held in their honor, O'Hara and the Melrose boys chattered and cracked wise throughout a speech given by the university president, whose wife fixed them with an icy glare. Other recruits were advised to steer clear of the Minnesotans.

It was not exactly like being wooed by UCLA. "Normally they take recruits to a party or something," Sieben recalls. "They took us to the local mall to see a movie." Feeling a bit churlish themselves after a forced viewing of *Grumpier Old Men*, the Minnesotans ditched their Wolf hosts, bought a case of beer and iced it in the bathtub of Tom and Ben's hotel room. While shooting the shit late into that Friday night, the trio agreed that they would never in a million years come to Northern State.

"So," said O'Hara to the Melrose boys, "where you gonna go?"

All three recall what Linnemann said next: "Let's go to St. John's and win a national championship." It was agreed.

Linnemann's last, best shot at fulfilling that dream ended with the pop of a spiral fracture in the first quarter of the third game of his fourth year at St. John's. It is a severe blow to Tom. For all of his extracurricular activities—the student senate, the radio gig—his identity is wrapped up in being the star quarterback. In front of the team and coaches over the next few weeks, he will present a brave face. On the phone with Carla one afternoon, he will show his true feelings:

"No more football at St. John's," he said, softly. "It's real hard."

It will be no less difficult for the rest of the squad. While they never quite replace his leadership, the Johnnies do immediately begin avenging his loss. Two plays after he is carted off the field, Phil Barry pins the home team on its 8-yard line with a sixty-eight-yard punt. Senior linebacker Brandon Novak picks off St. Thomas quarterback Greg Kaiser, and Moore scores two plays later. That's how it's going to have to be without Linnemann. The defense that nearly gave away the first game will have to carry the squad.

★ ★ ★

Sieben sets up a touchdown with a spectacular, leaping catch on the Johnnies' next possession. As he gets off the ground, I see him running smack past a Tommy defensive back. Gagliardi insists that his players comport themselves with class, and they usually do. His best friend just having had his career truncated, however, Ben cannot restrain himself from standing over the Tommy he'd just burned and shouting, "You are my bitch!"

With the score 13–6 at halftime, Roney, the Tommy coach, is in the dressing room telling his players that they're in a tie game, basically. "We felt like we could play with them," St. Thomas cornerback Nick Halvorson tells me later. "Our coach has two mottoes: We're gonna outhit and outhustle everyone we play."

If you think about it, Nick, that's only one motto, which is one more than Gagliardi abides by. His players snicker behind his back when he breaks out his Nike jacket, across the back of which is written: JUST DO IT. During slow moments at practice, some Johnnies bat around Gagliardiesque variations on that slogan:

"I guess we could think about doing it. What do you think, Jimmy?"

"Criminy, Pantzke, just do it. It's not that complicated!"

"Let's say an Our Father, then get out there and just do it."

And while he's all in favor of hitting and hustling, Gagliardi would rather, given his druthers, *outscore* everyone he plays. It helps to be loaded at quarterback. Stanger comes out of the locker room and completes four of five passes, driving the team ninety-two yards for a touchdown. He is throwing on the run, putting balls in tight spots. One local high school coach is highly impressed. "Here is a guy who hasn't played quarterback in about four years, coming into the game and beating St. Thomas. Someone put up a statue of this guy." It is Mike Grant, an ex-Johnny tight end who is the head coach at powerful Eden Prairie High, and whose father, Bud, also did some coaching in this state.

On a long pass to the 5-yard line, Sieben climbs the free safety's back as if it were a ladder. He makes a miraculous grab, then jogs into the end zone.

It's 28–12, but the Tommies are driving. Kaiser drops back to pass. Before he can find a receiver, Corkrean the redheaded Iowan gets to him, wrapping his legs, holding him for the marauding Zirbes, who graduated from Melrose a year behind Linnemann. Zirbes pile-drives Kaiser into a hash mark, into the land of Nod. Standing over Kaiser's inert form—the Tommy quarterback is unconscious and done for the day—Zirbes cannot resist a non-Gagliardi-approved pump of his right arm.

On the Johnny sideline, someone shouts, "Go, Dutchmen!"

Reporters scrum around Corey Stanger after the game: Heather Burns of the *St. Cloud Times*, Ray Richardson of the *St. Paul Pioneer Press*, Jon Roe of the *Star Tribune*. I edge in close. Now that he's bailed the team out, I wonder, does Stanger pop off? Does he ask out loud why he's been looking up at Linnemann on the depth chart all this time?

What Corey says makes me want to cry: "I love to play quarterback, but I also know that we're a better team with Tom in there. He's not only a great quarterback, but he's a great athlete and a great leader. That's the part that hurts. I felt pretty sure I could do the job, and I knew all the other guys on the team would step up and help me. But we're going to miss all the other things Tom does for the team."

Stanger is my new hero.

After shaking hands with Roney, Gags sits on a bench in the shade by the bus, looking his years. Hot days, especially, take it out of him. He has expended as much energy over the last four hours as he does during the rest of his workweek. Brother Mark brings him a Sprite.

"Boy, that's tough on Tom," says Gags, sorrowfully. There may be a few things he could do better, says the coach, "but in the end, I look at this: the guy went 13–1 for us."

As the players trickle out of the dressing room, John carries out one of my favorite Johnny rituals. As each player walks past,

Gagliardi shakes his hand and gives him a ten dollar bill. It is meal money, which is why two dozen guys nearly fall down laughing when moon-faced freshman center Josh Dirlam takes his ten-spot and asks Gagliardi, "Is this for winning?"

"Yeah, Josh," says Spencer. "When we lose, we pay him."

Tom is groggy with painkillers when Jimmy gets him on the phone that night. He accepts Jim's kind words, but it's obvious something is bugging him. Finally, he spills: "This *sucks,* man. I never got my ten bucks!"

On the bus back to St. John's, the guys seem a little off-balance, elated to be 3-0, but sad about Tom. Each player feels a little guilty for being happy that Corey will get a chance to play. We arrived in Collegeville a few hours before a ripsnorter of an electrical storm. That night, Laura and I lie in bed watching the free show: wind-whipped trees and tridents of lightning piercing the sky. We don't get thunderstorms in the Bay Area. At the first roof-rattling thunderclap Devin had come sprinting down the hallway, leaning into the turn, hurtling through our doorway, a pulling guard in miniature. After hurling himself between us, he insisted he was not scared, his wide eyes and racing heart telling a different story. (Willa slept through it.) We assured Devin that because we had our big, strong house, and one another, the storm could not hurt us.

The three of us watched the storm for a while in our shelter within a shelter. This sabbatical is a temporary bulwark thrown up against the storm of our normal lives, the lives to which we will return. Our big breakthrough this week was that Devin no longer cries during the day-care drop-off. He isn't exactly whistling when I take my leave of him, but at least he isn't bawling. I am ever so slightly less anxious about the book. We four are slowly finding a routine in this place. Tonight's thunder notwithstanding, the volume is being turned down on our lives. As it starts to feel more and more like a sabbatical, as Laura and I rediscover each other, it is becoming clear to us that the forces buffeting our marriage are external: a pair of wonderful but active young children, combined with the chronic absences (and exhaustion-induced crankiness) of their father. If Laura and I can hang on until the kids learn just a *little* common sense, and enter grade school; if I scratch and claw and wheedle and plead for as much time at home as possible, we'll be okay. The storm cannot hurt us.

6

AUGSBURG

While it is great fun hanging with a D-III team—hell, Brother Mark gave me my own sack lunch for the bus ride back from St. Thomas!—I must admit the time away from the NFL has left a void in my life. I long for the choreographed celebrations of the pros: Deion's little soft shoe; the Saints who play leapfrog in the end zone following touchdowns that whittle their team's deficit to twenty-one points; and the late, lamented Dirty Bird, which the Falcons did to death in 1998, before nose-diving into the tank from whence they'd come.

This is what it's all about, kids. Run through a hole cleared by teammates, catch a ball thrown by a teammate who was protected by still more teammates—and what do you do? If you're in the NFL, you do a dance calling attention to yourself. You make an ass of yourself for doing what you're paid a fortune to do.

The truth, of course, is that those celebrations make me want to vomit, and are just another aspect of big-time sports I have fled to the heartland to escape. When New England Patriot Larry Whigham blocked a Philadelphia Eagles punt late in the season, he launched into his celebratory dance . . . while an alert Eagle scooped up the ball and ran for a first down. The Patriots lost and were eliminated from the playoffs.

Not that the Johnnies don't have their celebratory routines. Whereas Krych holds the ball by one of its points and hands it to the nearest official after he scores, Sieben opts for a short lateral. After his touchdowns, wide receiver Jeremy Forsell goes with a jaunty, overhand toss to the closest zebra. Following his game-sealing interception against the Tommies, LaBore propelled the ball to the referee as one would shoot a foul shot, complete with a nice follow-through—an audacious flourish, for a Johnny. Gagliardi is down on celebrations. "We *expect* to score," he says. "We *expect* to make big plays. We do it all the time. It's not like the Second Coming."

He made the point more emphatically to a defensive lineman named Tom Sullivan, who once recovered a fumble on the opponent's 5-yard line, rolled into the end zone, then stood and jumped for joy, celebrating what turned out to not be a touchdown.

Gagliardi was merciless in the ensuing film session, replaying Sullivan's gaffe over and over. "We spent five minutes watching him roll into the end zone, then back. In, then back," one of Sullivan's teammates told me. "And the whole time John is just *riding* him: 'Christ, Sullivan, don't you know the damned rules? You can't advance a fumble. And what the hell is this? We don't dance when we score. We expect to score!'"

The understated celebrations of the Johnnies stand in vivid contrast, this afternoon, to the behavior yesterday of the American Ryder Cup team. When Justin Leonard drained a forty-five-foot putt on the seventeenth hole, capping the greatest comeback in Ryder Cup history, he was engulfed on the green by a small mob of players, wives, caddies, girlfriends, and spectators. That boorish display was rendered still more embarrassing by the hideousness of the Americans' shirts, cannibalized, apparently, from someone's rumpus-room drapes. Doing a slow burn during the melée, still waiting to putt, was the dour Spaniard José María Olazábal, who is cranky at the best of times, as you would be if you had a history of feet problems, still lived with your parents, and bore a name that only Jim Nantz is able to pronounce correctly.

Little wonder the Yanks are being eviscerated in the European press, which found the jingoistic comportment of Minnesota's own Tom Lehman, in particular, over the top. Lehman might have spared himself this criticism, had he listened to Gagliardi. "He was all set to come up here and play quarterback," says Gags. "Instead, he decided to go to Minnesota on a golf scholarship. I said, 'Who goes to the University of Minnesota to play golf?' Thank God he didn't listen to me."

Tom's father, Jim, remains one of the top two running backs Gagliardi has ever coached. There he is in mid-fifties film clip, swinging out of the backfield, latching on to a screen pass, then turning upfield. Four opponents fall to the downfield blocks the Johnnies steadfastly refuse to practice. Three more opponents converge on Lehman; he is trapped.

I saw this footage in the spring of 1992, sitting in on the class the monks allow Gagliardi to teach, "Theory of Football." With Lehman surrounded, John froze the tape. "How can any mere mortal escape this predicament? He's trapped, right?" No takers. The kids know John too well. He rolled the tape. Lehman stops, sidesteps the defenders—who collide like the Three Stooges—and runs for six.

Gagliardi challenged the class. "What was it that enabled him to get away?" Dramatic pause. "Great coaching! *I'm* the one who said, 'This guy is a hell of an athlete, let's give him the ball.'" The class cracked up. "That's right," said Gagliardi. "Great coaching." No one disagreed.

He is not here today. None of the coaches are. They are forbidden to be with the team. For the first time in the history of the program, St. John's is being punished by the MIAC. Excuse us, Notre Dame. Could we squeeze in here, Minnesota? The simon-pure squad I drove cross-country to lionize turns out to be an outlaw program. The Johnnies are on probation.

Did a female booster embezzle funds, treat players to madcap Vegas weekends, have sex with them and bear one of their children, as Kim Dunbar did at Notre Dame? No. Did tutors write hundreds of term papers for the athletes, à la the "U?" No.

The Johnnies' sins are rather less interesting.

Basically, they showed up for practice three days early.

It was an honest mistake. NCAA rules stipulate that a team is allowed twenty-seven "practice opportunities" before the start of the academic calendar. While the Johnnies had just twenty-six practices in that time, they had thirty-three practice *opportunities*.

Confused? So, apparently, were the Johnny coaches. In the Jabberwocky world of NCAA bureaucratese, every day a team convenes, it is charged with two practice opportunities. Doesn't matter whether you practice once, twice, or, as in the case of many teams, three times. Those August Saturdays when the Johnnies practiced in the morning, then—unlike virtually every other football team in America—took the rest of the day off, counted for two "opportunities." The Monday when John gave the team the afternoon off so freshmen could make it to orientation? One practice, two opps.

Conference commissioner Carlyle Carter was unmoved by the fact that the Johnnies didn't *use* those extra opportunities; that the players spent that time golfing or splayed in front of their televisions or wolfing down Mom's lasagna. Carter could not have cared less that the squad was in violation of the *letter*, rather than the spirit of the law—a stricture instituted, ironically, to curb the foaming-at-the-mouth members of the coaching fraternity opposite Gagliardi on the football spectrum.

The commish *did* care that this was not the sole NCAA guideline those renegades from Collegeville had trampled. Another rule mandates that teams not wear shoulder pads for the first three days of practice, a law the Johnnies ignored, forgot, or never knew about. Since they barely hit one another anyway—since their workouts "have as much contact as a checkers tournament," wrote the *Star Tribune* in a piece mocking Carter and the MIAC—the Johnnies were again in violation of the letter, if not the spirit, of the law.

In addition to placing the entire Johnny athletic department on three years' probation (the MIAC later relented and applied the probation to the football team alone), the squad was stripped of one practice per week for six weeks. It no doubt disappointed the commissioner to learn that the Johnnies don't practice on Monday anyway, rendering that sanction moot. (It did mean, however, that

Monday film sessions became players-only affairs, resulting in a predictable surge of bad jokes and audible flatulence.)

The violations are so penny-ante, why hammer the program with three years of probation? Notre Dame only got two years for *L'affaire Dunbar.*

John doesn't trust himself to answer; he's afraid he'll say something that will get him in more trouble with the conference.

Jimmy shrugs and says, "That's Carlyle."

Carlyle Carter was hired in 1993 as the MIAC's first-ever executive director, or commissioner. Up until then, those duties had been handled (quite competently, by most accounts), by a part-time commissioner.

He and Gagliardi clashed from the start. "When I was hired," says Carter, "we had faculty reps, athletic directors, coaches, but no one who had the luxury of focusing on the day-to-day business of the conference. It was the coaches who controlled things.

"I come along, and all of a sudden we demand some accountability, that all the rules are followed. When there is a change, you can look at someone as an agent of change, or as the grim reaper."

The coaches in the league who dislike Carter don't see him as the grim reaper so much as they view him as a career bureaucrat who has saddled them with additional red tape. "I can be pretty anal about procedure," says Carter.

Despite his professed anality, his devotion to "the day-to-day business of the conference," it is said that the conference office has actually become less efficient, more sclerotic, since Carter took over. A few years back, Gagliardi sent a letter to the MIAC presidents, making this case, complaining about lengthy delays in reimbursements for conference-related expenses. One gets the feeling it's personal between these two. Is this a feud?

"John feels it is," says Carter, "although I take pains to tell him, it's not personal with me. In every conversation we have I make sure he understands that I am amenable to him."

Slapping a three-year probation on a program for petty violations—using a firehose to extinguish a votive candle, basically—is an odd way of demonstrating one's amenability. Why the harsh sanctions?

It turns out Gagliardi is a repeat offender, a recidivist. This otherwise kindly gentleman has a famously low tolerance for incompetent officials, and has been known, during the heat of battle, to snipe at them. "That's it!" a zebra finally said to him some years ago. "One more word and I'm throwing the flag!"

"Can you penalize me for what I'm thinking?" Gags asked him. No, came the reply.

"Good," said John, " 'cause I think you're horse——."

In a trice, to borrow from Keith Jackson, "The laundry was on the carpet."

Gagliardi was not sanctioned for expressing that opinion, or for telling reporters on another occasion that he actually liked officials, and would send them Christmas cards, if only he could find such cards in Braille. Several years ago, however, he was quoted in a newspaper criticizing a conference official by name. That the fellow richly deserved to be ripped did not stop Carter from forcing Gags to write a letter of apology, which was later judged insufficiently contrite. "The compliance committee felt [Gagliardi's apology] was as close to a non-apology as you could get," tut-tuts the commissioner. "I felt the conference should have sanctioned him at that point. I felt this was an issue of institutional control. Without institutional control, a minor offense could be a major offense."

One is reminded, in Carter's fixation on finding "lack of institutional control," of a generalissimo seeking any excuse to declare martial law and seize the radio and TV stations. No wonder John won't say boo about this guy.

Senior wide receiver Steve Lynch kicks off the first coachless film session of the Probation Era by laboriously ascending the three steps to the stage, then leaning against the blackboard until he has recovered from that exertion. By now it is clear to every Johnny in the theater that he is impersonating Gagliardi. Lynch shuffles to the middle of the stage and says, "All-right-okay. Nice win. Got a tough game coming up. Augsburg. These guys aren't choir boys."

Someone raises his hand and poses the question: "Excuse me,

John, but I was wondering, do the Augsburg coaches just pull these guys out of the corridor?"

"Those Augsburg coaches don't just pull these guys out of the corridor," says Lynch, playing along.

The lights are dimmed, tape of the Tommy game starts rolling. Now the boys are back to business. "Krych, you're supposed to block that guy," says Sieben, laser-pointering a linebacker who is about to blow up a running play. "And O'Hara's supposed to reach a little more."

Moore is cheapshotted at the end of a punt, but doesn't retaliate: the Johnnies draw a lot of personal fouls this way. Several guys say, "Nice walk-away."

When Linnemann drops back and starts scrambling, then is pinned from behind, Sieben recognizes what is about to happen and fast-forwards through the carnage. He has zero desire to see his buddy go down again. As trainers and coaches bustle around the fallen quarterback in fast motion, everyone in the room observes a moment of silence.

And then life goes on. This is still St. John's football. The boys will have their fun. Grady McGovern, the cornerback, is the holder on extra points. When the team lines up to kick the conversion after a second-half touchdown, he picks the ball up and runs around left end, flipping acrobatically into the end zone for a two-point conversion. The fake is a designed play called "Beaver." As the play unspools on video, I realize that fifty guys have been waiting for this moment. In unison they announce,

"N-i-i-i-ce Beaver."

"Corey has a cannon," Spencer Sokoly is telling me. "He throws a beautiful ball. What we're going to miss from Tom is his leadership."

We are driving back from the Linnemann residence in Melrose on Monday night. A half-dozen guys had driven the half-hour from St. John's to lift Tom's spirits, express condolences, and stuff their faces with the victuals Mary Linnemann, Tom's mom, keeps bringing into the rec room, where Tom is on the couch, his leg elevated on some pillows. There is a cheese plate, two pizzas, chips, and a cooler of sodas. When Mary heads upstairs for more food, Tom voices a complaint:

"With my mom around all the time," he says, "it's, like, impossible to beat off." I think he may be serious.

The extent to which today's youth baffle me is nothing more than a reminder that I am morphing into my father. I remember a time when it was considered a *bad* thing, a plea for an Atomic Wedgie, if your pants rode down below your crack. And I remember, before the pioneering dialogues of Joycelen Elders, when masturbation was something *shameful*. I don't remember being quite so open with my college buddies about our periodic need to evacuate the hostages.

Tom and the boys are watching *Monday Night Football* when Steve Young gets his bell rung and stays down. "He should just retire," says Brandon Vonderharr, another Power House resident who is the starting center. Easy for him to hang up another guy's spikes for him.

Easy for all of us. In our heads, in fact, we've all written Tom off for the rest of the season. But Linnemann, I am noticing, is not so anxious to admit that he is finished. "I'll heal fast," he says. "I'll be back in time for the playoffs. You wait, I'll be running plays at flanker." No one says anything, pro or con. We all just let that one drift.

Linnemann is on crutches in the corridor outside the football offices the next day, the coaches gathered round. Normally, this would be a time for them to be shifting their weight and looking at the floor. But Tom won't allow them to feel the discomfort coaches customarily feel around the walking wounded. He speaks about the upside of his condition—"I don't have to feel guilty about using the handicapped shitter," he says—and of his intention to borrow his grandmother's Lark 2000, the same kind of electric cart *Seinfeld*'s George Costanza is issued when he claims a bogus disability.

"It's got two speeds, Turtle and Jackrabbit," says Tom. "I'm gonna open 'er up, see what she can do at Jackrabbit."

Coming out of Peg's office, John sees Tom for the first time since he was carted off the field.

"How's the pain," says Gags. "Are you in much pain?"

"It comes and goes," says Tom. He's got a bottle of Percocets in his pocket. He's got no worries.

Gagliardi is the one who is in pain. It genuinely bothers him to see his players injured. With effort, he makes small talk: "I see you painted your toenails red."

"Johnny red," says Tom, wiggling the digits. He doesn't tell the coach that the paint job was a consolation prize. When Becky came to visit him in the hospital Sunday morning, Tom somewhat wolfishly suggested that she shut the door behind her and lock it. She painted his toenails instead.

"Tough break, Tommy," says John before disappearing into his office. To Gagliardi, the call of the video monitor, of the unscrutinized Augsburg tape, is a wild call and a clear call that cannot be denied. Tom may be finished, but everyone else has a game Saturday. The undefeated Auggies will visit the Natural Bowl, hoping to spoil the Johnnies' homecoming. When John disappears into his office, I follow him. I don't want to crowd the legend, but I am anxious to know what he does in there all day. He is spot-welded to his most comfortable swivel chair, squinting at Augsburg video. The Auggies are beating a team called Mayville State. The Mayville State fullback runs a dive. Using a little joystick remote he works with his right hand, Gagliardi watches the play eight times. I counted.

He has had opportunities to take higher profile jobs. West Point was interested in him in the fifties. (Can you picture Gagliardi working for a bunch of generals?) In the midsixties, a successful Minnesota lawyer named Joe Robbie flew John and Peg to Miami. Robbie wanted John to coach the AFL team he'd just bought a stake in, the Dolphins. Gagliardi was reluctant to change jobs, so Robbie hired George Wilson, who was fired after four seasons, and replaced by Don Shula.

Ex-Vikings head coach Bud Grant once wooed Gagliardi, as did the University of San Diego. John and Peg got a nice trip out of that one. He has always said thanks, but no thanks. "My problem," says Gags, "is that I've never been an assistant to anybody. I've always been a little afraid of that. I like to come and go when I want to. I don't want to have to feel guilty about going to the bathroom. I don't want someone looking over my shoulder, making sure I watch five hours of film a day."

"But John, you do that anyway," I point out.

"Yeah, but it's *my decision*!" he says. Then he turns his attention back to Augsburg.

"This is where you go blind," he mutters. "Trying to see where people are lined up." Is the defensive tackle heads up on the guard? On his outside shoulder? On his inside eye? Plucking an index card from a ready stack, Gags prepares to write on it. Each card comes with the offense already diagrammed on it. Gags fills in the defense, then concocts a play he thinks might work against it. A lot of head coaches are the football equivalents of CEOs—figureheads to trot out on the sideline or at the shareholders meeting. Gagliardi is as far as you can be from that, as hands-on a head coach as I've seen.

Fasching twice reviewed the Eau Claire tape, only to have John point out two subtle but telling defensive mistakes. "I hadn't caught either of them," says Gary. "John is an incredibly keen observer. He misses *nothing*."

In each of its three games this season, the Johnny offense has come out strong in the second half. Someone is making some highly effective adjustments. "That's John," says Lynch. "He'll ask someone, When we ran that 52, was the end playing you inside or out? Based on the answer you give him, he'll say, 'All right, run this.'

"Sometimes he can't think of the name of the play, so he'll describe it, or draw it up on a card, and it will work. It's eerie how often it works."

The work looks tedious; Gags does not find it tedious. He is thankful for the video revolution. He spent thirty years wrestling with projectors, enduring the infernal staccato every time he wanted to see a play a second (or third, or eighth) time. He is grateful for the chance to rewind in silence, to dissect the opponent, to find some nuance that will give him an edge. He has spent a solid decade of his life doing this.

It is raining hammers and nails in the video. A few dozen

Augsburg parents stand under umbrellas. When play comes to the near sideline, the camera picks up peeling paint in the press box. Beyond the stadium is a field of wheat stubble. Such a tableau would fill many a Minnesotan with a longing to grab some decoys and a firearm and settle into his favorite slough. Personally, I find it depressing. That is why I am leaving after twelve minutes, I tell John. Not because I do not find his work riveting, but because the rain and the peeling paint are getting me down. He smiles as I take my leave, his eyes never leaving the screen.

That evening Laura and I drive over to St. Ben's to hear the poet laureate, Robert Pinsky—precisely the kind of date we never go on during a normal football season. During a normal season, I cab home from the airport on Monday and am on the road again Wednesday or Thursday. While Laura is desperate to don something tightfitting and black and to get the hell out of the house, I want to stay in, roughhousing with the kids, embracing them and inhaling the scent of them before it is time to once again abandon them.

Pinsky is funny, accessible, a joy. In a work called "Poem with Refrains," he sets a scene in which his mother sees Louis Farrakhan, the minister of the Nation of Islam, on television:

His bow tie is lime, his jacket crocodile green.
Vigorously he denounces the Jews who traded in slaves,
The Jews who run the newspapers and banks.
'I see what this guy is mad about now,' she says,
'It must have been some Jew that sold him the suit.'

After reading a poem of twenty-six words arranged alphabetically—"your zenith" is how he neatly brings it home—Pinsky talks about the pleasure of problem solving. "One of the things humans love is difficulty," he says. "The animal craving for difficulty has enabled us to evolve. The thrill is not necessarily to overcome a difficulty but to engage it."

A synapse fires, and Gagliardi suddenly makes more sense to me. Other than some animal craving, what would keep a septuagenarian squinting at video until eyestrain forces him to the restroom to splash water on his face? Yes, Gagliardi is closing in on Eddie Robinson's 408 career victories. And no, he does not have a bunch of hobbies to divert himself with in retirement. Still, what keeps Gags coming back year after year, I will conclude during my season off the brink, is the pleasure of problem solving, the jolt he gets out of that weekly battle of wits.

While I see precious few poetry readings in my travels for *SI*, I do occasionally patronize what is known in the sportswriting fraternity as "the ballet." These dancers aren't wearing toeshoes. If you ask them to do a plié, they might just tell you when they get off work, and how much extra it will cost.

I'm sure you can be a sportswriter *and* stay out of strip joints. I just haven't figured out how. Not long ago I was in Florida reporting a feature on a football player, one of the league's good guys. Driving back after dinner, the fellow blew past the exit for my hotel. "Gotta get you out of that hotel room," he explained. He was taking me to Thee Doll House. After one dance, I excused myself, explaining this was the time I usually called my wife.

"Hey, Laura," I said, from a phone booth outside the club.

"Where are you?" she asked, hearing traffic noises.

"The subject has taken me to a gentlemen's club."

"Behave yourself," she said. Laura is the coolest. "Your daughter would like to say hello to you." Willa had cut her head on the playground at preschool and taken five stitches. "Be sure to mention how brave she was," Laura whispered.

As cars whizzed by and simian bouncers eyed me dully, I asked Willa what happened; if the stitches hurt ("They gave me a magic shot, Daddy—the stitches didn't hurt at all!" she said). I asked her where she learned to be so brave. Back inside, they were running a special: for twenty dollars you got four dances and a denim Doll House baseball cap (which Laura now jogs in). The subject was treating. My first dancer was Isis. She was twenty-four and above average. By the end of four dances, I was feeling vaguely nostalgic for breasts that had not been surgically augmented. I was thinking that the purpose of the strip joint is defeated if the patron cannot stop reflecting on the fact that each of the dancers is someone's daughter.

John is in high spirits coming off the practice field on Wednesday. (You can't really call Wednesday "Humpday" at St. John's. There's something about a sixty-minute practice that starts with a Standing Beautiful Day Drill and ends with a Cherry O'Harey—a trick play designed for Chad O'Hara—that fails to conjure the image of a hump.) He asks a pretty trainer what perfume she is wearing. "Strawberries and Champagne," she says. "Jeez," says Gags, "I gotta get some of that for myself."

He lowers himself into his car with a startlingly loud sigh. I have never met a person who sighs with more gusto. "I like to give a little moan when I take a load off," he says. "It feels good." He makes no move to turn the key in the ignition. He is savoring being off his feet.

"I don't know how I ever did this for so long," he says. "In '63 there were just two of us. I was all over the place trying to get the offense ready, the defense ready. In '65, my two assistants were just players who were ineligible. One of 'em was a noseguard, and he didn't know anything about any position but noseguard.

"We did okay, though, I guess." He won national championships both seasons. One of the few concessions he has made to the march of years is the size of his staff. While relatively skeletal, at half a dozen—the Tommies have twelve assistant coaches, for instance—Gagliardi's staff is three times the size of what it used to be. His postpractice rambles through the locker room have become less frequent. "It used to give me a chance to get to know some of the guys a little better," he says. (It gave him a chance to try out his new material, is what it did.) "Now, all I can do at the end of the day is get to that La-Z-Boy."

I express interest in the La-Z-Boy, for he has bragged on it before. He decides that I must experience it. We drive the seven hundred yards to his house.

This is another concession to his senior status. The three places

Gags spends most of his life—home, office, practice field—form an isosceles triangle no point of which is more than a six-minute walk from the other two. Yet, if you see John walking on campus, offer him a ride, because it probably means his car has broken down. He is not being lazy, he is being time-efficient. You say a six-minute walk, but what about the round trip? That's twelve minutes. Do that five times, you've burned an hour. Who has an hour to burn? What if a man wants to sneak home to . . . to do some thinking on his favorite throne? Must that become a twenty-five-minute investment of time? What if John painstakingly makes Jell-O, following the instructions, pouring the mix into the mold, and then puts it in the freezer to harden? This happened a couple weeks ago. Upon learning that the Jell-O goes in the fridge, not the freezer, it was nice for him to be able to speed home and salvage dessert.

He pulls into his driveway—the monks have actually named it Gagliardi Drive—arrives at the end of the drive . . . and pulls a Fred Magoo, keeps right on going, up the concrete sidewalk, stopping at his doorstep. The sidewalk is actually wide enough to accommodate a midsize car. This must be by design. Parking *at* his front door may only save Gagliardi six or seven steps, but factor that out over the course of several decades. Those are miles that never make it onto his odometer. He is not lazy so much as he is rationing his heartbeats.

A guest is ushered into a space that, at one time, probably resembled a conventional living room where an ordinary couple might have entertained company. *No mas.* An enormous white screen, six feet high, ten feet across, obscures tasteful draperies. A satellite dish anchored to the back of the house is wired to the hi-tech entertainment system that projects images onto the screen.

"Peggy didn't like it at first," says Gags of his decision to sacrifice the living room. "But I said, 'If you're gonna watch TV, you might as well do it in *style*.'"

A pair of recliners faces the screen. While both are plush, one is clearly dominant, the alpha chair. John ordered it out of a Sharper Image catalog, and I'll be damned if it doesn't do everything but say "gesundheit!" when you sneeze. Beneath its leather dermis, right where your back hits the chair, lurk a half-dozen massaging balls.

From a menu on a handheld remote, you select the type and intensity of your massage. Gagliardi hits a few buttons, and all of a sudden it feels as if I am being rolfed by a 250-pound woman named Helga.

He fires up the television and surfs to the Travel Channel, where a despairing tourist is pleading with a horse on a mountain in New Zealand. He swings over to the History Channel, where they are building the Hoover Dam again. "I spend a lot of time watching these two," he says. I ask Gagliardi a question about his own history, and find myself traveling with him, backward in time . . .

John's older brother, Frank, was wounded behind enemy lines. An advance scout for the 5th Armored Division in World War II, he'd been shot through both legs in an ambush, and was hiding beneath a hayrick somewhere in France. When he looked out, he could see the boots of German soldiers, who periodically thrust their bayonets into the straw under which he was hidden. If German steel finds Frank, you are not reading this.

"Had he been killed, or badly wounded," says John, "I would never have gone into coaching. As the next-oldest son, I would have taken over the body shop."

Frank cheats death. He is rescued by members of the French Resistance, returns to Colorado and takes over the family business, freeing his little brother to revolutionize his little corner of the football world, to wage his own quixotic battles against misanthropic coaches and unquestioned loyalty to dumb ideas.

Until 1865, Trinidad, Colorado, was little more than a trading post at the spot where the Santa Fe Trail crossed the Purgatoire River. That was the year vast fields of soft, clean-burning bituminous coal were discovered beneath it. Word reached Europe that skilled miners were in demand in southern Colorado. Within a few decades, Trinidad's population had swollen to 20,000. In 1910, Ventura Gagliardi kissed his mother goodbye, knowing he would never see her again. He left his native Grimaldi, in the tip of the Italian boot, and set sail for New York City, from where he made his way to Trinidad. He mined coal, then opened a blacksmith shop.

When the need for his blacksmithing services waned, he opened a body shop. Ventura's ability to change with the times made a deep impression on his second son. The first and cardinal "No" on John's list: "No single way to coach football." Gagliardi's midsixties squads won with defense; the '76 national championship squad won with Gags's mystifying quadruple option. It is a mystery to him why coaches limit themselves to one system.

John was the fifth of Ventura and Antoinetta's nine children. In the summer of 1943, John was preparing for his senior football season at Trinidad's Holy Trinity Catholic High, when suddenly it looked as if there would be no season. Head coach Dutch Clark was called to war, and Father Sebastiani, the principal, decided to cancel football for the year. But Gagliardi and some of his friends begged for permission to coach themselves. The priest agreed.

Practicing on a cinder-strewn field across from the Schneider Brewery, the Tigers scrapped the drills that Clark had been so keen on. They lined up and ran the plays. When they could run them well enough, they went home. Holy Trinity opened with Florence High. "John says they barely beat us," says Charles Latuda, a 135-pound center on that team. "But I think they whomped us. But then we beat Aguilar, Canyon City Abbey—we'd never beaten them before, and I still remember the score, 19–9—and St. Mary's of Walsenburg." Holy Trinity clinched the school's first-ever league championship.

The Tigers lost to Regis, a Jesuit school in Denver, in their final game of the season, but Gagliardi had found a calling. "I thought I'd spend the rest of my life in Trinidad, welding and sanding and painting in the shop," says Gags. But Father Sebastiani was impressed, and asked his player-coach to stay on. While attending a local junior college, Gagliardi coached Holy Trinity to two more league titles. Word of the wunderkind's success reached Colorado Springs, 126 miles away. The priest-director of St. Mary's High in Colorado Springs arranged for John to attend Colorado College while coaching all sports at St. Mary's. As would happen wherever he went, John turned the football program around, winning a championship within two seasons.

As it happened, legendary Notre Dame coach Frank Leahy ran

a football camp every summer out of Colorado College. When one of Leahy's assistants arrived in the city, Gagliardi was asked to show the fellow around. "I got him a few dates with some of my friends," he recalls. "I didn't hurt my cause that they were very nice-looking girls." Before long, Gagliardi found himself in Leahy's inner circle. In 1949, the year he graduated from Colorado College, John applied for the head-coaching job at Carroll College in Helena, Montana. He was asked to supply references. Was there anyone in the coaching fraternity who might write him a letter of recommendation?

In fact there was, said Gagliardi. Perhaps they had heard of Frank Leahy? "After Leahy wrote that letter," says Gags, "that was it."

Gagliardi got the job, becoming Carroll's head coach of all sports and athletic director just as it enjoyed a surge in enrollment from ex-servicemen. Thus did the twenty-two-year-old find himself in charge of a pack of jaded, twenty-five-year-old veterans. "Waitresses would never give me the check," says Gags. "They'd always give it to Ed Dennehy." Still, he had little trouble getting the players to listen to him. Incompetence and apathy had nearly resulted in the cancellation of Carroll's football program shortly before Gagliardi was hired in 1949. From 1950 to 1952, they did not lose a conference game. "It was evident," according to *Scoreboard*, "that the bigger schools would soon be after Gagliardi."

Why not one of those bigger schools? Why St. John's?

By 1953 Johnny (Blood) McNally had just about had it trying to coach the Johnnies out of their .500-level mire. That's when Father Arno Gustin, the president of St. John's, took a call from an ex-Johnny named Bill Osborne, who was coaching high school football in Billings, Montana. He advised Father Arno to give Gagliardi a look. But John was enjoying himself at Carroll. He loved western Montana, and got along splendidly with his coworkers. The school's faculty representative for athletics at the time was Father Bernard Topel, who later became the bishop of Spokane. His assistant coach was Father Ray Hunthausen, who later became the archbishop of Seattle. But Gagliardi was swayed by Osborne's infectious passion for his alma mater, and the prospect of nearly doubling his $2,400 salary. "*And* I wouldn't have to coach all sports," he adds, "although they did slip hockey in on me a few years later."

Gagliardi arrived at St. John's at the dawn of a period of ferment, in the Catholic world in general and Collegeville in particular. The election of Pope John XXIII—Good Pope John—was still five years away, but the spiritual and liturgical renewal he would call for in the Second Vatican Council were already subjects of intense discussion among the bellwether Benedictines of Collegeville.

It was the Bulldozer Epoch on campus, as the monks busily carried out Marcel Breuer's Bauhaus makeover. With the election of Abbot Baldwin Dworschak in 1951, the university had placed a renewed emphasis on the appreciation and creation of art. Its newly minted "department of sacred art," says Barry's *Worship and Work*, called for "the power of creative intuition," developed through "experimentation."

It is easy to see how a self-made, self-taught maverick coach would have been a good fit in such an environment. The early returns on Gagliardi were excellent. In that first season, 1953, he brought the MIAC title back to St. John's for the first time since 1938. That campaign included a 21–7 upset of Gustavus—the Golden Horde's first conference loss in four years. "John came up with a stunting, 4–4 defense we'd never heard of," recalls Jim Sexton, a lineman on that team. "It totally baffled Gustavus. We beat them handily, even though they had far superior material."

Gagliardi's first season in Collegeville also featured a nonconference visit to South Dakota State, a much larger school the Johnnies had no business scheduling. One paper predicted the home team would prevail "by four to six touchdowns over this unknown team from central Minnesota." But Johnny tailback Casey Vilandre scored four touchdowns as the "unknowns" spoiled the Jackrabbits' annual Hobo Day.

Gagliardi's future was as luminous as his social life was leaden. Billeted in St. Mary Hall on this remote, all-male campus, he might have been much lonelier, were it not for the friendship of Father Adelard Thuente. Adelard was a crack biology professor who'd played halfback for the Johnnies in the early thirties. While he showed a patience with football players that was not shared by all of his colleagues, Adelard was no pushover. In a reminiscence included in *A Sense of Place*, a collection of essays about St. John's, professor emeritus William Cofell recalls a weekend night when a student returned to his dorm room "under the influence of too many steins." The inebriated undergraduate unwisely took a swing at his prefect—Adelard—who sent him to bed with the warning, "I will see you tomorrow."

At a bright and early hour, the student was awakened by Adelard, who escorted him to the gym. After helping the dehydrated and increasingly contrite young man lace on a pair of boxing gloves, the priest stepped into the ring with him. It occurred to the student, as he sparred with Adelard, "that his belligerence of the night before had been a serious and dangerous mistake," writes Cofell.

Alcohol was forbidden in the dormitories, of course. Taking Gagliardi's unusual circumstance into consideration, however, Adelard would smuggle an occasional six-pack into John's room. The thoughtfulness of the gesture was scarcely diminished by the fact that Adelard often put away most, if not all, of the ale. "John never liked beer," says Peggy.

Peggy Daugherty was a student at the St. Cloud School of Nursing when John was introduced to her. She was smart, good-looking, brassy. Gagliardi fell hard for her, but kept a foot on the brakes. This is, after all, a cautious man, a man who agonizes at length over which coat he should wear on the practice field; a man who will drive back to his office from the field if he feels he has chosen incorrectly. Now, faced with the biggest decision of his life, the bachelor from Trinidad . . . froze.

Normally, he would have introduced Peg to his parents and siblings, then carefully weighed their advice. The counsel of his family unavailable, Gagliardi turned to his best friend, Father Adelard, with whom John and Peg frequently socialized. Asked for his opinion, Adelard gave the answer that entered Gagliardi family lore:

"I think you better sign her before she jumps to another league."

John and Peg were married on Valentine's Day in 1956 and had four children: Nancy, John Jr., Gina, and Jimmy. In 1962, Peg was pregnant with John, whose due date fell not far from Adelard's birthday.

"If he's born on June 6," he cried, "you *have* to name him Adelardi Gagliardi!"

John Jr. was, in fact, born on June 6, and was not named Adelardi, though that is what the priest joshingly called him.

Football custom at St. John's had long held that a different monk would ride the bus to each away game. Adelard decided that a better custom would be for *him* to ride the bus to all the games. He was a welcome fixture around the team and in the Gagliardi household. "One day he was walking around in a new pair of shoes I'd bought," says John. "He really admired those shoes. He said, 'These are great. Can you get me a pair of these in black?'"

"The next morning they found him in his room, dead of a heart attack. The day before he'd been stomping around in my shoes. Boy, that was tough." As his voice trails off and he looks straight ahead, you see that some of the hurt has followed the old coach down the decades.

He is both friendly and elusive, receding like a mirage when you get too close. The wall is there for a reason. Gagliardi is as much of a celebrity as you will find in this region, unless Garrison Keillor or the poet laureate is in town. Strangers want to meet him, wish him well. He needs to be able to guard his privacy, to ensure quality control. It is a practical barrier Gagliardi has put up. I wonder if it wasn't easier to erect after the death of his close friend.

A couple of senior citizens are sitting in John's car during Thursday's practice, fogging up the windows. I wander over to introduce myself. Next thing you know, we're talking about transsexuals.

The visitors are the above-quoted Chuck Latuda, John's best buddy from grade school, and Dr. Bob Leonetti, a psychiatrist and a professor at Trinidad Junior College. Every year, a few of the guys from John's old Colorado crowd fly out for the St. John's homecoming. These two are only too happy to provide details about the young John Gagliardi. Latuda recalls that there were thirty-two girls and seven boys in his and John's high school graduating class. The school was run by Jesuits and the Sisters of Charity, nuns from an order based in Cincinnati whose good favor Gagliardi cultivated. "He wasn't above misbehaving," says Latuda, a wiry rancher with a ready smile, "but he was clever and subtle about it. He stayed out of harm's way. And you should've heard him with those nuns. He was like a Philadelphia lawyer. 'Oh no, not me, Sister.'"

John, meanwhile, is out on the field, unable to defend himself. While the Johnnies prepare for Augsburg under threatening skies—the autumn's first cold snap upon us—my new friends provide a Cliff Notes version of the history of Trinidad. "You've heard of the Ludlow Massacre?" says Latuda. In 1914, strikebreakers set fire to a tent encampment in Ludlow, fourteen miles north of Trinidad, killing forty people, including at least a dozen women and children.

The last of the mines closed years ago. Since then, Trinidad has carved a niche for itself as one of the world's foremost places to have a sex-change operation. Leonetti frequently counsels candidates for such adjustments, men who have come to Trinidad to become women. The transgenders often stick around for weeks and months after their surgeries, adjusting their medications, trying their modified organs out for size. Which is why it's not unusual, says Latuda, to sit down at a restaurant and have your order taken by a six-foot-three waitress.

Some are captivated by Trinidad's live-and-let-live attitude, and its mild, dry climate. They can't bring themselves to leave. "Like Trannie Annie," says Leonetti. "Big, rawboned gal, guy, whatever. She's been around a long time."

One wonders what O.P. McMains would make of all this. McMains, a Methodist minister who composed verse under the nom de plume A. Bach, wrote a poem about Trinidad in 1872. It is on display in Trinidad's Santa Fe Trail Museum, and reads, in part:

Where a village sits on a bed of coal,
And the billowy hills around it roll . . .

Where the hills are green and with cedars, clad—
That's Trinidad.

Where the girls, (tho', alas, few of them you'll see),
Are just as pretty as girls can be,
And almost drive a bachelor mad—
That's Trinidad.

Inspired, I am fairly certain, by McMain's old muse, I jot these updated verses:

Where the loveliest lass in all the mundo,
Speaks in a gravelly basso profundo;
Where that slimwaisted, head-turning burgher's wife,
Is the hormone-drenched product of a surgeon's knife;
Where that cute mom (who knows?) might be someone's dad—
That's Trinidad.

Latuda and Leonetti figure to see a good game. St. John's and Augsburg are both undefeated. Long a MIAC cellar dweller, Augsburg has reached respectability under head coach Jack Osberg. The Auggies will earn six victories this season, achieving a winning record for the third straight year, a streak they last accomplished from 1927 through 1929. Augsburg is a Lutheran-affiliated school whose stated mission is to provide an education "based in the liberal arts and shaped by the faith and values of the Christian Church."

About four seconds after the second play from scrimmage has been blown dead, mild-mannered Chris Moore is leveled by an Augsburg cornerback. The personal foul is so flagrant that the perp is lucky to just be flagged, and not thrown out of the game. After being tackled in the same series, Moore is buried and helpless in the pile when he feels the familiar sensation of Augsburg hands squeezing his testicles—the same thing happened last season, he tells me.

"Again?" Moore shouts. "You're doing it again? You guys are pathetic!"

Brilliant. Give the best back in the conference a reason to run harder against you. By halftime Moore has three touchdowns and 119 yards rushing, and the Johnnies are up 42–0. Moore was right. Those guys were pathetic.

The final was 55–nil, although a review of my notes from that day tells me that my attention wandered long before the Johnnies' final, window-dressing touchdown. After Sieben takes an end-around twenty-two yards to set up the St. John's third score, I have scribbled something about a gaggle of Canadian geese flying overhead in boomerang formation. There follows a description of the foliage beyond the visitor's bleachers—"scarlet, light green, goalpost-yellow." Be afraid when sportswriters take it upon themselves to describe nature. Be very afraid.

At halftime I am invited into the President's Suite adjacent to the press box, and introduced to the serendipitously named Bob Spinner, a trim ex-tailback in a dapper sweater who played for the Johnnies in 1963, making him part of one of the greatest upsets in college football history. Spinner informs me that some of the guys from that '63 team are getting together that night in Albany, ten miles up the freeway. We chat awhile, but it is Homecoming Weekend and Spinner, who chairs the school's Board of Regents, has flesh to press. After he leaves me, I am unattached in the luxury box, an uncomfortable feeling for a sportswriter among the brokers of power, the cultivators of philanthropy, the clean-shaven and well groomed. I would like to introduce myself to Brother Dietrich Reinhart, the university president, but he is deep in conversation. Oh well, I can always make his acquaintance some other time. I head for the exit, but not before sinking my hand like a backhoe bucket into a bowl of expensive mixed nuts.

So it is an *in*opportune time for Brother Dietrich to glide over and extend his right hand, which I cannot shake because mine is full of cashews and filberts. Instead, I offer him some of his own mixed nuts. At the top of the pile is one of those gorilla toes, a Brazil nut. "Go ahead," I urge him. "Take the big one. It's yours."

It really is. Still, he demurs. After an exceedingly brief conversation with the president, I am free to go.

7

PRAIRIE VIEW

They are his friends, his neighbors, his employers, his black-cowled comic foils. Back in the days when the entire monastery would turn out for Johnny games, the Benedictines would congregate in the stands behind the team, darkening the bleachers with their robes and the atmosphere with cigar smoke. "Check that smoke," Gagliardi has told his quarterbacks for nearly five decades. "If it's coming out nice and smooth, you're fine. If it looks like a four-alarm fire, throw the ball!"

Over the years, a little of the humor has leaked from that Gagliardi perennial. As Gags's legend grew—as his teams racked up conference titles, playoff berths, and national titles—it lost plausibility. I recently read that there have been an estimated twenty-five thousand college football coaches. Seven have won more than 300 games; two more than 350. One gets the sense that Gagliardi, who as of this week is 357-105-11, could string together a few sub-.500 seasons and *still* escape the ax.

That's not how he sees it. "John has always been driven by insecurity," says Dienhart, his old, friendly Tommy nemesis, "by the near certainty that no matter how well things were going, the knack for winning would desert him, the world would forget about him, he would never win another game."

Nowadays his handwringing, Chicken Little shtick—*These Hamline kids, they do some things very well*—is cause for covert laughter. There was a time, long ago, when Gagliardi had *grounds* to be worried about job security. The Johnnies' surprise MIAC championship in 1953 would not be duplicated in that decade. Gagliardi's teams won three games in the '56 season, four apiece in '57 and '59, and opened the '60 season with three straight losses.

The fourth game was at St. Thomas, and Gagliardi's pregame speech lives on as a classic:

"Guys, when the monks hired me they told me, 'We don't care if you lose every other game on the schedule, as long as you beat St. Thomas,' said Gags, looking around the silent room. "Well, men," another pause, "this could be that year."

A roar of laughter went up. The Johnnies went out and did a tap dance on the Tommies, winning 34–13.

In those days before the glaciers of the Ice Age had retreated from central Minnesota and Gagliardi was still fine-tuning his philosophy, the Johnnies held one, full-contact preseason scrimmage: freshmen against varsity. In 1960, for the first time ever, the freshmen prevailed, causing Gagliardi to grouse, "Jesus Christ, I've either got really good freshmen or a really lousy varsity."

It was the former. Bernie Beckman was a five-foot-seven, 170-pound halfback out of Elbow Lake, Minnesota, who would go on to pancake future Purple People Eater Gary Larsen. John McDowell was a huge, quick tackle with great feet and a lackadaisical attitude. He would go on to play briefly with the Green Bay Packers and for many years in the Canadian Football League. Tight end Ken Roering ended up at St. John's after turning down multiple Big 10 scholarship offers in order to stay close to his ailing mother in St. Cloud. Hardy Reyerson, a rangy end out of Mankato who caught a pair of touchdown passes in the biggest win in Johnny football history, is now teaching at a Jesuit high school in San Jose. When I tracked him down, he'd just finished a 540-mile bike ride down the California coast. Speedy and sure-handed, Reyerson had been wooed by Minnesota and Wisconsin. How on earth had he become a Johnny? "My mother was a Benny," he said. "She took me to St. John's one summer day when I was ten, and I fell in love with the place."

After the Johnnies opened the '60 season with three defeats, Gagliardi figured: what have I got to lose? He played the freshmen. The team didn't lose another game that season. It lost two close contests the following season. In 1962, the Johnnies *won* those close games, going 9–0. (They were not, alas, one of the four teams chosen to participate in the NAIA playoffs, which, in those pre-Division III days, determined the small college national champion.) In 1963 the team simply didn't have any close games, outscoring regular-season opponents 298–45 and allowing 12.9 yards rushing *per game*, a national record. This time the NAIA could not ignore them.

The Eastern semifinal pitted the Johnnies against the likewise undefeated Presbies (their actual nickname) of the College of Emporia, in Kansas. (We've got Presbies, we've got Lutes; why not dub St. John's the Mackerel Snappers and have it done with?) The Presbies boasted the nation's most prolific offense (517 yards per game) and one of its most ghoulish rituals. Vanquished foes were "buried" in a "football cemetery." A headstone bearing the date and score of the game was erected as "services" were conducted by pre-ministerial students.

By this time the Johnnies had not lost a game in two and a half seasons, and had about them an aura of quiet confidence. Informed of their impending interment in Emporia's "cemetery," they suggested to one another that perhaps it was time the Presbies got their own asses buried.

The game was played at Bloomington's Metropolitan Stadium—since razed to make room for the Mall of America—with the nation still in shock. Eight days earlier, President John F. Kennedy had been assassinated. "There was some question about whether we should even play," recalls cornerback John McCormick.

Gagliardi played reserves in the second half as the Johnnies scored fifty-four points and hung a goose egg on the vaunted Emporia offense. Next stop: Sacramento for the small-college championship game, the Camellia Bowl.

Overshadowed in its own state by Los Angeles and San Francisco, Sacramento has always been a self-conscious state capital, a sweltering, flood-prone city in search of nice things to say about itself. The Johnnies and the Panthers of Prairie View A&M—their opponents in the championship game—may or may not have known, upon their arrival, that they were in the self-styled Camellia Capital of the World. (It is unknown how much, if any, competition Sacramento faced for the title.) In those days, Sacramento had a new reason to puff its chest. The backwater once served by Pony Express and riverboat had carved a niche for itself in the missile industry. The chamber of commerce that dubbed its city the Camellia Capital also proudly declared itself "the Missile Center of the Free World."

This was a formidable mantle, indeed, fewer than fourteen months after the Cuban Missile Crisis. Aside from being played at the dawn of a fast-freezing Cold War, twenty-three days after the murder of the most popular president in the nation's history, the '63 Camellia Bowl called to mind the other major story of that era: the civil rights movement. The Johnnies had not a single black player; the Panthers, not a single white one. This would be the first-ever college football game between an all-black team and an all-white one. To learn more about it, I called the sports information director at Prairie View, who gave me the phone number of a remarkable gentleman named William Downey, an ex-Panther player who has devoted much of his adulthood to researching the life and career of former Prairie View head coach W. J. "Billy" Nicks. "Yes, yes," said Downey when I phoned him and explained my reason for calling. It was as if he'd been wondering what took me so long to get in touch.

After the season I flew to Seattle and drove the twenty-five or so miles to Downey's home in Lakewood, Washington. An ex-Army colonel and paratrooper, he strikes me first and foremost as a man who does nothing halfway. He has made three thousand parachute jumps and collected ten thousand pages of documents on Nicks, who won eight national black college championships and fielded some of the best teams you never heard about. Downey's bright smile and powerful grip belie his overall condition. "I'm on a cancer journey," he tells me. "I woke up this morning. I'm vertical, and I'm ambulatory. That means it's a good day."

Downey started at center for Nicks and the Panthers in the late forties and early fifties. "The team never had more than nineteen helmets," he says. "If you were a second-stringer going into the game to replace someone, you just *hoped* his head was about the same size as yours."

Nicks died at the age of ninety-five on November 9, 1999—three months after he'd been inducted into the College Football Hall of Fame. Downey shows me snapshots of the ceremony, in South Bend, Indiana. There is the old coach, ashen and skeletal, wheelchair-bound, not long for this world. While ex-Nebraska Cornhuskers coach Tom Osborne was a bit standoffish, Downey says, Nicks and Don Coryell, the old San Diego Chargers head man, hit it off like old friends. Before Nicks was inducted, a researcher from the Hall of Fame had phoned Downey. The man wished to confirm the accuracy of the information he had on Nicks. He read the information back to Downey, who politely pointed out numerous errors.

Downey sits there, ticking mistakes off on his fingers. "They had his won-loss record wrong, they had him coaching in '51, when he was assistant. They didn't have him as head coach in '45, when he *was* coaching. They asked me how I knew he wasn't the head coach in '51. I told 'em, 'I was the starting center on that team!'"

The man from the Hall of Fame could not help wondering, what made Downey so sure his won-loss records for Nicks were more accurate than theirs? Because, Downey told him, he had spent four years traveling the country, camped out in libraries and archives, squinting at microfilm and wrestling onto Xerox machines bound volumes of black newspapers like the *Amsterdam News*, the *Atlanta Daily World*, the *Chicago Defender*, the *Dallas Express*, the *Houston Informer*, and the *Pittsburgh Courier*. Downey said Nicks had a career record of 195 wins, 60 losses, and 22 ties. On what did he base those numbers? Well, he had a photocopied account of every game the man ever coached. What did they have?

The Hall of Fame changed its records to match Downey's.

All I know of Nicks I learned from Downey, who describes the late legend as "my friend and coach, my mentor and *tor*mentor." Nicks was born in 1905 in Griffin, Georgia. He grew up across the railroad tracks from the local high school, the doors of which were closed to him. Half a century after the Emancipation Proclamation, the defeated South still begrudged blacks an education. "The opposition to Negro education in the South was at first bitter, and showed itself in ashes, insult and blood," wrote W. E. B. DuBois in *The Souls of Black Folk*, his searing examination of American racism. Says Downey, "Black people who finished eighth grade either enrolled in a private school or went into the cotton fields."

At the age of thirteen, Nicks walked across the tracks and into the school, attempting to enroll. His father was summoned at work. "You better come get your son," the caller said, "because he's lost his mind."

Bill Nicks's father drove with his son directly to a local bank, and asked to borrow fifty dollars. The loan officer told him he would have to speak to the bank president, who said, "Why do you need fifty dollars?"

"To send my boy to Atlanta to go to school," replied Mr. Nicks. The loan was approved, and Young Bill was on a train to the big city that day. He attended Morris Brown preparatory school, then Morris Brown College. As an undergraduate, he was all-conference in track, baseball, football, and basketball, and was all-American in football. He took over as the Wolverines head football coach in 1930, and within three years guided the team to the first of three national black college championships it would win under him. (There is some question whether Nicks deserves full credit for the second of those titles, won in 1940. He spent that season working on his master's at Columbia University, and would take the train from New York City to Atlanta every weekend to coach the team.)

Too old to be drafted for World War II, Nicks enrolled in the USO. "He felt it was his duty to serve," says Downey. "He always felt he owed it to his country"—the same country that refused to provide him with an education after eighth grade; the country in which he often slept in the homes of opposing coaches on the nights before road games, this man with a Columbia master's whose race made him unwelcome in the hotels of his native South.

The segregation that shamed the country also provided Nicks with a certain bounty—the talent he used to win eight national titles: three at Morris Brown and five at Prairie View. While serving as the director of the USO Club at the Tuskegee Army Air Force Base, Nicks met the man who, in 1945, hired him away to Prairie View, which played in the all-black Southwestern Athletic Conference. Although the Panthers had athletes good enough to play in the higher-profile Southeastern and Southwest Conferences, the SEC and SWC would not have them. The SWC—Texas, Texas A&M, Southern Methodist, that crowd—did not begin integrating its athletic teams until the midsixties. The SEC took longer still. Alabama coach Bear Bryant only broke down and recruited black athletes in 1970, after Southern Cal's great fullback Sam (Bam) Cunningham humiliated the Crimson Tide in a 42–21 win in Birmingham. As Jerry Claiborne—then assistant coach at Alabama—put it, "Sam Cunningham did more to integrate Alabama in sixty minutes than Martin Luther King did in twenty years."

Unwelcome at higher-profile programs, talented black players flooded into the Southwestern Athletic Conference or SWAC, whose member schools—including Jackson State, Grambling, Alcorn State, Mississippi Valley, and Texas Southern—have put scores of players in the NFL. And in 1963, the Panthers of Prairie View were the scourge of the SWAC. Eleven players from that Panthers roster would either sign free-agent contracts or be drafted to play professionally. All forty were on scholarship. The Johnnies, of course, don't award athletic scholarships. Prairie View was coached by Nicks, who would finish his career with a winning record against every other SWAC school, including Eddie Robinson's Grambling Tigers. His quarterback that year, Jim

Kearney, would go on to play nine years for the Kansas City Chiefs. Kearney was protected by future NFL linemen Carl Robinson and Seth Cartwright, who opened holes for future NFL draftee Ezell Seals. Sophomore linebacker Kenny Houston—you can read about him in the plaque under his bust in the NFL Hall of Fame—had not yet cracked the starting lineup, although he left his mark on the Camellia Bowl. Kearney's go-to receiver was a rangy junior from Houston by the name of Otis Taylor, now a member of the Chiefs Hall of Fame. Gagliardi reviewed two of Prairie View's game tapes, and decided not to allow his team to see them. He was afraid the Johnnies would be beaten before they stepped on the field. Did he see *any* flaws he might exploit? "Well, in one of their games, they lost the coin toss," says Gags. "I mean, those guys were *good.* Vince Lombardi would double-team Taylor, and we're out there covering him with Bernie Beckman."

McCormick, the other Johnny cornerback, also spent much of that soggy, foggy December afternoon in Sacramento's Hughes Stadium running with, and after, Taylor. At dusk, a few hours after the Johnnies whipped Augsburg, he joins me in the foyer of the Albany Golf Club. McCormick is a slight man in a Charlie Brown sweater, a real estate developer peering out from behind spectacles with Hubble telescope lenses. He is listed in the Camellia Bowl program at five-nine, 160, but confesses that when the game ended, he weighed 149. Try as you might, you cannot picture him rotating up to play bump-and-run with the six-foot-four, 215-pound, NFL-bound Taylor.

"I guarded Otis," he says. "Did I get smoked? Yeah, a couple of times." But then he smiles, and you know a couple things must have gone his way, too.

The Johnnies' charter flight stopped in Kearney, Nebraska, where the Panthers boarded the plane. The players mingled, and many Johnnies had their first prolonged conversations with members of the black race. The Panthers had just come from behind in a snowstorm to defeat Kearney State 20–7. They had been well treated in Nebraska, for the most part. "The headline of one of the newspapers referred to us as 'the Black Panthers,'" recalls Kearney, the quarterback. "Some of the guys were a little hot about that. They were saying, 'Man, they didn't have to write that. We know we're black.'"

"After that game our heads were high," recalls Walter Ford, Prairie View's middle linebacker, who had eighteen unassisted tackles in the game. "We felt good about ourselves. We got on the plane with these guys from St. John's, and we thought we could run 'em off the field."

"Not only were they fast and huge, they were extremely self-confident," agrees Roering, now the director of the Carlson School of Management at the University of Minnesota. "To the point of cockiness."

The Panthers could be forgiven a certain measure of self-assurance following their first play from scrimmage, after which they led 6–0. Kearney, who'd started at quarterback all season, had fractured his left thumb the previous week, and arrived in California with his hand in a cast. After two days of watching his teammates practice, he soaked the cast in warm water, then tore it off.

"It takes a lot to get a cast off," recalls Kearney, who now teaches high school biology and mentors urban kids in Kansas City. He has eight sons and a daughter, twenty-one grandchildren and some distinct memories from the '63 Camellia Bowl: "What I remember about those guys is how disciplined they were. How well coached. And aggressive. That was the best defense we saw all season. They were some *hitters*."

When Kearney showed up at practice without the cast on his wrist, Nicks dressed him down. "But his heart wasn't in it," says Kearney. "He tried to sound angry, but it wasn't genuine."

Fog cloaked the old horseshoe stadium at game time, holding attendance under 13,000 and forcing officials to turn on the lights during warm-ups. The gloom was compounded, for Johnny fans, by the result of the Prairie View's first play. Kearney did not start the game. Getting Nicks's nod was speedster and backup quarterback Billy Hall, who swept around right end on the Panther's first play. Seeing him run, McCormick sprinted up to make the play. Except . . . well, let him tell you:

"A 235-pound guard hits me, the fullback buries me. So now I'm on the ground watching their quarterback run for more yards than anyone's gotten against us in any three games all season."

Seven Johnnies played both ways that day, including quarterback Craig Muyres, who flew up from his safety position and overran Hall, who crossed the plane of the goal line like a sprinter breasting a tape.

Hall only had to run twenty-nine yards, Ken Houston having blocked the Johnnies' first punt. These twin calamities failed to induce panic on the Johnny sideline. "We had a quiet confidence," recalls Roering, the tight end, "a determination that we were going to be in this game, and if not win it, to make damn sure they knew they'd been in a fight."

The fight was joined early in the second quarter, with halfback Bob Spinner landing the Johnnies' first punch. The future chair of St. John's Board of Regents fielded an end-over-end punt on Prairie View's 40-yard line and promptly gave away five yards, looping back, giving the members of the return team time to draw beads on their blocks.

Spinner was the fastest guy in the MIAC. The previous spring, he'd run in the 100-meter finals at the NAIA track and field championships in Sioux Falls, South Dakota. As the sprinters limbered up before settling into their blocks, McDowell, the Johnny tackle, had wandered up to the track to cheer on his buddy. "C'mon, Spinner!" he shouted, with entirely too much gusto. "Let's go, Bobby! You can beat these guys!"

McDowell's antics gained the attention of the sprinters in the lanes on either side of Spinner: Bob Hayes, who later came to be known as the world's fastest human, and Roger Sayers, Gale's brother, who outleaned Hayes at the tape to win that race. "Everyone on the track starts looking at John, then looking at me, like we're from another planet," recalls Spinner, the sole Caucasian in the race. While he finished out of the money, Spinner recalls, he did not finish last.

Just because he couldn't beat Hayes didn't mean Spinner couldn't fly. The first Panther down the field on that punt was end Norris McDaniel, who was softened up by fullback Rich Froehle, then rubbed out by special teams commando Jim Dey. Spinner was at the 10-yard line before McDaniel hit the ground. St. John's missed the extra point.

"After I scored," Spinner tells me, "I remember thinking, 'This is going to be kind of fun.'"

McCormick, the corner, was not having fun. Seventeen seconds elapsed on the game clock between St. John's' first touchdown and the Panthers' second. Kearney entered the game in the second quarter, after an interception earned Billy Hall a seat on the bench. In his first series, Kearney called a pass play to the best athlete on the field. Although Otis Taylor would be his teammate for another nine years with the Kansas City Chiefs, Kearney would no longer be throwing passes to him. The Chiefs had Len Dawson, and conventional NFL wisdom dictated that the mental demands of the quarterback position would overwhelm a black.

With Roering roaring down on him, Kearney completed a deep pass to Taylor, who with three successive moves juked McCormick, Muyres, and Beckman onto their butts. By the time Taylor reached the 5-yard line, he was overtaken by a hustling McCormick, whom Taylor stiff-armed by the facemask into the mud before completing the sixty-two-yard touchdown. As he throttles down after scoring, slowing to a lope, the future Chief puts the ball behind him and lets it drop, a subtly arrogant gesture that packs far more punch than, say, a spike or a dance routine; an act that says, *Oh, man, this is too easy.*

"So now it's 14–6, and I'm starting to feel a little inadequate," recalls McCormick, who stood a half-foot shorter than Taylor. The Panthers liked that matchup. In trying to exploit it, however, they pushed their luck. Midway through the second quarter, McCormick stepped in front of a ball intended for Taylor and retraced Spinner's steps up the left sideline and into the end zone, bringing the Johnnies within a point of the lead.

The halftime score was 14–13, the halftime question: how was St. John's not getting run out of the stadium? The dominance of the Prairie View defense forced Muyres to conclude that the Panthers could hear him calling the plays. He spent the second half whispering in the huddle. In the locker room at halftime,

Beckman had bad news for the defensive line, "You *have* to get some pressure on the quarterback," he said, " 'cause we can't cover these guys."

Beckman later lent me a (no pun intended) black-and-white video of the game. In it, I see a thirty-yard promenade of humanity awaiting the Johnnies as they emerge from the locker room to start the second half. Among the throng are a dozen or so Gagliardis who have taken a puddle jumper from Colorado Springs, a suspicious-looking aircraft with propellers and patches. Watching the Panthers and the Johnnies go through their pregame paces, John's older brother, Frank, had confidently predicted, "We're going to get killed."

As usual, Gagliardi figured a few things out at halftime. Held scoreless in the first half, the Johnny offense is suddenly moving the ball. Capitalizing on a Panther fumble, Muyres marches the team down to the 23-yard line, where the offense stalls, and Hardy Reyerson speaks up.

Under Gagliardi, the St. John's offensive huddle has always been a hotbed of democracy. "Because we called our own plays," recalls Muyres, the quarterback, "I always encouraged the other guys to make suggestions." During that undefeated season, things had sometimes gotten out of hand. "I'd have ten guys talking to me at once: 'Try this,' 'No, try this,' 'This is a sure thing.' Sometimes I had to just tell 'em all to shut up," he recalls.

No one had much to say against Prairie View. Nothing was working. The Johnnies had run over opponents all season—Beckman and Spinner slicing through holes cleared by McDowell and 313-pound center Jack Hickey, an ex-prison guard who was the oldest, meanest player on the team. "You mean that big guy with no teeth?" Ford, the Panthers linebacker, asked me. Indeed, Hickey practiced and played without his bridge. "I went up against him all day. He moved pretty good for a big guy." But Ford got the best of Hickey in the first half. "I called dive plays, sweeps and options, trying to find their weakness," recalls Muyres. "But they had no weakness."

There was this scarcely discernible fissure in Prairie View's armor: *they pushed their luck.* So eager were they to stuff the run that this eagerness came back to bite them. With the Johnnies stalled on the 23, Reyerson made a suggestion.

"Hey, Craig," he said in the huddle. "Fake the off-tackle play and throw me the ball. I can beat this guy." Muyres faked to Froehle, the fullback, and Reyerson found a seam between the corner and free safety. His seemingly effortless touchdown catch gave the Johnnies a 20–14 lead.

Muyres then indulged in a bit of Gagliardi's trademark flimflammery. Beckman lined up in the left slot but took a handoff on a double reverse, then looked for Roering in the back of the end zone. Roering was well covered—"I should have just tucked the ball and run," Beckman recalls. Instead, he threw at the rapidly closing window between converging Panther defensive backs, one of whom called the other off, like a centerfielder dibsing a pop-up. "I got it! I got it!" But the fellow merely tipped the pass, which Roering caught for a touchdown, putting the Johnnies up 26–14.

Here's what jumps out at me, watching the game on tape: Every other play in this game, it seems, goes for big yardage. You keep waiting to see guys pop off the turf and pantomime hitting a baseball over a fence or shoveling dirt on a grave or slashing their throats, but they just pat one another on the butt and walk back to the huddle.

"They were great sports," recalls Kearney. "There was no trash talk, nothing racial. Just two good teams out there trying to kill each other.

"Now you got a defensive lineman making a million and a half dollars, every time he makes a sack, he's gotta go through his little routine. Hey man—you just did your job! Now get back to the huddle."

Here's what else jumps out at me. Despite Prairie View's decided advantage in team speed, Beckman and Spinner keep getting around the ends for big chunks. The keys? (A) Those two can fly; (B) the Johnnies are successfully executing the chop blocks Gagliardi is so adamant they not practice. With the score 26–21, Muyres flips a quick pitch to Beckman, who breaks three tackles at the left corner and is off to the races before Seals, closing like a cheetah, takes him down forty yards later. After reviewing the tape, says Beckman, "I've calculated that Seals is running exactly twice as fast as I am."

No matter. Beckman's gallop sets up another play-action pass to Reyerson, a play the Johnnies concocted in the huddle. Muyres faked a handoff to Froehle—"This has to be the best fake of your life," he whispered as they broke the huddle—and threw high to the middle of the end zone. Reyerson made a spectacular, leaping catch between two defenders, giving the Johnnies a 12-point lead with five minutes to play.

A Panther touchdown with two and a half minutes to play makes the score 33–27. Everyone knows what's coming next: an onside kick. Everyone knows but the camera operator, who whips his instrument left, then right, creating a nauseating, Zapruder-film effect, and missing the kick, which Roering recovers and returns to the Panthers' 31-yard line, where he is all but ignored by his teammates. Fellow end Joe Mrozinski claps him on the shoulder; bone-weary Ken Voss walks past him enroute to the huddle, a horse to the barn.

C'mon guys—I know you're the Johnnies, you expect to make big plays, but *Christ*, Roering just clinched the Johnnies' first-ever national championship, and arguably the greatest upset in college football history. Somebody give this man a hug!

As the clock hemorrhages its final seconds, the Johnnies cross the line of scrimmage to shake hands and drape their arms around the Panthers. These meetings are interrupted when the players are mobbed from behind by teammates and classmates. Watching the film thirty-seven years later, I want the interlopers to back off. Leave these guys alone for a minute, I would like to ask them. They're Minnesotans! It's not every day they get a chance to talk with black people.

The crumbling, yellowed newspaper accounts of the game that I come across all dwell on the heroics of Beckman, Muyres, Reyerson, Roering, and Kearney, who in defeat was named the game's outstanding back. Not only do these stories bury the lead, they leave it out of the paper completely. The most noteworthy aspect of the contest is consistently and studiously ignored. No one mentions that for the first time in college football history, an all-black team played an all-white team, and not a single player on either team struck a blow in anger. *No trash talk, nothing racial. Just two good teams out there trying to kill each other . . . They were great sports.*

The 1963 Camellia Bowl took place at a time when race relations were an open wound on the body politic. It took place fourteen months after the Supreme Court ordered that black Air Force veteran James Meredith be admitted to the University of Mississippi. When Meredith tried to enroll and was repeatedly rebuffed, President Kennedy federalized the state's National Guard and sent in hundreds of U.S. Deputy Marshals, thirty-five of whom were shot in ensuing riots.

It took place less than a year after Alabama governor George Wallace pledged "segregation now, segregation tomorrow, and segregation forever"; seven months after Birmingham police turned dogs and firehoses on black protesters, many of whom were children; four months after two hundred thousand blacks and whites marched on Washington, D.C., where they heard Martin Luther King's "I Have a Dream" speech.

Sitting at Downey's dining room table six months after the end of the 1999 Johnny season, I found a clip that did not bury the lead. An editorial in the *Houston Informer*, a black newspaper, said:

"The game was above all a real tribute to interracial good will. Prairie View's all-Negro eleven . . . was matched against the top ranked all-white team of St. John's. This type of situation was the first of its kind in the nation's history, and it worked beautifully."

What did the game prove? It proved that a black team and a white team could oppose each other without a riot breaking out. It served as a reminder that black guys could think, in addition to running and jumping; that white guys could run and jump, in addition to thinking. As I tracked down and spoke to the men who played that day, I kept hoping that one of them would speak of an epiphany earned that afternoon, of a life-changing experience in the mud and mist. Just because nothing quite so romantic or dramatic was forthcoming does not mean the game did not open some eyes.

"Most of the guys hadn't been around black people," Reyerson recalls. "I mean, we're from Minnesota. But once the game started, you forgot about [race] altogether. They were out there trying to do a job, and so were we. After a while you realized, 'Hey, these guys are just like us.'"

Millions of such minor revelations push us toward "the morning"—this again is DuBois, with whom Nicks was casually acquainted—"when men ask of the workman, not 'Is he white?' but 'Can he work?' When men ask artists not, 'Are they black?' but 'Do they know?' Some morning this may be, long, long years to come."

Another *Informer* clipping shows a photograph of a good-looking black high school player. The clip is from 1964; the story announces that the player, from Houston, is considering a scholarship offer from Southern Methodist, the Southwest Conference having just announced that it would integrate its athletic teams.

"Coach Nicks went to see that boy," Downey tells me. "He said, 'Well, Coach, what can you do for me?'"

"He said, 'I can get you a job.' And that boy said, 'Coach, SMU already gave me a convertible, and promised my dad a job.'"

The young man went to Southern Methodist. After winning his final black college national title in 1964, Nicks watched his team lose three games the following season, then retired. "He saw the handwriting on the wall," says Downey. Bereft of the finest black talent in the Lone Star State, Prairie View's football program endured a long, dry spell that continues to this day. The school was much in the news for a fortnight in 1998. On September 19, the marching bands of Prairie View and Southern engaged in a tuba-denting, trombone-pretzeling free-for-all that resulted in four hospitalized musicians and $32,000 in damaged equipment. A week later, the Panthers beat Langston University, ending an NCAA-record eighty-game losing streak.

I recall my initial delight upon reading about that "battle of the bands." Now it makes me sad to think that Nicks lived to see it.

★ ★ ★

Among the Nicksiana I find on Downey's table is a program for the coach's funeral. On either side of a yellow rose are printed the dates of the great man's birth and death:

Sunrise *Sunset*

August 2, 1905 *November 11, 1999*

Downey sees me admiring the program. A scowl crosses his face. "See, Bill actually died on November 9," he says. "They even got that wrong."

"A lot of people think if we played Prairie View a hundred times, we would only win that one time," says Roering, now sitting on the sofa McCormick has vacated. "I disagree. We were more closely matched than that. Prairie View was a very talented group, but we played better as a team. For St. John's that afternoon, the sum was greater than the parts."

Gagliardi's own analysis is slightly less in-depth. "We didn't know who Otis Taylor was. We didn't know he'd play ten years in the NFL. We didn't know him from Adam! Had we known, we would have switched our plan. We would've been scared to death and screwed everything up, see? What we had on our side that day is the most powerful thing imaginable, the greatest force in the universe. Ignorance!"

Beckman, now a credit manager at General Mills, follows Roering into the foyer. Against a bunch of guys ticketed for the NFL, this modest, modestly proportioned gentleman rushed for fifty-two yards, threw a touchdown pass, made a dozen tackles and recovered a fumble that led to a touchdown. He was the quintessential ordinary person doing ordinary things extraordinarily well. He was the game's MVP.

Camellia Bowl talk rivets me but leaves Nancy Beckman cold. She is Bernie's good-looking wife, and she has left the reception to eavesdrop on our interview. She ends up interviewing me. In about seven seconds she has me read.

"Be sure you enjoy St. John's," she commands. "It is a truly blessed place. Enjoy this time with your family."

Nancy, I am trying. The following night we are scheduled to attend a concert of the St. John's Boys' Choir. No, no, no, we tell the children when they kick and scream: it's a *treat*! First of all it begins *at* bedtime, so that's a sweet deal right there. Second, the choir is directed by our friend, Brother Paul, the guy who showed us St. Lawrence, the patron saint of outdoor barbecues.

"That's Paul with the stick," Willa whispers, moments before the show begins. Indeed, there is the Naughty Monk—Laura's coinage—baton in hand, looking tense. The theme of the show is "Boys on Broadway," and Paul has been busting his butt in the last few weeks to get his kids ready.

While the band warms up I peruse the surprisingly slick program. This is quite an operation: the choir has been around nineteen years, is sixty members strong and tours extensively. It's got a junior varsity. Each boy gets his mug shot in the program, along with his name, age, school, instruments played, and a quote about what they most like about the choir:

> *Brother Paul's different quotes are the funniest thing about choir: 'You're not the brightest bulb on the Christmas tree,' etc.—Donny Codden, age 13.*

> *Kokomo was my favorite tour because there were five tornadoes and two floods in two days.—Matt Potter, age 12.*

> *It was funny when, to get us to smile for the viewbook pictures, Brother Paul told everyone that his middle name is Herman.—Jason Lutz, age 12.*

> *I like learning all the different languages in songs. I also like going off the platform at the pool during our breaks.—Corbin Chaffee, age 11.*

So *these* are the little shits doing cannonballs while I'm in the next lane trying to swim laps. Good to know.

All is forgiven when the show begins. One moment we were looking at a bunch of fidgety adolescents and preadolescents adjusting the cummerbunds of their rented tuxes, the next they were blowing us away with their sweet sound. I've divined that Paul is something of a perfectionist, a smiling but stern taskmaster. His discipline is evident in the choir's timing and pitch; the boys are all business, hitting the notes where and when they're supposed to be hit.

Between "Les Miz" and *Rent*, the jayvees nearly steal the show with their choral sampler from *Joseph and the Amazing Technicolor Dreamcoat.* Their medley takes some funky turns—what is this trio of cowboys on stage, dancing to country music?—none so surreal as the sight of a swivel-hipped, adult Elvis impersonator in a white jumpsuit. In this case, the "King" is Pharaoh, ordering Joseph to interpret his dreams. This windfall Elvis is made more hilarious, and scandalous, by the fact that he is none other than Brother Paul, who, come to think of it, never did return from intermission, and is now gyrating his pelvis to beat the band. Look, we tell the children, it's Brother Paul! But they don't believe us.

Maybe the kids have been reading *St. Benedict's Rule*, which in Chapter 55 suggests that "the following dress is sufficient for each monk: a tunic, a cowl (thick and woolly for winter, thin or warm for summer), a scapular for work, stockings and shoes to cover the feet."

No mention of a form-fitting, sequined, white jumpsuit.

A few days later, I run into Paul on my way to football practice. He asks me, "Are you going to rehearsal?"

"Well, the players usually refer to it as *practice*, but yes, I am," I say. I cannot resist ribbing him over the white jumpsuit. "What kind of monk are you, anyway?" I say. I'm joking. I know what kind of monk Paul is: an extremely devout one. He is one of the first Benedictines asleep every night. He rises at what is, even for a monk, an ungodly hour, because he actually enjoys meditation and prayer.

"I know," says Paul, "I've brought shame on the order." He is smiling, smoking a Marlboro Light. He is not in the least bit concerned.

When things go bad for the Johnnies in the days that follow, I will cast my memory back in search of cosmic causes. I will think of Benedict of Nursia, gazing with mortification from his heavenly perch upon the monk in the Elvis costume. I will suggest to several people, "Maybe it's Paul's fault."

8

BETHEL

Gagliardi is stoking that big game furnace at this Tuesday practice, finding fault, going off. Today's victim is Pantzke, who blocks the wrong way one too many times. "Goddammit, you block it just like a 52!" sputters John. "Jesus Christ, that's first-day-of-practice stuff."

With Gags on the warpath, I wander over to the defensive side of the field, where linebacker Brandon Novak says, "Let me tell you what the opening scene of your book's gonna be. Me and Trier, stripping off our uniforms after the Stagg Bowl, streaking across the field in Virginia after we win the national championship." The D-III national championship, known as the Amos Alonzo Stagg Bowl, is played every December in Salem, Virgina. "We'll get a keg on the field and drink from the tap doing naked handstands," says Novak. "John will be getting ready to yell at us"—his rasped, Gagliardiesque "*jay*sus *christ*!" is spot on—"but then, he'll be so happy that he'll just say, 'Whatever.'"

"It's important to have goals," I say, "and to visualize yourself achieving them."

Novak turned my head before I found out he was a returning

Division III all-American. There is something leonine about his chest-out walk, the directness of his gaze, his supreme self-assurance. He is the unquestioned leader of the defense, the best athlete on the team and, incidentally, the one most inclined toward exhibitionism. From what I hear of his performances in the locker room, he may also be the Johnny likeliest to moonlight as a Chippendale. He is a terror at linebacker: cat-quick, a superb diagnostician and sure tackler (he was recruited by several Division I schools as a wrestler). "He can take over a game," I am told by several rival MIAC coaches. What kept Novak out of Division I, off your television on Saturday afternoons, was his size: he goes five-eight, 205.

And that was before he became the Incredible Shrinking all-American. Plagued by a mysterious stomach virus he picked up on a trip to Colombia after his junior season, he began losing weight right around the time the season started. He found himself a despised figure at film sessions, where his gastrointestinal distress manifested itself in episodes of eye-watering flatulence.

He is still feeling lousy this week. Although he won't confess it until afterward, when doctors finally figure out what's wrong with him, he plays the Bethel game at 184 pounds. He thinks it best to conceal his condition from the coaches, who might just decide that a guy who's dropped twenty pounds since late August probably shouldn't be playing. There is no way he is missing the Bethel game. Just because the Royals recruited him hard doesn't mean Novak doesn't enjoy sticking it to them. When the game is over, Novak tells me, grinning wickedly, he wants to crack open a cold beer, then rumba across the field with one of the female trainers.

I trust that he is joking, since such a licentious display would deeply offend the host team. "Bethel is a ministry of the Baptist General Conference," says the football brochure sent to prospective Royals. "Academic excellence in a distinctly Christian environment" is what it seeks to provide. That environment should feature no dancing, no intoxicants, and certainly no skipping those two and proceeding directly to the Main Evil, the Tube Snake Boogie. An oft told joke about the Royals:

Q: Why can't Bethel students make love standing up?
A: They're afraid it will look like they're dancing.

Bethel students must agree to a covenant, or contract "to live holy lives according to the values, expectations and goals of the Kingdom of God." The covenant prohibits "malice, rage, sexual immorality, impurity, adultery, evil desires, greed, idolatry, slander, profanity, lying, homosexual behavior, drunkenness, thievery and dishonesty."

So if you're a Bethel student you *definitely* wouldn't want to, say, steal cash from your roommate in a drunken rage, then spend it on a prostitute whom you profanely slander upon discovering, too late, that the hooker is a (married) transvestite.

Or, having *done* those things, you wouldn't want to lie about it.

In order to leave as little as possible to chance, the author of that litany of iniquities—which reads, for the most part, like a Saturday-night checklist for a Barry Switzer-era Oklahoma Sooner—has erred on the side of redundancy. "Lying" appears to fall under the rubric of "dishonesty"; likewise, the big tent no-no "impurity" should cover "sexual immorality," which, to the college elders' way of thinking, would certainly include "homosexual behavior"—although that gray phrase could encompass everything from your basic buggery to an affinity for the films of Merchant and Ivory. The sobering truth is, you could abide by every other condition in the covenant, but harbor a single evil desire—*I sure would like to go clog dancing with Lena*—and fall afoul of it.

One of the MIAC's unique charms is that all of its schools are least loosely affiliated with a religious denomination. Usually the religion is back-burnered, an optional part of one's collegiate experience, a quaint vestige from a pre-*Animal House* era when gentlemen removed their hats indoors. At Bethel, the religion is front and center. It's easy to poke fun at such a straitlaced place. But give the Royals credit. They have the courage of their convictions. As head coach Steve Johnson tells me a few days before the Johnnies visit, "We've got a bunch of kids who love football and love the Lord."

They will beseech God with added frequency this week. They've never in their history beaten St. John's.

★ ★ ★

I visit Gags in his office the next afternoon. Just to see him wince, I mentioned his perfect record against the Royals: 20-0. He begins nodding vigorously, as if that will ward off the bad juju I have unleashed by mentioning the streak.

"How long can we keep beating them?" he asks, suddenly miserable. "The odds aren't good. I just saw some guy throw a hell of a pass, unbelievable pass. Watch this." On the video monitor, Bethel quarterback Bart Becker takes a three-step drop and throws a strike to his wide receiver. Touchdown. "That's just a perfect throw," says Gags.

"They've got a lot of good players," he says. "I don't know." He heaves a deep sigh, and you can only smile at this man who has cried wolf so many times. In the world according to Gags, all of St. John's' opponents are strong, never so strong as the week they play St. John's. They are formidable on Monday, damned good Tuesday, scary good Wednesday, indomitable Thursday, all but invincible Friday.

Then the ball is kicked off and the other guys turn out to be Johnny fodder, grist for the Classics they watch in the pre-season, and Gagliardi makes his joyless trudge to midfield, thinking about everything his team did wrong while shaking hands with some guy who, at that moment, despises him for allowing his fourth-string quarterback to throw play-action passes into the end zone late in a game the Johnnies already led by, say forty-two points; a coach who wishes Gags would develop a hobby or a heart murmur—anything that would convince the living legend to hang it up, so that the program could backslide a bit, so the MIAC could take its revenge on these Nebraska Cornhuskers-in-miniature.

I have been hearing about Bethel since my first day on campus. Sitting on a reasonably comfortable, 67–12 lead in the 1993 game at Bethel, Gagliardi decided he could not risk injury to his kicker, the Royals having injured his kicker the previous year. So the Johnnies went for two. They went for two following their next touchdown, as well, winning the game 77–12.

Regardless of whether Gagliardi in his heart believed his own excuse for going for two—whether he was guilty of poor sportsmanship or merely the *appearance* of it—that unpleasant postscript took some of the luster off a milestone: that win over Bethel was the 300th of his career.

It was appropriate that number 300 was a blowout, for Gags has a reputation around the MIAC for pouring it on. You would think that a guy with such compassion for his players might have a dollop for his opponents, too. Throughout the season, coach after coach complained to me—never for attribution, of course—of the Johnnies' habit of routing opponents. It is cold comfort to these men that the Johnnies pushing those point totals into the fifties, sixties, and beyond are often third-, fourth-, and fifth-string players. Gagliardi's take on it is: it's not his job to hold the score down. Says Jimmy, "Our backups work just as hard as everyone else, and when they go in, they should be able to run the offense."

There is a rumor that it was a Bethel assistant coach who informed the MIAC office of the Johnnies' illegal practices. Whether it is true or not—Bethel wide-receivers coach and sports-information director Greg Peterson assures me he can "one hundred percent, truthfully say" he knows nothing about such an insinuation—Grady McGovern can be overheard telling his teammates in the days before the game, "These are the little bitches who turned us in."

Whether they narced on the Johnnies or not, the Royals are good. Upset by Concordia in the second week of the season, they are 3-1, coming off a thrashing of St. Olaf. Jerry Haugen and Gary Fasching are watching Bethel video in Jerry's offense. I can tell Gary wants this game: he's got a competitive thing going with Steve Johnson, who preceded him at St. Cloud's Cathedral High. It's also personal for Jerry, who says, "They give you all that religious stuff up front, but then they run picks with their receivers! That's cheating."

On film, they see Bethel's barefoot kicker, Seth Olson, drill an extra point about sixty yards in the air. The Johnny coaches are envious. Placekicking has been a glaring weakness this season, every extra point an adventure. Kicker Joe Linhoff has a strong leg but drives the ball out on a low trajectory. Says O'Hara, the tackle, "We're all waiting for the day he kicks it up one of our asses."

Gagliardi, the architect of so many prolific offenses, cannot seem to muster up any passion for placekicking. It is one of his few blind spots. His attitude toward the field goal is similar to my father's mistrust of e-mail and the call-waiting feature offered by the phone company. Did John lose faith in the kicking game because it let him down, or does the kicking let him down because he has no faith in it? Either way, this Achilles' heel could cost his team a game, which could cost him the conference championship.

"It will be sunny Saturday," Novak had predicted. "Their God'll give 'em nice weather."

Novak got that right. Bethel is a handsome campus on a wooded, lakeside parcel in Arden Hills, a St. Paul suburb. After filing off the buses, the Johnnies don't find the visitor's dressing room right away. Poking his head through a door, Spencer Sokoly stumbles upon a room where some Bethel coaches are sitting in a circle. One has tears running down his face. "I think it was a prayer meeting," says Spencer.

I think these guys are tired of losing to St. John's.

It is a five-minute walk from the dressing rooms to the surreal pregame environment of Armstrong Stadium. No AC/DC for the Royals. The stadium is bathed in soothing Christian music. The home bleachers are bright with the white of the students' tee shirts. Unlike the Tommies' tees, which tend to advertise current intoxication or imminent intercourse, the Bethel kids opt for Scripture.

While standing on the sideline near the visitor's bleachers, I feel water seeping into my shoes. Why would the field be soaked on such a bright, shiny day? Could the Royals, the slower team, the team that is 0-for-20 against the visitors, have watered it down? What the heck, they must have figured. The Lord helps those who help themselves.

It was not at that wet-socked moment I knew in my bones that the Royals would finally have their moment in the sun against St. John's.

It was not on the Johnnies' first offensive series, when Sieben was mugged running under a long pass, but did not get an interference call from an overmatched crew of officials. It was not while watching the Johnny secondary give up not one, not two, but three long completions on wobbling throws of which Father Wilfred would later say, "I could have run down on the field and knocked those balls down myself!"

It was not when Moore, the most irreplaceable talent on the team, was lost in the first quarter with two torn ligaments in his left knee; not when Ryan Danielson, the only guy in the secondary willing and able to blow people up, crumpled after a crackback block chipped a bone in his ankle, knocking him out for the season.

I knew my friends would lose their first MIAC game since 1997 after Stanger drove them thirty-one yards for the game-tying touchdown late in the third quarter. Except that it turned out to *not* be the game-tying touchdown. McBroom's snap was low, and although Grady's hold was heroic—he vacuumed the ball on the short hop—the timing was off: Linhoff's kick hovered unsteadily like an upright zeppelin, and would have missed by thirty feet had it not been swatted away.

"I don't care who you are, you're gonna get knocked down," Gagliardi had told his inexplicably listless troops at halftime. "The mark of a champion is the guy who gets up when no one thinks he can get back up."

Directly behind John, Moore is on a desk getting his leg wrapped in a temporary cast. He is done for the day. Seeing this, the Johnnies deflate a little further.

"We're not used to being behind," Gags continues, "but we've had some great rallies. Let's make another one today. These guys are fired up, well we're gonna put the fire out."

Not only do the Johnnies not extinguish that fire, Gagliardi hands the Royals a couple cans of kerosene when he refuses to kick a field goal in successive drives to open the half. Both times, the Royals make a fourth-down stand. Both times, the home crowd erupts, Bethel fans jumping up and down on the aluminum bleachers in a rhythmic fashion that could be construed—accompanied as it is by lively numbers from the pep band—as dancing.

The offense can't get out of its own way in the fourth quarter. Stanger is indecisive—he will end up taking ten sacks on the day—and the Johnny offensive line looks, at times, overmatched. Crazed with frustration, Linnemann crutches over to the linemen and tears one a new orifice. "If I was out there," he screams, "you'd have f—— whiplash right now because I'd be yanking your facemask all over the place. You're like a goddam wind sock out there!"

While executing the two-minute drill, Stanger is picked off with thirty-nine seconds left in the game. As the clock ticks down, Jimmy goes after the official nearest him: "You have no conscience. You GAVE this game to them."

A purple wave crashes onto the field. Students, players, coaches are crying and embracing—albeit chastely. It is impossible not to feel happiness for the Royals, out from under the ugly and oppressive red 0-fer; victors over the Johnnies for the first time in twenty-one tries. Johnson is a headless chicken, shaking Gags's hand, putting Fasching in a friendly headlock, taking time to tell Linnemann, "You made my job a lot easier today."

There is a congregation around the south goal post, and I wonder if it will come down. Of course it won't come down. Goalposts are traditionally toppled by drunken students, which are in short supply here. Johnson takes a knee and leads the team, and a hundred or so onlookers, in the Lord's Prayer.

I once took a half-dozen Boston College linemen to dinner a few hours after they'd beaten the University of Pittsburgh. After gorging themselves on *SI*'s nickel, they pushed themselves back from the table and unbuttoned their pants. What are you guys doing later tonight, I asked.

The consensus reply: Get (1) drunk; (2) laid, or failing that; (3) in a fistfight.

One weary defensive tackle—let's call him Jim Biestek—was the exception, announcing: "I'm gonna go up to my room, lock my door, lie on my bed, and give it to myself."

What are the Royals doing tonight?

None of the above, I'm thinking.

One of the things that blew me away about seeing Gagliardi in August was that he looked exactly as he had in 1992, which was eerily similar to the way he looks on the cover of the program for the 1980 Homecoming game against Bethel: thin, graying hair slightly disheveled; the vulpine grin, the perpetual squint. It is as if the wunderkind coach awoke one morning in 1977 looking very much like what he looks like now. "His tribe is famous for that," says Chuck Latuda, his oldest friend. "The way he looks now is the way he looked twenty years ago."

Right now, none of that applies. Right now, as Gagliardi contemplates life without his starting quarterback and one of the best running backs he's ever had, he looks every hour of his seventy-two years and eleven months. After a long walk off the field, where some of the Royals fans had not been able to resist gloating and shouting in his face, he retreats to the bus. He seeks solitude, but mostly, he seeks an upholstered seat. "God," he says, "it feels good to sit down."

As always after a defeat, he lists three things that it takes to beat St. John's: "They better play a hell of a game, we better not play up to our level, and they better get some monumental breaks."

After a brief rest, John summons the team into a kind of cul-de-sac behind the bus. The Johnnies' backs are, literally, against the wall. Someone makes a crack about a firing squad. Gags tells the guys forget it, move on, fight back. "Worse things than this happen every day," he says. "We're still a damned good team, and we can still be champions."

They will need help. This loss drops the Johnnies into a second-place tie with the Royals. The Concordia Cobbers, ever formidable, are undefeated, and travel to Collegeville in a week. Even if the Johnnies defeat the Cobbers, even if they win the four games remaining after that, they are in the uncomfortable position of needing someone to knock Bethel off for them.

"Someone will," Zirbes predicts during the bus ride home. We are cruising past millponds and stubbled cornfields, the scenery somehow less alluring now that the squad is no longer undefeated. To the north, the twin stacks of the Becker power plant belch scrubbed white smoke. On the video monitor, Matt Damon is outwitting John Malkovich in a movie about playing cards. "I think this'll be good for us," says Zirbes. "Now we'll get our heads out of our asses."

Walking over the Stumpf Lake bridge on my way home, I cross paths with the other John. This is John Parente, the bearded and Buddha-like watercolorist and religious studies teacher who lives across from us in the Ecumenical Institute. Like the other John, John the painter periodically takes my breath away with his wisdom. He doesn't know whether a football is blown up or stuffed, but has this to say about the team's loss, news of which has preceded it to campus. "I'm sure this will be good for them," he says. "Adversity can be a good thing. To be denied something you want is to find out what it really means to you."

At Monday's players-only film session, a miserable silence descends on the room as Grady falls down and Bethel's Eric Carlson scores on an eighty-yard touchdown, after which the camera lingers momentarily on some coeds beyond the end zone.

"Virgins," says Novak. "That's why I couldn't concentrate. All those virgins, ripe for the picking."

"Gotta keep it light, guys," he says, once the laughter subsides. "That's the only way we're gonna win the rest of 'em. Gotta run the table now."

9

A WALK IN THE WOODS

The silver maples beyond the practice field are balding quickly now; the oaks still clinging to leaves going orange, blood orange, rust. “Could you ask for a prettier setting?” Wilfred asks on a mid-October afternoon.

“It’ll all be gone in a week,” says Gagliardi, stirring nascent panic in my bowels.

Didn’t the autumn color show just start? Have I missed most of it for note taking? The whole point in coming to St. John’s had been to get in the right lane, slow down, immerse myself in the change of season. As the adversity mounted—probation, key injuries, a surprise upset—I backslid into old, familiar behaviors. I started covering the Johnnies as if they were the 49ers, as if it mattered, in the grand scheme, *what* Stanger saw the free safety do before throwing his interception against Augsburg.

Moved to action, I looked up Father Paul Schwietz and made a date to go on a hike with him. A few years ago, St. John’s designated its 2,400-acre greater campus as an arboretum, of which Father Paul is the director. The beauty of living among Benedictines is that you can call them out of the blue and ask for help—*and they have to give it to you!* ("Let all guests who arrive be received like Christ"—the *Rule*, Chapter 53.)

I meet Father Paul in his office. He is wearing a flannel shirt and well-worn blue jeans. After graduating from St. John's in 1976, he tells me, he earned a degree in forestry at the "U." He has been in charge of managing the land up here since 1985.

The forest beyond the bleachers of the Natural Bowl is a conflagration of yellow and scarlet. Father Schwietz explains to me that the maples turn first, then the oaks. When I ask for a refresher on what, exactly, *makes* the leaves change colors, he seems momentarily embarrassed for me—this is, after all, seventh grade-level stuff—but dives in. (Again, what choice does he have?) "When days start getting shorter, the trees pick that up," he says. "Nutrients going out to the leaves are sealed off. As the chlorophyll is burned out of the leaves, different pigments—the yellows and reds beneath the greens—are exhibited."

He throws in a geology lesson at no extra charge. Kicking a rock in his path, Paul explains that, ten thousand years ago, the glaciers came down through the middle of the state and stopped here, leaving behind terminal moraine, gravelly ridges, and depressions that would become ponds and lakes. Mostly, the glaciers left rocks, which is why this land is difficult to farm.

It is interesting to note that these lands, among the university's richest legacies, were purchased with monies that had been sent to a convent of impoverished Benedictine sisters in St. Cloud by the kindly King Ludwig of Bavaria, but were intercepted by Sebastian Wimmer, one of the founders of St. John's. According to *Worship and Work*, Wimmer questioned the sisters' future in the area, and resented their independent decision to settle in St. Cloud. He took their money and spent it as he saw fit.

Because he did, I am enjoying this informative hike, which takes Paul and me to a modest promontory that the monks have puckishly dubbed "Mt. Carmel." A rope-tow has been erected to haul skiers up this hill. Across the valley is Pine Knob, whose aspens have turned, splashing gold among the evergreens. Pine Knob is a thirty-acre plantation begun by the monks early in the century.

"I'm told that, from the air, the pines in Pine Knob appear to form a capital *B*," says Paul.

I gaze blankly at him.

"For Benedictine."

None of the pines are native to this area: each was planted by some selfless monk. Among the deciduous hardwoods that have been here forever—your elm, basswood, ash, maple, aspen, birch, hickory, and black walnut, to name a few—the oaks are dominant. Trudging along, Father Paul tells the story of Brother Ansgar, a tough old Kraut who used to supervise the sawing of the firewood that area farmers have long harvested from these lands. One day a man got his arm caught in a giant saw, and was bleeding profusely. Ansgar bound the wound with his belt, then told the fellow, "You walk over that hill, then you'll be at the Waltzes' place. Tell them to help you." He did, and they did.

The arboretum contains 120 species of birds; 40 species of butterflies. None of God's creatures seems to be thriving so well as the white-tailed deer I am constantly startling during runs on the school's twelve miles of wooded trails. Because the deer have no natural predators here, other than the automobiles of speeding students, the animals (deer, not students) have become too numerous. Every year, twenty or so are hit by cars on the front road alone. Equally perilous for the deer—unbeknownst to the deer—is their insistence on availing themselves of the fruits, flowers, buds, and bark of the flora planted by the monks.

That, frankly, means war. For the third straight year, there will be a deer hunt on campus. Forty permits will be issued. On consecutive autumn weekends, the woods will be closed to nonhunters, the better to ensure that only the deer population is thinned. Anticipating a backlash before the inaugural hunt two years ago, Father Paul set up a fenced-in protest area, to help prevent animal-rights activists from wandering into the woods and becoming animal-rights martyrs.

On the morning of the hunt, the cordoned-off area contained three protesters: a doe and two fawns who'd jumped the fence during the night. They were released, their opposition to the hunt duly noted.

Thinning the deer falls under the heading of stewardship of the land, on which Benedict of Nursia was very big. Sometimes, such well-meaning stewardship falls on its face. On Earth Day in 1972, Paul recalls, he was an eager, shovel-wielding St. John's freshman, helping to plant thousands of pine seedlings along the front road from I-94. Once these trees matured, it was hoped, the two-mile drive from the freeway would become a verdant promenade, so beautiful that perhaps the students wouldn't feel compelled to push seventy-effing miles per hour on their way to and from campus.

Alas, those trees were "all wrong for the soil," says Paul. Most withered.

Sometimes, the monks get it exactly right. Before returning to Paul's office, we linger under the Swayed Pines, those towering monuments to the importance of doing one's homework. Once they'd kiln-baked a few thousand bricks, erected some buildings, and settled into a routine, the pioneer monks of St. John's sought to re-create the flavor of their coniferous German homeland. "They wrote home," says Paul. "They said: this is what our soil is like, this is what the weather is like." The good volk back in the fatherland sent seeds of trees that would thrive. The seeds that grew into these stately Scotch pines—*Pinus sylvestris*—came from Riga, Latvia.

Thus do the old trees lording over the football stadium repeat the lesson of the old man lording over the football program: it's important to work hard, but more important to work smart.

No one told me that Father Paul had a history of heart problems; I had no way of knowing, as I walked ahead of him up Mt. Carmel that afternoon, that he made the ascent with an artificial valve in his ticker. Six months later, as he exercised alongside Timo in the fitness center, Father Paul said he wasn't feeling well. He was taken to the monastery's infirmary, and was loaded onto an ambulance. Just before the right turn to get on the freeway, the front road reaches its apex. This spot commands the finest vantage of the arboretum Paul had been so instrumental in preserving. It was on this spot, as Abbot Timothy pointed out in his eulogy, that Paul went into full cardiac arrest. The paramedics could not bring him back.

"I look at it this way," one of the monks told me. "Paul knew what was happening and saw what was coming: open-heart surgery, lots of tubes and fluids and convalescence and perhaps living like a forty-eight-year-old octogenarian with slippers and cardigans. I think, when the ambulance rounded the corner, he sensed where it was and said, 'No thank you, I'll just get out here.' And that, to this day, is where you feel his presence the strongest."

10

CONCORDIA

The children have already been put to bed on this Monday evening when there comes a knock on the door. It is Linnemann, who has motored over to show off his sweet new ride. Behind him, bathed in the carport light, is a golf cart on steroids, a souped-up rig painted in camouflage motif: it resembles a miniature, half-track troop carrier. After reading of Linnemann's injury in the newspaper, the owner of some local company lent him this vehicle. Standing on his bed and looking out his window, Devin spies the cart and sprints out of his room to investigate. Even though it is past his bedtime, we take him for a spin around the grounds.

Devin sits in Tom's lap, his hands on the steering wheel, his mouth frozen open in a rictus of ecstasy. "This truck is camouflaged, Devin," Tom tells him. "That means right now, we're invisible."

When the three of us return, Laura flashes Tom a tight smile. For me, she reserves a look that I might expect upon returning from, say, a two-week-long drinking and gambling binge. She's not pleased. Once again I have shown reckless disregard for the routine.

After five and a half years of parenting, Laura and I have settled into a familiar pattern: she establishes domestic routines, and I wreak havoc on them. While I am on the road, eating room service fare, not bothering to make my own bed and wondering exactly how long it takes the hotel chambermaid to fold the end of the toilet paper into a neat little triangle, Laura is home running a tight ship, restricting the kids' intake of sweets and Nickelodeon; enforcing bedtimes, dispensing time-outs with the hard-heartedness of a distaff Captain Bligh.

Then I walk in the door and the children descend on my luggage, foraging through it like customs agents. They're looking for loot: they know I often return bearing gifts—a truck for Devin; a book or Barbie for Willa, a guilty smile for Laura, who unfailingly says, "You *have* to stop buying them junk." Their closets and toy bins are overflowing with detritus, yet, I can't stop myself.

I am similarly spineless, on those nights when I am in charge, in denying them television—"*One* show" I say, caving—and getting them to bed on time. In every sense, I lack the strength to resist them. Upon returning home I am often exhaustion-addled, having stayed up most of all of the previous night to make an *SI* deadline. During my absence I have missed them fiercely. Who wants to let a little disagreement over television policy, a little bedtime disobedience, interfere with our joyous reunion?

They walk all over me, in other words, so that by the time I leave again, Laura must don her Bad Cop's hat and reestablish the routine. The more time I spend at home, however, the more I realize the importance of the routine.

The Johnny defense has its own Tuesday routine: Gary Fasching, the line coach, reads off the names of the upcoming opponents' offensive starters. He includes their heights and weights. Concordia is in Moorhead, Minnesota, just across the Red River from Fargo. The Cobbers do much of their recruiting to the west, stockpiling burly farmboys from the Dakotas and Montana. "They're big and physical, typical Concordia," says Gary. "They're gonna try to pound the ball, control the clock. They're undefeated in the conference and probably feeling pretty good about themselves. Let's get ready to play our best football of the year."

Jerry Haugen, the defensive coordinator, takes over. He wants to talk about something dear to his heart: reading keys. "No more shortcuts," he says. "No playing by the seat of your pants. Last week we took some backdoors, and it got us out of position.

"Last year we gave up two plays over forty yards. This year we've given up seven in our first five games. We've *got* to eliminate that. Because great defense can carry us."

Indeed, it will have to. Chris Moore's MRI revealed a partial tear of the medial collateral and posterior cruciate ligaments. He'll miss at least three weeks and possibly the rest of the season. Moore shows up for Tuesday's practice with crutches and an immobilizer on his leg. He is standing next to Linnemann when Gagliardi walks by. "What did I ever do to deserve this?" he asks, gesturing at the damaged limbs of his injured stars. "I've led a clean life. Even in my childhood I never got in trouble."

Standing close by is Father Wilfred. Gagliardi has a few words for him, too: "You monks need to pray harder."

Wednesday's practice is over. Gagliardi is sitting in his car with the engine off. I tap on the window and ask him, "Are you praying in there?"

"No," he says, "but I should be." He motions me in. I sit in the passenger seat while he free-associates. This is our routine.

He wonders about Moore. "This kid is a great, great player," says John. "But he gets hurt. I don't really know what we've got behind him, but we're gonna find out."

"This type of stuff makes me wonder how I ever did it for so long," he says. "Teams have caught up to us a little bit. We've been beating 'em pretty good for a while, and these guys aren't dumb, and they've got good players. I don't know if we can do it this year. I don't know when we've been this badly beat up. Hell, it's tough enough to win with your *best* guys." He heaves a profound sigh, a sigh freighted with the fears and anxieties of a man who has coached long enough to know when a season is slipping away from him.

"I could easily have been a body man," he says, "sanding, matching colors, making the customer happy. Sometimes I wonder if I need all this.

"But what the hell, if I wasn't doing this, I'd probably be twiddling my thumbs somewhere."

I suggest that he would be reposing with his friends in the monks' cemetery.

"It's probably very peaceful up there," he says.

After ordering the construction of a blacksmith shop, a new slaughterhouse, and a two-story laundry, Alexius Edelbrock, the second abbot of St. John's, turned his attention to the need for a cemetery. In 1875, we are told in *Worship and Work*, Alexius instructed that a knoll just south of the monastery, overlooking Lake Sag, be cleared of timber "and a worthy monastic cemetery laid out on its eastern slope."

It was here, amidst the tombstones of departed Benedictines, that my children romped after dinner most of the evenings we lived in Emmaus Hall. Yes, I found it a bit ghoulish, and yes, I worried, as the kids sprinted across the granite slabs commemorating deceased abbots, that some in the community might find their choice of venue for hide-and-seek somewhat inappropriate.

By six in the evening, Laura and I were so spent from running after them and trying to get them to if not actually *eat* their dinner, at least not chuck it on the floor, that we let them do anything, short of playing with steak knives or holding each other's heads under the lake's glassy surface.

Now Gagliardi and I decide to take a walk in the cemetery. A thunderstorm percolates in the west as he pulls up its oak-lined drive. As we walk past the headstone of a man who died in 1876, a crow takes wing from it. "Believe it or not," says Gags, "I didn't know that guy."

Laid out in precise rows, under identical, rectangular granite headstones, as ordered in death as they are in life, are the monks who have gone to their reward. We move toward the rear of the cemetery, where the abbots lie in a row on a bluff overlooking Stumpf Lake.

"There's Baldwin," says Gagliardi of Abbot Baldwin Dworschak. "He was the abbot when I was hired. Good guy. Didn't like TV, though." Baldwin was opposed, you will recall, to the idea of Gagliardi getting a television in his room in St. Mary Hall. Thus the coach's smile at the memory of counting Baldwin among the seventeen monks who jammed his cell for the broadcast of the 1958 NFL championship game. As that contest went into overtime, the abbot stood rooted in the doorway, riveted in spite of himself. Baldwin died three years ago, and is now presumably free to discuss with Alan Ameche and Big Daddy Lipscomb the finer points of the Baltimore Colts' sudden-death victory over the New York Giants.

"There's Jordan Stovik," says Gags, tapping a headstone with the toe of his shoe. "Ahh, he was a great guy. There's Emeric—he used to watch TV in my room and read at the same time. I'd ask him, 'How can you do both at once?'"

At a recent funeral, the old coach stood with Abbot Timothy and the monks. On the far side of the hole in the ground were the graves of many old acquaintances of Gagliardi, who whispered to the abbot: "How come I know more guys over there than I do over here?"

Gags taps another headstone. "This guy, Ignatius, he was the business manager—the procurator—and just tight as hell. But a great guy. He did a good job. I used to go listen to his sermons at a church in east St. Cloud."

Down the hill, closer to the lake, seven rows of small gravestones tell the saddest stories:

AMANDA LEE VAN SCORK, JUNE 19–21, 1986

To her left:

JOAN MARIE MURPHY
FEBRUARY 14, 1956
APRIL 21, 1956

ROBERT J. EIYNCK
NOV. 20, 1951
NOV. 22, 1951

Marlene Douvier lived six days in 1946; born in the summer of 1938, Elvira Mary Louise Eisenchenk died in the winter of 1948. Into the tombstone of Mary Ann Ida Salzer (1924–1925), a dove has been engraved: it is presumably bearing her soul to heaven.

Hard by the driveway, a sad surprise:

BABY JOE GAGLIARDI
SEPT. 10, 1970

"We had a little stillborn," John explains, leaving it at that. I don't want to push him, but there are times when I wish Gags would reveal more of himself to me. When you most want to reach out to him, he tends to turn inward.

Oblivious to the rain that has begun falling, John is walking diagonally among rows, swiveling his head. He is looking for his best friend, dead these thirty-seven years. "Where's Adelard?" he wonders. "They've buried so many new people I can't find Adelard."

A few years ago, the monks rearranged some of these gravesites to make room for more. Adelard has been lost to Gagliardi in the shuffle. "Oh well," says John, giving up the search. "I always thought, a guy like Adelard who enjoyed life so much—his spirit isn't here in the cemetery, anyway. He's someplace less depressing. He's in the bleachers during a game, or on the team bus.

"I used to come down here more often, but I finally figured, he's not here."

Thunder peals on the horizon. It seems to me to be at a safe distance, but Gagliardi says, "Let's get out of here."

When he was a boy in Trinidad, John had a baby brother named Jim, who had blond ringlets and a sweet disposition. He died while still a toddler. Nearly seventy years later, Antoinetta is still mourning her lost angel. Years after the death of her son, Antoinetta regularly dragged the family to the boy's grave. John grew to dread those visits. "I came to the conclusion that the poor little guy wasn't there, in the cemetery," he tells me. "He was in heaven, or someplace he'd always liked being." To this day John cannot quite see the point of visiting cemeteries.

In a couple weeks he will pop out of his office chair on a Monday morning, realizing that if he doesn't hurry, he will be late for the funeral of his old buddy Kenny Borgert, who'd run a local concrete company and been a good friend to St. John's. Borgert had donated the red bricks for the walkways on the campus, and had once showed up at the Gagliardis' house with a giant, heavy picnic table. "I could just barely budge it," says John, "and he muscled it out of the truck like it was nothing. Great big brute of a guy—I can't believe that he could be dead. Course by the end he was all skin and bones."

This is what spooks Gagliardi, the wasting away, the earthly manifestation of death. In 1997, Gagliardi's dear friend Mike Augustin was hospitalized with the cancer that would kill him. Augie, as he was known, covered the MIAC for the *Pioneer Press*, and loved Johnny football with all his being. Gags went to visit his ravaged friend in the hospital room and . . . froze in the doorway. He had to be coaxed to Augie's bedside. When Ventura died at the age of eighty-seven—largely because he balked at checking into a hospital—John would not look into his father's open casket. He doesn't do open-casket viewings. "He wants to remember people the way they *were*," says Peg.

He may be preserving his memories. My suspicion is that he is also, in his mind, preserving himself. I suspect he fears that when he sees Death—in a dying friend or open casket—Death might see *him*, and remark to itself, Now how did I miss you?

Gagliardi showed up at Borgert's funeral in his electric purple ski jacket with pink shoulder panels—the one that, unbeknownst to him, cracks his players up. "I was gonna go home and put on a nicer coat," he said, "but I was already late, and I thought, What the hell, Kenny won't notice. By the time they're putting a guy in the ground, it's a little late to be showing concern for him."

★ ★ ★

Beau LaBore is working the morning shift at the Fitness Center when I drop in to break a sweat on my favorite Life Cycle. Nate Kirschner, the happy-go-lucky tight end who will relieve him in fifteen minutes, is also behind the counter. The guys earn six bucks an hour to sit there and make sure everyone signs in. For as often as they look at the register, you could write *Johnny football players take it in the behind* and not have a care in the world. What they *are* diligent about is monitoring the presence of nubile Bennies on the premises.

"Very tight butt on the last Pre-Cor," says Kirschner when I show up. "If you get a chance, check out the panty line."

"She's thongin' it," Beau confirms. It is a service they provide, these two: when I show up, they update me on the pulchritude quotient in the room. Although the news is irrelevant to a happily married man such as myself, I feign interest in their reports, sometimes offering my own analysis and commentary. Distasteful as I find it, this base, sexist banter helps me bond with my subjects.

Beau is feeling grim, in the wake of the Bethel loss, but also vindicated. I remind him of our conversation from the previous Friday. We'd stopped to talk on the sidewalk under the Swayed Pines, and I could tell something was eating at him. Practice had been shabby all week, he'd admitted. The defensive huddle had been sloppy. A slovenly huddle can only lead to slovenly execution—anathema to Beau, who prides himself on never screwing up. He detects complacency in this 1999 Johnny dee, which has already surrendered more big plays than St. John's yielded all of last season.

Beau is not complacent. He prepares for games and class with equal intensity. He lives a couple doors up the street from the Power House in an apartment that is, if possible, more frightening and less sanitary. This bacteria-rich abode—into which I stepped, unannounced, one Sunday morning bearing newspapers and donuts, only to find hours-old vomit on the sofa—is called Chubby's. Beau shares it with, among others, Nate and cornerback Andy Hover, whose uniform number informs his nickname, The

Dirty Deuce. Whenever I dropped in at Chubby's for a wrestling tutorial with Professor Hover—the Deuce is the team's reigning WWF expert—the response to one of my questions never varied: "Beau's at the library."

I think of Beau when Mark Dienhart shares with me the baseball metaphor that applies to so much of the MIAC. "One of the discouraging things" about his time at St. Thomas, Dienhart had said, "was that you saw a lot of kids who were born on third base, and when they crossed the plate, they thought they'd hit a home run."

St. John's has its share of smug and comfortable young swells. Beau is about as far away from that kid as you will find in Collegeville. During his first week of school, while many of his classmates bitched about their tiny dorm rooms, Beau exulted at only having to share a room with one other person. To meet and shake hands with Tom LaBore, Beau's dad, is to be suddenly conscious of the soft, uncallused texture of one's own hands. Tom works as the "right-hand man" (Beau's words) for a construction magnate. He knows his way around a backhoe. He does not look like a guy you would want to spill beer on in a bar. I tried, but never got a smile out of him all season.

Tom married his longtime sweetheart, Carol Arnold, in 1980. Beau is the second of their seven children. After starring in two sports for the South St. Paul High Packers—meatpacking is one of the area's staple industries, as becomes clear when one stands downwind of its stockyards—LaBore was offered scholarships at numerous Division II schools, and was invited to walk on at the "U."

Because he wanted "to go to school to go to *school*," as he says, Beau ended up in Collegeville. He is a social science major with a minor in secondary education and coaching. His future is mapped out. He is not screwing around. There is a hunger in Beau, a seriousness of purpose, that I don't see in all of his teammates (and which, as an undergrad, I lacked myself). Watching LaBore handle himself on the field, and on campus, for that matter, I am reminded of a line from Raymond Chandler's *The Big Sleep*. A grifter says of the hit man Lash Canino—one of the great handles in American literature—"There is a guy who is tough the way some boys *think* they are tough."

Ditto Beau, a laborer's son in this league of upper-middle-class white boys. Toughness in this case does not equal recklessness. While Novak is the all-American and vocal leader of the defense, Beau is its tongue-clucking parent. While Novak goes freelancing, taking backdoors, playing hunches, Beau stays at home and cleans up the mess. He had been the voice of caution before the Bethel game. As it turned out, he was right. Now that the Johnnies are playing with no net, Beau will command even more respect.

Biting cold on the day of the Concordia game necessitates that, for the first time this season, the press box windows in Clemens Stadium are closed. Forgetting this, our intrepid announcer, Father Tim, can't for the life of him figure out why he cannot hear the chorus when it launches into the national anthem. The speakers must need more juice, he figures, cranking the volume. The deafening and feedback-laced cacophony that ensues causes the seven thousand-plus people in this Family Weekend crowd to cover their ears, wincing, and sets the tone for the Johnny offense, which sucks out loud for most of the afternoon.

If it isn't Stanger getting picked off on the Johnnies' first possession, it's backup halfback Ryan Tritz blowing out his knee or Sieben dropping an easy pass or Krych missing a block.

The Cobbers, meanwhile, are playing exactly how they must to wear down the more talented Johnnies. Gutsy and gifted quarterback Jeff Hertel is chipping away with short passes and options. Concordia's first possession results in a long, clock-eating drive that ends in a field goal. (The kicking-challenged Johnnies can only look on in wonderment and awe.) The Cobbers' second possession looks like a carbon copy of the first, Hertel driving the offense methodically upfield. Not only is the Johnny defense bending, but it appears ready to break when Hertel takes the center's snap at St. John's 5-yard line, fakes a handoff to his halfback, then pivots right, handing the ball to fullback Nathan Reiff.

The season turned on the next instant. Reviewing the video,

you see Reiff look down when he arrives at the line of scrimmage, noticing belatedly that he is no longer holding the ball. After shooting the gap between the left guard and the center, defensive tackle Brian Zirbes broadsided the quarterback just as he was making the handoff. "I hit him at the mesh point of the handoff," Zirbes told me later. *The mesh point.* I knew there had to be some coach-speak term for it.

The mesh mashed, the ball hits the grass at the 7-yard line and is immediately covered by Marc Jerzak.

"I thought we screwed up," Concordia head coach Jim Christopherson told me later. "Reviewing the tape, you see that [Zirbes] hits the 'A' gap just right and makes a great play."

Christopherson is a spring chicken on the far sideline. He is in only his thirty-first year as a head coach—two decades shy of matching Gagliardi's college-coaching tenure. They are old friends who know each other's playbooks by heart. "We caught 'em when they were vulnerable," Christopherson would say. "Moore was out, Stanger—although he played well—was still feeling his way. And we were pumped up. Had we won, the Johnnies would've had two losses. It would've knocked them out of the conference race."

But Stanger sends Sieben wide to the right. The Concordia corner comes crowding up tight to play bump-and-run, but forgets the "bump" part. Sieben sails around him and into the end zone, where Corey's perfect pass hits Sieben in the sternum. The score is 7–3 after two quarters, 7–3 after four quarters. The most dramatic moment of an artless second half comes during a stoppage of play, as Timo runs down scores from around the MIAC.

"In the fourth quarter," he says, pausing dramatically, "Gustavus 19, Bethel 10."

A cheer goes up. That is precisely the help the Johnnies needed to reclaim first place in the conference. Gustavus will hold on for the victory, putting the Johnnies back on track for the automatic playoff berth that goes to the league champion. The Gusties' final touchdown in the game was scored on a perfectly executed hook-and-ladder play up the right sideline—a wide receiver catching a short pass, then pitching a lateral to a running back, who scored.

I love this league.

★ ★ ★

After the game I congratulate Christopherson on his team's effort; Gags on his 358th win, and my parents for having flown seven hundred miles to see, basically, two guys punt the ball back and forth on a cold, windy day.

They'd flown out from Rhode Island on Friday afternoon. They wanted to see the campus, find out what all the fuss was about. My father wanted to see what was so special about a place that would keep me from writing articles for *SI*, forcing him to repeatedly explain himself to golfing buddies, who'd noticed the absence of my byline and arrived at their own conclusions:

I guess they finally shitcanned young Austin?

At five o'clock we drive to Swanson's Day Care. The children are frolicking in the fenced-in "play yard." (When kindergarten ends at 3:00, Willa joins her brother at Swanson's.) Rex has an idea. "Let me go ahead alone," he says. "I'll surprise them!" The sight of this strange old man leaning on the fence and peering intently at the children did indeed surprise the day-care providers, who were about to call the police, until they saw me.

This is my father distilled to his essence, an old salesman limping through life willfully oblivious to the fact that we live in an America less friendly than the one in which he grew up. His pathological congeniality—he often startles complete strangers, tollbooth attendants, for instance, with effusive greetings—is as embedded in his character as, paradoxically, his volcanic temper. He can no more curb it than he can control his need to tailgate and spew Rexisms—the name my seven siblings and I have assigned his distinctive figures of speech. An incompetent could "screw up a two-car funeral"; someone who takes a pratfall goes "ass over teakettle." When hungry, he is apt to exclaim, "I could eat the ass off a goat."

That won't be necessary tonight. Obeying the chromosome she possesses that commands her to perform frequent selfless acts, my mother had "zipped" out the morning of the game to purchase ingredients for a pot roast. Come dinner time, Willa takes a few desultory pokes at the beef, pronounces it "gross" and fills up on goldfish crackers. By everyone else's reckoning, the roast is a hit.

You won't catch Rex clearing anyone's plate but his own, or, for that matter, wiping the table and counters, or sweeping the kitchen floor. (The bending to sweep jetsam into the dustpan might tax his titanium hip and knee.) Emptying the dishwasher, if it is full, is clearly not his responsibility: he would be a week finding the proper drawers and cabinets.

What the hell is this?

That's a garlic press, Dad. Second drawer.

Even loading the dishwasher is a bit much to expect from this former captain of industry, this decorated veteran who has already done so much for so many. But it embarrasses him to immediately fire up the television while everyone else is pitching in, so Rex rinses. He is a rinsing fool. Rinsing is his thing, which is why he is a bit miffed, after dinner. He cannot rinse. Something is in the way. There is a pan in the sink full of grease from the pot roast. "What the hell is this?" he says crossly.

From down the hall, where she is gamely bathing my children, Pat explains the grease would gum up the DisposAll, and so must be scooped manually into the garbage. Her husband has no intention of undertaking such a disgusting, menial, *unfamiliar* task. He rinses the plates over the greasy pan, leaving upon it a Close Encounters of the Third Kind-mountain of scraps. It falls to me to scrape mountain and grease into the wastebasket while Rex eats frozen yogurt and checks out the evening game on ESPN.

It is so easy for me to snipe at his flaws and petty tyrannies. (Rex, as in *tyrannosaurus*, is not his given name but, rather, his children's nickname for him.) It is not so easy for me to avoid duplicating that behavior. Some of this minor-league misanthropy—Laura calls it my "black Irish"—was passed down, some of it is spawned by the pressures of my profession. When the season is in full swing, I am not a happy, centered person. I am increasingly tired, increasingly cranky, increasingly stressed. I am, in short, Rex.

That, in fact, is what Laura calls me when I devolve into a grouch. Here in Minnesota, I have avoided the kind of behavior that earns me that nickname. Here in Minnesota, I help out in the kitchen. (In our old lives, I never cooked.) Here in Minnesota, I'm home for dinner every night. For these brief, golden weeks, we are actors in a production about a normal family.

In real life, during a normal autumn, I phone home at 7 P.M., California time, and say goodnight to the kids. I have a longer conversation with Laura after they have gone to bed. My ear is a vessel into which she decants her woes: Devin head-butted his bedroom window; it cost $120 to replace; Willa behaved abominably after school. Laura has gone the entire weekend without speaking to another adult. She is beyond tired. She is lonely.

"Don't have an affair," I plead with her.

"I don't want to have an affair," she says. "I want *time* to have an affair."

During the season, we backslide into survival mode. Problems are not solved so much as they are shelved, put on hold until after the Super Bowl, much the same way manically depressed people put off suicide until after the holidays. Here, problems crop up, and they are dealt with. One morning earlier this week I was feeling sorry for myself and being a jerk to Laura, who finally said, "You know what, Murph? We're all here for you. Please try to remember that."

I digested the rebuke, quelling the familiar urge to draw inward, to brood, to don the old frown-mask. I apologized, sincerely. Laura accepted my apology, and I had the sense of having rescued the day.

After brushing his teeth, Rex emerges from the powder room in boxers and an XXL-sized Barcelona Dragons tee shirt. His left knee is a scarred and knotted lumpscape, a vestige of his own football career, stunted by a Princeton blocking back who ended his junior season with a clip forty-nine autumns ago. When arthritis in the knee became too advanced, Rex had it replaced with a titanium joint (to be complemented later with a titanium hip). If you're ever seated next to him on a flight or in a restaurant and have a half-hour to spare, ask him about his fake joints.

The ravaged knee and the Dragons tee sum up who he is: an

ex-ball player who lived to see his sons play the game. I was twenty years old and a sophomore in college when my desire to please my father was overtaken by my desire to be shut, at long last, of organized football. After two seasons as a junior varsity wideout at Colgate, I quit, and the world opened up for me.

I wrote for the school paper, worked for the campus TV and radio stations. I took up rugby, then became the rugby correspondent for the *Colgate Maroon*, which led to my becoming the paper's sports editor, which led to a career. It may have devastated my father, but quitting football was one of the smartest things I ever did.

Rex wasn't down for long. While I was enjoying my first fall in memory without the temple-to-temple carbuncles known as "helmet acne," my younger brother Mark was emerging as a prep monster. Mark stood six-two and weighed 190 in the ninth grade. He could dunk, fight, hit a curve. He was the best athlete our family has ever produced, and he came along just in time to blunt the old man's disappointment in me.

By the time he was a senior at Bishop Egan High in Levittown, Pennsylvania, Mark was six-five, 225, and looked like one of those sculptures on the Parthenon. He had quick feet and a mean streak, and was named all-Pennsylvania on both offense and defense. He sifted through scores of scholarship offers and decided to attend Boston College. In camp during two-a-days, he roomed with senior quarterback Doug Flutie, who would go on to beat the Miami Hurricanes late in the season with a last-second Hail Mary pass to Gerard Phelan. Flutie won the Heisman Trophy, and the Eagles accepted an invitation to play in the Cotton Bowl, where they defeated Houston. A redshirt freshman, Mark did not play in the game, which is not to say his week was uneventful. While doing his best to give the defense a "good look" in practice, he fought with all-America noseguard Mike Ruth, who punched Mark in the kidney, causing him to piss blood.

In addition to spending the week as Ruth's personal ragdoll, Mark provided at least one teammate with a shoulder to cry on.

With the game still five days away, the Eagles were bused to what the driver called "the belly-rubbin'" part of Dallas. The boys had been given $200 for incidental expenses—snacks, postcards, cheesy belt buckles. The stipend was to last the entire trip. Much of that cash, not surprisingly, was spent on beer, or ended up in the G-strings of the dancers whose acquaintance the Eagles made that night.

The bus was scheduled to return to the team hotel at 2 A.M. When Mark and some of his goombahs stumbled aboard, they found a teammate sitting in the back, blubbering to himself. It was Buford, a 330-pound offensive tackle from Lynn, Massachusetts. He was inconsolable.

"Buford, what's wrong?" asked Mark, concerned.

"I spent my whole two hunnert dollars," Buford wailed, *"and I ain't even drunk!"*

Patting his teammate on the shoulder, Mark soothed him, saying, "Believe me, Buford, you're *plenty* drunk."

BC's head coach at the time was Jack Bicknell, one of the profession's all-time good guys. "Cowboy Jack," as he was known, didn't go in much for curfews. A bowl game was a reward, in his view. When the team traveled to Tampa in December of 1986 for the Hall of Fame Bowl, he did not set a curfew, trusting his players to use their own good judgment. Unlike in Texas, where last call came at 2 A.M., the bars in Florida closed at four in the morning. The bus left the team hotel for practice exactly three and a half hours later, posing a problem for many of the Eagles, who, when it came time to take the field, had yet to metabolize the alcohol in their systems.

In addition to playing defensive tackle, Mark was the team's snapper for punts and field goals. Upon leaning over the ball that morning, he discovered that the already difficult task of longsnapping is made harder when one is afflicted with a savage hangover. So Mark sat cross-legged on the grass and threw balls back to the punter. Bicknell took note of Mark's compromised condition, just as he took note of the death-warmed-over appearance of wide receiver Tom Waddle, whose pounding headache was exacerbated by the sun's glare. To ease his pain, the future Chicago Bear asked around for sunglasses, finally borrowing a pair from the son of an assistant coach. They were oversized, Elton John shades. Waddle taped the shades to the outside of his helmet, then commenced fielding punts, several of which caromed off his helmet and sailed ten to fifteen feet in the air. Halfway through a very sloppy practice in which, according to Mark, the smell of booze was discernible in the team's perspiration, Bicknell teetered on the edge of a tantrum.

Renowned for his easygoing demeanor, Bicknell was nonetheless susceptible to periodic eruptions. Aware of this, Eagle veterans occasionally bungled drills deliberately, knowing that, in cases of extreme pique—forecast by throbbing of veins in his forehead, aka as "the Bick-o-meter"—Bicknell was apt to scream, "Get the [hell] off the field!"

There was no method to their shoddiness on this day. The team simply felt like shit. What finally pushed Cowboy Jack over the edge was the tardy arrival of starting linebacker Blake Galvin, whom careful readers will remember from an earlier chapter as the insolent, police-baiting guest at Mark's wedding. Having found female companionship the previous evening, Galvin had arisen in a panic in Tarpon Springs, several towns away, with practice already underway. He frantically hailed a cab, which took him to the team hotel, where he donned his practice togs. As reporters and television crews looked on, the taxi pulled *onto the practice field* before discharging Galvin, whose teammates accorded him a lengthy ovation. When Bicknell finished chewing him out, Galvin looked down at the turf and said, "Umm, Coach, there's still the, uh, matter of paying the cabby."

"That was it," says Mark. "Bick lost it. He screamed, 'Everyone down on the goal line!' We thought he was going to run us, but instead we had goal line offense on goal line defense for about twenty-five minutes."

Despite that inauspicious start to the week's practices, the Eagles beat Georgia, 27–24, then descended into an interval of mediocrity. Mark was a defensive cocaptain his senior year, a season highlighted by a trip to Ireland, where BC faced Army in the Emerald Isle Classic. With four Murphys on its roster, including "Mean Sean"

Murphy, a backup tight end who vowed only to drink "on days with a *'d'* in 'em," Boston College won the hearts of the locals, then won the game, 38–24.

In addition to providing the victory-starved Eagles with some I-AA pickings, "the match," as the locals referred to it, provided an excuse for half of my family to descend on the old sod. We spent six days touring the country by van and developing a taste for viscous black beer served at room temperature. Stopping for lunch at a Killarney pub early in the week, my brothers Chris and Matt—both large enough to pass for American gridiron players—approached the bar. "Are ye here fer the match, then?" a local asked them.

Yes, we are, they replied.

"Ye're big enough to be playin' in it!"

In fact, we are, they lied.

"Well, have a pint on that!"

"If it happened once, it happened ten times," recalls Rex. And there were Chris and Matt after "the match" at Lansdowne Road rugby stadium, comfortably ensconced in their roles as imposters, signing autographs for clueless Irish fans. They signed the names of various retired Pittsburgh Steelers: Franco Harris, L.C. Greenwood, and Mean Joe Green. Nor was Mark, for his part, above forging an autograph. He happily signed for kids. Requests from adult men, on the other hand, aroused in him a certain mean-spiritedness. *"Everyone screws your wife but you,"* he might write. *"Get a life—Doug Flutie, #22."*

The win over Army was the high-water mark of a disappointing season. The meatier postseason honors somehow eluding him, Mark was selected as an alternate to the Japan Bowl. He went undrafted, but was contacted by several teams immediately after the draft. He signed a free agent contract with the Detroit Lions, the worst of the three, figuring he had the best chance of making their roster. Some rookies spent portions of their signing bonuses on sleek cars. In keeping with the size of his bonus, Mark treated himself to a shopping spree at Waldenbooks. He had finished two Tom Clancys and was halfway through a Clive Cussler when his NFL career was terminated.

Mark lasted five weeks with the Lions: they cut him on August 18, 1989. For the first three weeks of camp, he'd handled the Lions' longsnapping duties. As it turned out, he was first-string only because the team's deep snapper for the previous three seasons was holding out. The day that vet reported to camp, Mark was back on the scout team.

That longsnapping helped earn Mark an NFL shot vindicated one of Rex's lifelong tenets: Special Teams Play Is Next to Godliness. At Colgate, he played end and longsnapped for punts and extra points, in addition to pulling straight C's. On countless autumn afternoons throughout my youth, our yard became the site of Rex's special teams clinics. "If it comes down to you and another kid for the last place on the traveling squad," he would say, "they're going to take the one who can do more on special teams." The clinic invariably ended with Rex shanking a punt onto the roof of the garage. Cursing and clutching at some freshly pulled muscle in his right leg, he would hobble indoors, calling it a day.

"Stay in shape," then-Lions head coach Wayne Fontes had advised Mark while relieving him of his playbook. "You never know when someone's going to need a longsnapper."

He got that right. A year and a half later, Mark was sitting in his Boston apartment, circling want ads, when the phone rang. It was someone claiming to be Terry McDonough, assistant general manager for the Barcelona Dragons, coached by Bicknell, who with a heavy heart had made Mark his final cut in the preseason. In three days, the Dragons would be playing the London Monarchs in the World Bowl, the inaugural championship game of the World League of American Football. The Dragons' longsnapper had just wrenched his knee in practice, McDonough said. Could Mark be on that night's red-eye to London?

"Nice try, Kwitcher," said Mark, who more than once had been the victim of practical jokes played by his BC teammate, Jim Kwitchoff. "How's your love life. Still oh-for-'90s?"

McDonough was not amused. "Murph," he said, "this is serious." Thus did Mark end up on a flight to London that evening. His first snap in the World Bowl, for a chip shot field goal, was on the money. Alas, Mark was so excited that he sent the ball rocketing back to the holder, who failed to hang onto it, leaving kicker Massimo Manca to reprise the panicky dance of ex-Miami Dolphins kicker Garo Yepremian. Upon slinking to the sidelines, Mark was greeted by Bicknell, who told him, "Good snap. The holder mishandled it."

"Being a team guy," Mark recalls, "I blurted, 'Thank God!'"

Mark got on the field three more times that day, without incident. To fill dead air late in the game, an insipid, 21–0 Monarchs victory, ABC's Brent Musburger spent a minute talking about Mark, whom he described as "a great human-interest story."

I will always have a soft spot in my heart for Brent, for the WLAF, and for Bicknell, who tossed Mark that bone. Getting the ax from his old college coach had been a cruel blow to my brother. While his seventy-two hours as a Dragon was not a substitute for a season, or career, this windfall professional experience, however fleeting, provided a grace note to his football days.

More important, it enabled his father to offhandedly drop in conversation the fact that one of his sons had "a cup of coffee in the pros."

Or, in Mark's case, a cup of tea.

As much as they looked forward to seeing a Johnny football game, my parents have anticipated every bit as eagerly attending mass in the renowned Abbey Church. They are ready to leave for the 10:30 mass twenty minutes ahead of me and my children. While they wait, I begin to recognize in my father the irritable fidgeting that telegraphs his dual fears that (1) the parking lot will be full, and (2) the pews will be full. "Why don't you go ahead of us, and save us some seats," I say.

Before mass, a monk stands at the front of the congregation to explain how they do things here at St. John's. The Benedictines observe longish pauses during the liturgy, the better to reflect on the Word. The monk also reminds congregants that the bulky, hardwood kneelers should remain *down at all times*, since raising them creates a racket, and might also damage the speakers that were installed at great cost after it was discovered that Breuer's concrete masterpiece was the acoustical equivalent of a Costco.

I must give credit where it's due: when I arrive at church with the kids, it is standing room only. Thankfully, my parents reserved a pew. When it becomes apparent that not all of us will squeeze in, however, Rex volunteers to move up a few rows.

While riffling through the hymnal in search of the opening song, I am startled by a series of booming reports, a cannonading that sounds like a reenactment of the Battle of Trafalgar. Querulous at the interruption, the monks in their choir stalls look up from their hymnals . . . and see my father, squeezing past stoic Minnesotans, nodding and grinning like a coolie as he works his way down the pew, heedless of the crashing of the kneelers he is raising as he goes.

11

HAMLINE

Having salvaged their season, the Johnnies sailed into the safe harbor of their schedule, successive games against Hamline, St. Olaf, and Carleton. Victories against those eminently beatable opponents would set up a regular-season-ending showdown with always-tough Gustavus Adolphus, with the winner clinching the MIAC title and claiming the league's automatic berth to the NCAA Division III playoffs.

My notebook is not exactly crammed with rich detail from the weekdays preceding the game against the Hamline Pipers, as that time was spent as a single parent, preparing meals, reading aloud from the canon of Dr. Seuss, wiping Devin's bum, that sort of thing.

I am a widower for a week. The day before the Concordia game, Laura flew to California for her mother's surprise sixtieth birthday party. While she was eagerly anticipating the bash, Laura told me before leaving, what she was really looking forward to was the *cleaning out of the linen closet* in our California home (italics are mine). We are all, ultimately, strangers to one another.

I have had the kids to myself before, never for quite this long. It is good practice for me. Many is the evening I am sprawled on some overstuffed chair in a $250-a-night hotel, holding the phone to my ear with one hand and the TV remote in the other while Laura fills my ears with her tribulations. I am often damp with perspiration from a just-completed workout in the hotel's health club, and eagerly awaiting the delivery of my room service dinner. Laura's workout, meanwhile, consisted of eight hours of intermittent stoop labor—a day bent over, picking up after children who leave rooms looking as if a tsunami has just swept through them. While I wait for some waiter to roll a table into my room, there to pull a silver cover off my entrée and announce, "Your herb-encrusted filet of beef, sir," she is boiling hot dogs, or standing at the sink doing battle with some gunk-encrusted pot.

There are times when I delude myself into thinking that we are working equally hard. Nothing cures me of that delusion faster than a few days in Laura's World. And so I am spending the week as Laura would if I were gone: obeying the commands of the children—not immediately, but eventually: *I didn't hear the magic word!* —and trying to steal a quarter-hour here and an hour there to write.

Three days in, neither the writing nor the parenting is going particularly well. Fiercely as I love Willa and Devin, they are wearing me down—*Daddy, this milk isn't warm enough! Daddy, my omlin fell on the floor! Daddy, do electric eels have real electricity?*—as a lower-seeded NHL playoff team defeats the will of its more skilled opponent with grit and a relentless forecheck. Devin, the nudist, must be dressed half a dozen times a day; his sister, the nascent Georgia O'Keeffe, leaves a trail of artsy detritus—scraps of construction paper, markers, paintbrushes, small white ponds of Elmer's Glue. They create mess roughly twice as fast as I can clean it up.

Little wonder that I find myself missing Laura far more keenly than I do when *I* am the one on the road (and I do long for her then). The parent who stays behind is doing the more important—and more thankless—task; the labor less valued by society, the work whose finished product is not a magazine story or a closed deal, but, rather, a little person. In her wonderful 1993 essay, "A Woman's

Work," Louise Erdrich described the love of one's child as "uncomfortably close to self-erasure"—an overwhelming welter of emotions that shove aside one's "fat ambitions." She was writing about her infant daughter, but anyone who spends a day in rank servitude to a three- and a five-year-old; who goes two days without bathing or doing a lick of work on a book that he is contractually obligated to deliver in four months—that person can agree that Erdrich's sense of "self-erasure" may apply to the parents of older children, as well.

What about this notion of self-erasure, I have asked Laura. As someone who spends half the year as a single mother, do you feel as if you are losing your identity? "No, and that's the problem," she says. "I still *have* my identity. My life would be much easier if I *could* lose it." Laura is a writer; sees herself as such. She clings to her "fat ambitions" despite not having enough hours in the day to realize them. Because of the travel demands of my job, Laura is forced to work at home. If she worked in an office, Willa and Devin would most likely be raised by a matronly Guatemalan or El Salvadoran woman from the Canal District near our little town. "That wouldn't be fair to the kids," says Laura, never, ever complaining that our current arrangement isn't fair to her. She deserves a holiday from children as richly as I deserve this week alone with them.

As I type these words, some fifty minutes after reading my children one final book (*The Berenstain Bears and Too Much Junk Food*—how droll) and putting them to bed, my left elbow is jostled by a three-year-old who has crept from his room and joined me on the coarse wool couch. The "routine" I routinely sabotage upon returning from road trips—the strict regimen of dinner at 5:30; playtime till seven; reading time till 7:30; kids brush teeth then go to their rooms; lights out at eight—is, in Laura's absence, my most valuable ally. In theory. What I am finding out is, when the Bad Cop leaves town and the Good Cop tries, all of a sudden, to play the hard-ass, his bluff is merrily and repeatedly called. Devin says he will go back to his room if I let him type his name on the computer. Holding his right index finger in my hand, we hunt and peck:

DEVIN JACOB MURPHY

Still, he won't go. "I want to do the trash can," says my coauthor. Together, we drag an old file down to the "trash." Devin gets a bang out of watching the "can" swell up. Having reminded me who is in charge, he takes his sweet time wandering back to his room.

More and more this week, I find myself taking the path of least resistance. Look at the nourishment they are taking. My instructions are clear: bring a snack when I pick them up at Swanson's. By getting food in their stomachs—especially Willa's—we can prevent the hypoglycemic meltdowns that make late afternoons at our place sound like a bad day at the Attica Correctional Facility. On Monday, I plum forgot the snack. To avert disaster, I popped into the SuperAmerica, scoring the kids chocolate donuts and chocolate milk. They were more than a little wired at practice, turning Gagliardi's head as they took delighted, shrieking, headlong leaps into the leaf piles at the edge of the field.

Dinner was pizza, washed down with the rest of the chocolate milk. Dessert was chocolate cookies. Laura phoned after I put the children to bed. (For some reason, they failed to immediately drift off.) The party for her mother went swimmingly. Now she is home, cleaning the linen closet. "I'm having a cleaning orgasm," she says, reminding me that no matter how long one lives with a woman, one stands no chance of ever really *knowing* her.

John Parente, our bearded and Buddha-like friend, drops in for *Monday Night Football*. He has become a regular visitor in the apartment, and his windfall friendship turns out to be one of the greatest gifts we take from St. John's. He is a little lonely and discouraged by the standoffishness of some of the Benedictines. It saddens him that some of the men with whom he has prayed three times a day for two months would still fail to return his polite greetings.

Remember, I tell him, a lot of these guys are of German descent. Painstaking reserve is in their genetic makeup. (It turns out they are simply slow starters; as the year goes on, he will feel much more included in the community.)

John recalls his years at the Weston Priory, a much smaller community of Benedictines in Vermont, where he found the liturgy far more vibrant, and where robust hugs were common. He is suspicious of people unwilling to return his embrace. Now, whenever John and I say goodbye after an extended period in each other's company, we hug. At first I was squeamish about these hugs. (Tonight's embrace, two guys awkwardly hugging during *Monday Night Football*, is more awkward than most.) Once you get one under your belt, they're easy. Kind of like apologizing to your wife.

Thrice daily, the monks gather in prayer. The Ecumenical Institute's resident scholars are expected to pray with them. Laura and I aren't expected to attend the services, but would be welcome if we cared to. With two young children our attendance at these services is sketchy at best. While Laura worries that we are squandering opportunities to immerse ourselves completely in the St. John's experience, John Parente has told her that her spiritual practice, right now, consists of strengthening her marriage and nurturing her children. He reminds us to look for the sacred in the ordinary.

Maybe it is in the pumpkin patch the kids and I visit before school on Tuesday. They select pumpkins that I would not have chosen; blighted, irregular pumpkins that Salvador Dali might have painted; homely, unround ones with a tendency to list. As I pull out of the driveway, the children are thrilled to see that one of the cats from the farm is still on the roof of the car. I pull over and get out; the cat retreats from my reach, but stays on the roof. Have it your way, cat, I say, punching the gas. Our stowaway springs to safety before I get it up to fifteen mph.

Maybe it is in the moments I drop the children off at school, and day care. The operation is not so simple as it sounds. In the staunchness of his opposition to Swanson's, Devin is a sawed-off Taliban warrior. Over the last few weeks, however, we have settled into a drop-off routine that eases his anxieties, somewhat. Once he releases my leg, allowing a resumption of normal blood flow to the area, I walk to the car while he races to the window overlooking the driveway. Rather than commence crying, he blows me kisses. As part of the game, I slap myself in the face, complaining that he is blowing the kisses too hard—literally making a smacked ass of myself in exchange for a tears-free drop-off. I wave to him while getting into the car, wave to him while pulling out of the driveway, wave to him while driving down the street.

Willa is dropped off at Kennedy Elementary, four blocks away. Some of her friends take the bus to school. The "bus kids," as she calls them, run the fifty yards from the bus to the door of the school. Willa likes to arrive just before the bus, so she can participate in this mass sprint. Every day I watch her grab her Bug's Life backpack, wait for the bus, then throw herself into the stream of screaming children, craning her head as she runs, scanning for friends, taking pleasure in the sight of herself among the bus kids. This morning she struggled with the heavy glass door, but got it open. Rather than enter right away, she held the door for the other runners—a small courtesy that, for some reason, took my breath away.

Fiercely determined, prone to tantrums, she is also a sweet, bright, generous girl. "That's what makes it so worthwhile," says Laura when I tell her the door-holding story. "It's actually working. They're turning out to be great kids."

They are great kids—and resourceful. After supper on Wednesday they erect a barricade against the front door: a stool, two kitchen chairs, their bikes. A babysitter is coming over, and they are not pleased. Tonight I am to accompany Corey Stanger to his hometown of Becker, twenty-seven miles southeast of St. John's. At halftime of this evening's game between the Becker Bulldogs and the Annandale Cardinals, the all-time Becker all-Star Team will be announced. Corey and fellow Bulldog alums Brandon Novak and John Treptau made the cut.

I'm pleased to have a chance to spend some time with Corey. We've had some nice chats, but nothing in depth. I know what everybody else knows about him: that he is an extremely nice guy with a big-league arm. An all-state quarterback for the Bulldogs, he considered attending Bethel, until Gagliardi came calling. It is only on extremely rare occasions that Gags leaves campus to recruit players, so his decision to drive to Becker to woo Stanger and Novak conferred instant-legend status on them. I know that

Stanger engaged Linnemann in a dogfight for the starting job before the '98 season, but didn't get it, even though plenty of people thought he should have. I know that sometime during Corey's freshman year, he and his girlfriend (now his fiancée) Amy conceived their son Andrew, who is now a cherubic two-year-old with his mother's fair hair and his father's density.

Earlier in the season I'd taken snide note of a big-time college football trend: in deciding whether or not to go pro, many of today's stars—Florida State's Peter Warrick, Wisconsin's Ron Dayne—took into consideration the welfare of their children. The sight of Corey's mother, Mary Jo, pushing her grandson in a stroller on the sidelines at Johnny games served as a reminder that D-I has no monopoly on unplanned parenthood.

The Becker Bulldogs are 3–3 this season, all of their losses coming in close games against strong teams. Becker's best player is Corey's brother Tommy, a six-foot-five, 250-pound two-way tackle with cannonball biceps. As we cruise past potato fields on Route 10, Corey recalls the final game of his senior season, a loss in the state championship to Deer River. "A cold front came in, it was zero at game time," he says, leaving it at that.

Before Corey can say, "There's the power plant," I am staring at the dual stacks of Sherburne County Generating Plant, their massive silhouettes accessorized by blinking red lights. The plant burns thirty thousand tons of coal *per day*. In this bedroom community of fewer than two thousand people, it accounts for more than 90 percent of the tax base. Those tax dollars—Becker's cut for agreeing in the midseventies to allow the construction of this behemoth—have paid for gleaming, spacious, modern schools; a state-of-the-art community center with library and pool, the pool featuring a couple big waterslides.

"This community was so poor," schools superintendent Dr. Jim Mantzke tells me, "we were looking to consolidate with other school districts." And now look at them. Proud. Flush with tax money. Yes, some area dairy farmers have complained that their cows aren't producing as much milk. True, there is an occasional flurry of fly ash. And the coal cars tie up traffic at railroad crossings. But there's no such thing as a free lunch.

Both Corey and Tommy have made the all-time Bulldog squad, so the Stangers are out in force tonight. Amy and Andrew are at the game, as are Corey's parents. His father, Chuck, is Becker High's director of buildings and grounds, and has a spacious, modern office in the school. The first people Corey encounters on the sideline are his grandmother and her second husband, Cal, who asks Corey, "You been pheasant hunting?" Corey, in fact, has not been pheasant hunting, but is now required, in accordance with hunting etiquette, to ask Cal if *he* has ventured out in pursuit of the wily ringneck.

"Went last Sunday," he said. "But all I seen is hens. Can't find a rooster."

"Why not harvest the hens," I said. I've been reading sports pages in this state long enough to know that duck season has been disappointing, and that outdoors writers like to use "harvest" when they mean "shoot dead."

"Ain't you ever hunted pheasant?" Cal asks me. I admit that I have not. I do not admit to never having discharged a firearm. To move the conversation along, I note that duck season has been a bust so far. "It hasn't been cold enough to bring 'em down," says Cal.

"The best season is coming up," says Corey's cousin Billy, who has joined us. "Deer season." Billy played some football. He recites for me his entire athletic history, slowly, as if I should be writing it down. He asks Corey if he ever hunts deer.

"I do, but I've never gotten one," he says. "Tommy's shot three or four."

"My brother's like that," says Billy. "Got a big horseshoe up his ass. He gets three, four a year. He's got a beard like Fidel Castro, stinks, and the deer just come to him."

Before long the members of the all-time team are summoned to the far end zone. At halftime, when they hear their name over the public address system, they are to walk to midfield—a fifty-yard promenade to bask in the crowd's appreciation for all they have done for Bulldog football.

But when the moment arrives and the first five or so names are called off—Jason and Regan Anderson, Bryon Bistodeau and the Borsts, Gary and Kevin—no one makes a move toward midfield. To do so would be to unduly call attention to oneself, to put on airs. Finally the Bulldog greats allow themselves to be shooed down the sideline, a herd of them migrating at once. It takes until the middle of the alphabet, the Knutsons (Jeff, Phil), Lindboms (Grady, Greg, Scott) and the Lundeens (Matt and Mike) for the Bulldog great walking up the sideline to correspond with the Bulldog great whose name has just been called.

"Uff da," says Corey as we cross the field after the game, "my toes are cold." This is a Margaret Mead moment for me. I fall behind, noting the time and place of my first overheard "uff da." We stop to talk to Tommy, the conquering hero, who played just a quarter in the Bulldog's rout. His girlfriend, a blonde cheerleader, has painted his number in blue marker on her right cheek. They are a Rockwellian portrait of wholesome, halcyon youth. Corey is just four years removed from this tableau, but his life will never again be quite so uncomplicated.

Back on Route 10, I tell Corey what a good-looking son he has. Our conversations so far have consisted of football, not fatherhood. I tell him he's probably the guy on the team with whom I have the most in common.

At that moment, with the blinking lights of the twin stacks receding behind us, Corey opens up to me. Conceiving a child, he says, "was a mistake at the time, but it's turned out to be one of the best things that's ever happened in our lives. I can't imagine my life without Andrew. He is so beautiful and innocent. He gives me a whole new view on the world."

I recognize exactly what he is describing: a windfall perspective superbly expressed by Bruce Springsteen, who speaks of how his own children are "a window to the grace that's in the world."

"I wanted to win in high school and I want to win now, badly," Corey continues. "But I also see a bigger picture. If we play hard and play well and things don't go our way, well, I can live with that."

★ ★ ★

More and more this week, the Boss's window is mirroring my inadequacies as a dad. While I soak in the tub on Friday morning, I hear Devin expel a toddler sigh and utter words I never thought would cross his lips: "I'm sick of watching television."

Wow. I mean, I knew I was cheating a little—Laura's no-TV-during-the-week policy has proved unworkable in her absence—but maybe I've been overly lax in this area. Maybe three hours of television per day is too much.

There will be no more boob tube for them this morning. I have planned a special treat, a junket that will divert the children and kill off the seven hours remaining until I can hand them off to their mother, whose flight arrives at 5:30 P.M. today. Before meeting her at the Minneapolis-St. Paul airport, we will park the family truckster in the world's largest parking garage, then worship at that gleaming temple of consumer culture, the Mall of America.

Throughout our sojourn I have sensed a kind of pressure, inchoate but discernible, to drive on down and see the mall. *You haven't taken the kids down there yet? Oh, you should.* On one hand, I know it is a gigantic, gilded trap, a false kingdom falsely promising fulfillment of all my earthly desires—a realm whose every inch has been designed to separate me from my money.

On the other hand, the pull to check it out is strong—not just because I've got a Banana Republic gift certificate that's been burning a hole in my pocket for months. Here, after all, is a tourist attraction we have not *toured*. To resist its lure is to risk offending our host Minnesotans—*You still haven't been to the mall?*—and to engage in behavior that is vaguely un-American. The mall's California analog is Disneyland, which Laura and I and our friends deride as offensive: a triumph of cloying corporate commercialism; unendurable unless toured under the influence of hallucinogens. Yet our friends have—as we probably will—burned a weekend and blown a small fortune to take their kids through it, because it is "something you have to do."

We are not mall-crawling, cruising aimlessly. We have a goal. We seek Camp Snoopy, the seven-acre amusement park at the core of this Hedonopolis. For the kids, it is a literally torturous trek. The mall does its job well. Walking past display windows designed to fill them with covetousness, Willa and Devin are reduced to pleading, frantic vessels of material desire: supercharged particles bouncing between the walls of these realities—they want everything and can't have anything.

Check that. They can eat. Lunch consists of hot dogs and cotton candy—foodstuffs that, taken in concert with the rides, seem designed expressly to coax vomit from overstimulated children. Only Dad comes close to ralphing. After a pleasant interlude on the seven-story Ferris wheel, we board the "Camp Bus," a deceptively innocuous-looking apparatus that reverses directions midway through the ride, thrilling my children and bringing me to within a Snoopy-whisker of hurling out the window of the "Bus." Lingering nausea is my companion for the rest of our visit.

So far we have steered clear of the "Big Kid" rides—the haunted house, the Screaming Yellow Eagle, and the Ripsaw Roller Coaster, which roars over our heads, the screams of its occupants wafting their way down to us. Willa won't watch a video of *The Lion King* because the hyenas scare her. No way is she going on that thing. She and her brother are quite content to take ride after ride on the L'il Shaver, a scaled-down roller coaster; and Truckin', in which they board miniature eighteen-wheelers replete with steering wheels, side-view mirrors, and shiny chrome exhaust pipes (the Camp will go just so far in pursuit of verisimilitude: you will find neither porn nor amphetamines stashed in back).

After a couple hours on these rides, I mention offhandedly to the kids that the Log Chute doesn't look so scary. You "float" in a hollowed out log through a "lumber mill," nod to the replicas of Paul Bunyan and Babe the Blue Ox, and you're done.

I say nothing about the ride's two, near-vertical forty-foot "waterfall" drops, figuring we'd cross that bridge when we came to it. We joined a queue, talked for a while, and before we knew it, we were being strapped into the log. As we rounded a bend and headed into the "mountain"—gradually gaining altitude she knew in her five-year-old bones we would lose much more rapidly—Willa became more and more afraid. Emerging from the "old mining tunnel" we saw that the track ended—simply fell into space. The first waterfall awaited. "Daddy, you said it wasn't scary!" shouted Willa, who was, perversely, in front (camp attendants forbade me to take the point). *"I want to get off!"*

We plunged forty feet, the nose of our vessel kicking up a splash that streaked Willa's face, the flume-water mingling with her tears. I had thought the ride might serve as a breakthrough; that she might think, Hey, that wasn't so awful. Instead, I have compounded her terror of amusement park rides and undercut any trust she might otherwise have been inclined to place in me. A year later, she still brings up my betrayal.

Back in our log, we still had one more waterfall to go. As we approached it, Willa turned and spat these words: "I'm telling *Mommy* you took us on this ride!"

She had to wait to rat me out. We didn't make it to Laura's gate on time. I couldn't find the car right away in the 13,000-space Mall of America parking lot. I was one floor off. While wandering the parking structure in search of his lost car, Daddy said some bad words. "I'm telling Mommy you said the 'f' word," vowed Willa, still plenty steamed at me. And she did.

We headed for Laura's baggage claim area, where Devin sat on the edge of the carousel, letting it nudge him along. I just let him do it. If he got his little buttocks pinched, well, he wouldn't sit on a baggage carousel again, would he? His little game ended when a businessman lifted him off the carousel. The guy gave me a look that said, *If my time were just a little less valuable, I'd report you to the authorities.* I almost told him to go shit in his hat. I was too tired to care.

Laura showed up in a black skirt and leather jacket, smiling, radiant, turning heads all over the terminal. We all tried to hold onto her at once. Willa narced on me in the car on the way home, but her heart wasn't in it. Her sense of betrayal and fear were trumped by her joy at being reunited with the one professional parent in her life, the authority figure with a clue. Sometimes it's good to be the Bad Cop.

★ ★ ★

Laura and I were awakend at 5:45 the next morning by the whimpering of Willa, who had been awakened, possibly, by a Log Chute-nightmare. I bounded to her aid. When parental duty calls in the night, there is no wee-hours game of rock-paper-scissors between my wife and me. We do not shoot fingers. She stays in the bed, I get out. It is immutable.

I get out because this is my penance for having a job that takes me away from home half the year. I get out of bed, combating darkness, disequilibrium, unseen sharp-edged Tonka vehicles and the occasional wee-hours Woodrow because there is a price to be paid for all those nights of interruption-free slumber in Marriotts, Hyatts, and Westins; for all the nights she must handle things alone.

Willa says she can't get back to sleep. I warm milk for her and tell her it's still the middle of the night, even though it's crowding six in the morning. With luck, we can all get another hour of shut-eye.

The clattering of matchbox cars on the hardwood floors tells us that there will be no more sleep: Devin has cast off his covers and is slouching toward the master bedroom. He snuggles up next to me and breaks wind. Twice. The kid is three. Reflexively, Laura accuses me. "Devin," I say, "what do you say?"

"I WON'T say excuse me," he says. He wakes up looking for a fight, as would any of us who slept in a bed with roughly thirty Lego pieces and woke up with several of them embedded in our flesh.

Willa is not far behind, and for a few minutes we are all four of us under the covers on this chill morning, like the hounds crowding the bed in *Go Dog, Go*. This bed is small, the manners of its younger occupants unformed and primitive, but the point is, unlike the past seven mornings—indeed, unlike so many mornings in football seasons past—we are together.

Beware the Hamline Pipers. Underfinanced, underappreciated, they scrap. They fight. They punt the Johnnies down and make them go ninety yards to score. They find a way to keep it close. Late in the second quarter against St. John's in 1994, they returned an interception 102 yards for a touchdown, giving them the lead at halftime. The Pipers hung on, snapping what was at the time the nation's longest home-winning streak at thirty games.

Nestled up against a freight yard, two thousand-seat Norton Stadium did not make *SI*'s preseason list of the Top Five Places to Watch a College Football Game. (Clemens Stadium did, the only non-Division I venue to be so honored.) It might have sneaked in, had the list been expanded to, say, the top 500 such sites. Little wonder visiting opponents sometimes refer to this underwhelming pitch as "Hamline High."

Still, the Pipers have much to be proud of. Despite the fact that Hamline is coming off a 16–13 loss to Carleton; despite the fact that the Pipers will finish the season in the MIAC cellar, their fans can lay legitimate claim to being "No. 1." Established in 1854, Hamline is Minnesota's first private university. The Pipers make the home-field advantage work for them. Before the game, Jimmy tells me the Pipers have been known to try to get the Johnnies off-balance by starting the national anthem while the visitors are still on the field, warming up.

This year they add a devilish new wrinkle. Gags has just concluded his pregame speech and launched into the Our Father when a voice comes over the loudspeaker:

"Ladies and gentlemen, please stand for the national anthem."

God or country? To which to pledge one's allegiance? Students at a school less grounded in Catholicism may have felt some momentary confusion. Not a Johnny budged before enunciating the words, "For thine is the kingdom and the power and the glory. Amen." In a contest between church and state, most of these guys will come down on the side of . . .

"Jesus Christ!"

That heartfelt epithet passed Gagliardi's lips exactly one second into the game, when he saw that Joe Linhoff's kickoff was abysmally short. If John felt even the slightest spasm of guilt over taking the Savior's name in vain (I think he did), that remorse had not passed before the Johnnies caught the only break they would need on this bright Saturday afternoon. Linhoff's kick bounced off the chest of some luckless Piper and into the arms of the hustling Andy Hover, No. 2, the Dirty Deuce, Chubby's resident, and my instructor for Monday night WWF tutorials.

Seven plays later, Stanger sneaked in for the only touchdown St. John's would need in a listless, 20–3 win.

In the dressing room at halftime, Jimmy carps at the offense. "I don't know why we're not able to chop these guys. Everyone else has chopped the heck out of this team."

His old man is worried. The Johnnies should be steamrollering Hamline, but are letting the Pipers hang around, a prescription for an upset. "We've really got to give it everything for the next thirty minutes," he says. "We've gotta fire up and give it our all."

I see a backup guard yawn.

The Johnnies score quickly—Sieben makes a leaping, circus catch, stripping the Piper's free safety in midair, then running for a forty-eight-yard touchdown—then stall on three straight possessions deep in Hamline territory. The frustration of the offense is palpable. Alas, the ugliness is only beginning.

A twenty-two-yard punt return by Grady comes back on a clip. As the return team filters resentfully off the field, mild-mannered sophomore Brad Beyer, of all people, strolls past the referee to deliver a little drive-by jab. I see the white cap register the remark, and restrain himself. *Okay, kid. Your first one's free.* But now Beyer is peeling back for another fusillade, and this time the yellow handkerchief takes wing. After throwing the flag, the ref turns, raises his index finger like the grim reaper and marks the perp. Beyer turns his head, groaning. As he should. He's in deep shit.

I'd already heard Gagliardi, on the Johnnies' previous possession, ask the side judge, "Do you have it in for me?"

No sir, came the reply.

Now the white cap tells him that on top of the clip, the Johnnies are getting another unsportsmanlike conduct—their second in as many series—because No. 4 popped off. ("All I said was, 'Nice call,'" Beyer protested.) John spins toward Beyer, then back to the ref. This Rexism springs to mind: *He doesn't know whether to shit or wind his wristwatch.* Gags doesn't know whom he wants to ream out worse.

Now Jimmy goes into pit-bull mode, storming up and down the sideline, ordering players to move back. "Even you, Novak!"

Brandon takes a step back. The instant Jimmy turns his back, he takes a step forward.

The Johnnies score, anyway. The extra point is blocked. A Hamline defensive back tries to run with the ball, zigzagging chaotically. The play goes on forever, the Pipers scrambling around like doomed Romanovs in the basement of the Winter Palace. It is a fitting conclusion to an ugly day's work.

As the Johnnies board the bus, Gagliardi shells out ten-spots. When a Hamline player walks past, minding his own business, Gags distractedly tries to hand him money. Player and coach smile at the misunderstanding.

Squandered opportunities, personal fouls, unsportsmanlike conduct, general slovenliness—this anarchy is at once entertaining and disturbing. The Johnnies are winning even as they seem to be imploding. If they keep playing the way they did today, someone is going to take their lunch money.

12

ST. OLAF

The Johnny coaching staff lunches together on Mondays, carrying trays through the cafeteria line, then gathering around a table in the deepest recess of the refectory. After Gagliardi poses a series of "What-happened" questions—What happened on that fake punt? That bungled extra point? That long pass surrendered?—the conversation can, and does, range anywhere.

Jerry Haugen, the defensive coordinator, fears that the absence of coaches at Monday's film sessions is hurting the team. A lot of teaching goes on in those sessions, he says. Jerry has not noticed in this team the steady improvement that is normally seen in a St. John's squad.

The Bethel Royals, a bunch of guys who love football and love the Lord, edged Macalester two days ago, 74–nil. The Johnny coaches note with mild surprise that Bethel's second-to-last touchdown was scored by its starting halfback. At least when the Johnnies run up the score, they have the decency to run it up with fourth- and fifth-stringers.

It is important for me to spend as much time as possible with the coaches. Spelunking in their heads, I will find out what's *really* going on. At the same time, I must take care not to interrupt their important work. Stopping by the cubicle of defensive line coach Gary Fasching on Tuesday, for instance, I overhear him and offensive assistant Mike Trewick discussing the Johnnies' kicking woes:

TREWICK: "Remember Super Toe? That was a great toy. Just hit him on the head and he'd kick the ball through the uprights. We need Super Toe."

FASCHING: "Sure I remember Super Toe. When I get an artificial knee, I'm gonna have them put a couple extra springs, so I can kick like Super Toe."

TREWICK: "Did you know that Super Toe got more distance if you put the ball on its side, like a watermelon?"

FASCHING: "Didn't they use to have Super Toe basketball?"

TREWICK: "*And* hockey!"

Like clowns piling into a VW Beetle, a half-dozen defensive players shoehorned themselves into Gary's cube on Wednesday to review tape of Saturday's opponent, St. Olaf. Gary heard something encouraging, one Johnny telling the others, "I don't think they can move the ball on us."

"I used to hear 'em say that all the time last season," Gary tells me later. "This is the first time I've heard it this year."

The offense remains in the doldrums. Linnemann's limitations—he lacked Stanger's arm strength—forced him to take the short stuff. Corey tends to miss or ignore receivers who flash open right away. And unlike Linnemann, he has no stomach for confrontation with his linemen. The offensive line tends to regard Corey as one of its own, a hog who made good. True, Stanger was a tight end, blocking only half the time. At six-three, 240, however, he *looks* like a member of their mesomorphic fraternity. "It's like he's one of us," says Vonderharr, the center.

Is it possible to be too much like an offensive lineman? Some of the coaches feel that Corey's mellow demeanor might occasionally be a detriment to a unit that needs a hot poker. Before the

Hamline game, Jerry told Corey, "Sometimes you've gotta be an asshole out there."

Linnemann admits he doesn't have the strongest arm. "But I think you'll find," he says, "I've got the asshole part down cold."

Willa—no scissors till Nov. 4.

So commands the Post-it note on the fridge. Sometime before dinner yesterday evening, our children cut each other's hair, emerging from Devin's room with guilty smiles and grotesquely serrated bangs. ("I needed hay for my horses," explained Willa.) Laura and I would like to assure each other that our children remain cute despite their hellish new 'dos. But there is no use lying to each other. They look like trailer trash, like kids who wander out of a junkyard in one of those postapocalypse, *Mad Max*-type movies.

We arrive late to the Abbey Church on Sunday morning, shushing our cranky, tonsorially mutilated offspring. Father Don Talafous bestows prayer books, greetings, and his kind smile upon us, despite our tardiness. All seems normal. This illusion belies the magnitude of this date in church history. It is 482 years to the day since Martin Luther nailed his ninety-five theses to the door of a church in Wittenberg, Germany. Among other things, Luther objected to the Vatican's selling of indulgences, by which Catholics could pay the church to have sins forgiven—an ingenious coupling of contrition and capitalism (and an early example of what we at AOL-Time Warner would call "synergy").

Today, after thirty years of negotiations, representatives from both faiths have signed the Joint Declaration on the Doctrine of Justification. "We're closer to healing the scandal of this rift," the celebrant tells us, "this terrible division with our Protestant brothers and sisters."

The new spirit of ecumenism had not trickled down to the Natural Bowl in time for yesterday's game against Lutheran-affiliated St. Olaf, whose junior strong safety Jason Carlson could be overheard promising Grady McGovern that he would leave the field "in a body bag" and addressing the Johnnies' top receiver as

"Sieben, you little bitch." But that's how it works in the church: it takes a while after the guys in the funny hats sign the paper for the goodwill to trickle down to the rank and file.

The school St. Olaf is named after King Olaf, the patron saint of Norway. It boasts one of the nation's finest Norwegian Studies programs, and what is believed to be the only fight song set to a waltz beat. We excerpt it here:

> *Our team is the cream of the colleges great*
> *We fight fast and furious, our team is injurious.*
> *Tonight* [opponent here] *will sure meet its fate.*
>
> *Um Ya Ya, Um Ya Ya,*
> *Um Ya Ya, Um Ya Ya,*
> *Um Ya Ya, Um Ya Ya,*
> *Um Ya Ya Ya.*
>
> *(Repeat).*

Less distinguished is the Oles football program, which has won but two of its seven games this season. Head coach Paul Miller ran an immensely successful high school program before joining the college ranks, where he has found the going more difficult. Both of St. Olaf's wins, however, have come in the last two weeks. The Oles—pronounced Ollies—are on a rollie.

They come out fired up, hitting hard. While making the tackle on the opening kickoff, Johnny freshman Cam McCambridge takes a helmet to the helmet, as it were. He leaves the field hunched over in pain. While inspecting himself for damage on the sideline, he draws a circle of interested onlookers. Jimmy curtly ends the carnival, saying, "McCambridge, put that thing away."

I try to make it to the pregame mass on Saturday morning. I sit in the last pew of the chapel on the right-hand side. Gagliardi sits in the last pew on the left. I am fairly certain, as he sits motionless in his pew, his chin resting on his right thumb, that he is thinking about God and football. What I don't know, and lack the nerve to ask, is how the percentages break down.

The celebrant is the friendly and eccentric Father Bryan Hays, who does this mass not because he is a genius—I am told he is a brilliant composer—but because he can zip through the service in eighteen minutes flat. I try to blend in, become part of the scenery. It didn't go so well this morning. Father Bryan is accustomed to Gagliardi being the last guy in line for communion—so much so that after handing John a host, he turned his back on me and walked away. I had to chase him halfway to the altar and tug on his cassock just to get a wafer. It was as if someone was trying to tell me something.

At the pregame mass a couple weeks ago, Father Bryan disturbed my reverie by doing a bit of freelancing during the Eucharistic Prayer, a part of the mass I'd always assumed was etched in stone.

"I always like to offer up a prayer for the injured," he said while glancing briefly but significantly—so it seemed to me—at Moore. I half expected a heavenly shaft of white light to pierce the ceiling and home in on the damaged left knee of the MIAC's finest running back. But no such miracle occurred.

Or didn't it? Astonishingly, on the Johnnies' first play from scrimmage against St. Olaf, No. 41 takes a pitchout and submarines for six yards around the right end. Timo deliberately (in my opinion) injects a joyous, incredulous intonation into his voice when he announces over the loudspeaker, "Chris Moore on the carry."

That's right, three weeks after tearing two ligaments in his left knee, Moore is back on the field. The first doctor he went to see told him he was done for the season. The second doctor told him that he might be able to play without the full use of the two ligaments he'd torn, the posterior cruciate and medial collateral. Guess whose opinion Moore heeded? To accelerate healing, he's been making frequent visits to a St. Cloud acupuncturist. He's got a brace on the knee and a roll of tape on his left ankle—which was badly sprained, incidentally, on the same play that saw him tear those knee ligaments. I knew Moore had talent, and I knew he had character. (He will spend his spring break ministering to alcoholics and drug addicts in Miami.) I didn't know he had stainless-steel cojones. It is an overused word in sportswriting, but I apply it to Moore because it fits: he is a *warrior.*

He is not, however, the same warrior who started the season. He has lost speed, and his cuts to the right lack their old crispness. "Chris Moore at 75 percent is better than any other back in this league at 100 percent," says Beau. I wouldn't argue with him. A month or so after the season, a running back from a rival MIAC school ended up at a Johnny party, where he was overheard saying, "I was better than Moore. I outrushed him." It was the visitor's misfortune to make this intemperate boast within earshot of LaBore, who got up in his face and ticked off seven reasons why he was wrong, those reasons ranging from "If I could choose any back in the MIAC, it would be Chris Moore," to "Before he tore up his knee, Moore led *the nation*, at one point, in rushing yards per game," to "You're not as good as you think you are."

Reason number seven: "Maybe we should step outside and figure this thing out once and for all."

The guest conceded the point.

Moore's second-quarter burst up the left sideline gives the Johnnies a first down on the Ole 23-yard line. After beating his block and stuffing Moore on the next play, Carlson, the extroverted St. Olaf safety, pops off the ground, whooping, arms upraised. Carlson, it should be noted, has painted around his eyes a kind of Zorro mask. He has tricolor hair, various body-piercings, and seldom stops running his mouth. The Johnnies *really* don't like him.

On the next play he is one of three Oles who run into one another in the back of the end zone, Three Stooges-like, as Stanger hits Kirschner in the navel with a touchdown pass. Despondent, Carlson stays on the ground for a few moments. A couple guys in the Rat Pak can't resist needling him:

"Hey, 48, where were you?"
"Hey, 48, don't cry, your mascara will run!"

★ ★ ★

The Rat Pak is the Johnnies troupe of male cheerleaders. Gagliardi doesn't care for their shtick—in the old days, their chants and cheers crossed the line into vulgarity—but everyone else does. Some of the guys cross-dress in traditional cheerleader garb. Others outfit themselves in seventies leisurewear and fright wigs. They lead sublimely ridiculous cheers—

Johnny fans, on your feet
Stand up and smack your seat!

—conduct halftime shopping-cart races, and unfailingly take up the cry after every penalty by an opposing team: "You gotta play by the rules!"—an admonition I found amusing, coming from the sideline of the team on probation.

To me, the Johnnies' lack of a traditional cheerleading squad is just another item to check off in the "What I Love about This Place" column. While I admire the athleticism of traditional cheerleaders, and have spent many pleasant moments on assignment for *SI* watching nubile and expertly waxed young women perform high kicks and back handsprings, I now see cheerleading as an anachronistic and silly activity that sends an outdated message to youth. *Okay, the boys will be over here, doing the important work, and the girls will be over here, shouting encouragement!*

I'm hoping Willa won't be a cheerleader. Let her guyfriends come by the pool or soccer pitch or softball field or track where she's competing and cheer *her* on.

The Oles fight back, and the halftime score is 14–all. For the fourth time in as many weeks, Gagliardi has a close game at halftime. In his stirring halftime oration, he relies once again on flame imagery. "They're gonna be fired up," he predicts. "Put the fire out, guys."

His players dutifully take up the cry—"Put the fire out!" "Put the fire out!"—and charge the exit, where equipment manager Leroy Henkemeyer pushes the wrong button, causing the automatic door to slide down rather than up, creating a dense bottleneck of Johnnies and diffusing the excitement of the moment.

Inspired by the lofty rhetoric of his legendary coach, Stanger throws a pick on St. John's first possession, causing Gagliardi to toss his index cards in exasperation. As the recipe cards flutter to earth, at least one alert Johnny alum has diagnosed Stanger's problem. "The plays are well designed, the receivers are open, but the quarterback overthrows them. It's clear that he has no depth perception."

This would be the opinion of Dr. Robert Hilgers—Laura's father—who has flown from Louisville, Kentucky, to visit us this weekend. Bob graduated from St. John's in 1958 as the covaledictorian of his class, and has gone on to become one of the nation's preeminent gynecological oncologists. (His brother Tom, Laura's uncle, is another Johnny alum, class of '65.) As it is for so many Johnny alums, this place is a refuge and touchstone for him. His job is difficult and high-pressured. When he returns to St. John's, the lines on his face soften. He disappears on long walks to the Stella Maris Chapel and the monks' graveyard, communing with the souls of men who taught him to love knowledge for its own sake. Early in our relationship, when he knew me as just some punk shacked up with his daughter, my conversations with Bob tended to be more strained than they are now. He was an unathletic brainiac, I was the converse. We found common ground talking football. Nothing improved my relationship with Bob like the decision to spend a season at his alma mater. St. John's has strengthened the bond between us—so much so that I can say, without fear of weakening it, that he doesn't always know what he's talking about when it comes to football. I disagree with his assessment of Stanger's depth perception, and remind him that it can be tough to put the ball precisely where you want to while ducking blitzing linebackers intent on bodily harm.

Stanger is about to silence his critics. Noticing how the Oles have been flying up to blow up the screen pass Stanger keeps calling, Ben suggests a ruse. Kirschner, the tight end, will fake the crackback—that is, he will pretend to block down on the outside linebacker, as if the Johnnies are running that screen again. Once the safety is suckered up, Kirschner will bolt for the flag. "He'll be wide open," says Sieben. The new play is dubbed DJ Brown. "DJ" is the name of the screen pass, "Brown" in the Johnny lexicon denotes "fake"—"'Cause we wanna make 'em look like shit," Sieben explains to me.

They do. Nate's thirty-six-yard reception puts the Johnnies on the 13. While he's hot, Stanger rolls right and throws low to Sieben, who makes a nifty, sliding catch for the game-winning touchdown. After lobbing the ball to an official, Ben seeks out his body-pierced buddy, Carlson, and gives him an earful. This unsporting harangue is overheard by a stern old back judge who makes a special trip across the field to instruct the Johnny coaches to tell number three to keep his mouth shut.

Talking to Carlson on the field after the game, I cannot help noticing the five safety pins in his left ear. Then again, he is a safety. He's got shoulder-length hair died purple and blue, with a fiendish yellow streak down the middle. Perspiration has melted his eyeblack-mask making him look like a collaboration between LeRoy Neiman and Henri de Toulouse-Lautrec. When I ask him if he has put all this effort into his hair and makeup for Halloween, he and his buddies laugh menacingly. "For me," he says, "every day is Halloween."

I am drawn to him because the homogeneity of the MIAC is beginning to drive me just a little crazy; because I think that a guy who goes so far out of his way to *not* conform in this conformists' sport is probably worth meeting. It turns out Carlson is a bit of an outsider even at St. Olaf. He comes from Tower, Minnesota, in the Vermilion Iron Range. "Five hundred people in the town, twenty-five in my graduating class," he says. He's majoring in bio and thinking about grad school, maybe getting into physical therapy or sports medicine. Although Carlson would not want this getting out, his coach tells me later that he is one of the most meticulous, anal students on the team.

I congratulate Carlson on a hard-fought game and ask him what he thinks of my boys. "Solid, maybe a little overrated," he says. Fair enough. Do the Johnnies talk much? "Not a lot," he said. "I personally do a lot of talking. I think it's fun. Makes it interesting."

What's it like down there at St. Olaf, I ask him. I hear the college is 70 percent female. Are you much in demand?

"Nahh," he says, modestly. "The girls there are all pretty strait-laced. Although," he says, smiling at his buddies, "there's a few of 'em that want to come to the dark side." A gale of sinister laughter erupts, during which I experience a burst of clarity. This is the guy who will be sitting across from me in my living room in a dozen years, lying through his teeth when I ask him, "So, where will you be taking my daughter tonight?"

After the game, a couple of my Johnny buddies want to know why I was talking to "that freak show." Their timing is poor. Even though Halloween proper is not until tomorrow night, the students will celebrate it tonight, meaning that in a few hours, half the team will be enthusiastically cross-dressing. It is noteworthy and, I think, ultimately encouraging that many Johnnies dress up as women for Halloween. Moore and linebacker Adam Switlick are French maids. Steve Lynch, the wideout, is a bunny, with pink tights and a fluffy ball over his backside. Josh Otto, a slim junior wide receiver, looks pretty damned good in a skirt and brunette wig. I find myself hoping, for his sake, that he is never remanded into custody in the state penitentiary.

St. John's has a proud history of imaginative Halloween costumes. The award for Most Warped Costume Ever goes to the Johnny who used as inspiration the disgrace of one-time Minnesota gubernatorial candidate Jon Grunseth, whose 1990 campaign was torpedoed by reports that he had skinny-dipped with teenage girls. The following October, one resourceful Johnny made the Halloween-party rounds wearing around his waist a kiddy-pool containing water and several nude Ken and Barbie dolls. When asked, the fellow would answer indignantly, as if it were obvious:

"I'm a Jon Grunseth pool party!"

The boys are raging tonight at various Halloween parties. I have been invited to join them, but that is out of the question. It's important for me to keep a professional distance. Besides, I don't have a costume, and lack the nerve to ask one of my monk friends if I can borrow a cowl for the night.

Also, I've got top-secret plans. A monk friend has invited Laura and me to join him on a forbidden, covert mission inside the Abbey Church.

Entering through the main doors, we pause in the baptistry, waiting while the mystery monk parks his car. This gives us a chance to commune briefly with the sculpture of St. John the Baptist. It is not a cheerful communion. His gaunt, grim aspect reminds us that life in the service of God is one of privation and persecution. Cast in bronze by Doris Caesar, this is a tall, skinny, and black St. John, the model for which might have been Manute Bol. I have heard stories about Agnes Ramler, a devout German woman who did housework in the monastery. She was a favorite of the monks, who did their best not to laugh when she proclaimed in her "tick" German accent, "Tanks to be God," when what she meant, of course, was "Thanks be to God." Agnes would stand in the baptistry on bitterly cold days, awaiting a ride home. The monks knew Agnes loved that statue of St. John, and gently provoked her by poking fun at it.

Why is he so skinny?

"You'd be skinny, too," she would say, "living on honey and locusts."

Why so dark?

"He roamed the desert. He was always in the sun!"

Why so tall?

Agnes's reply to this question is much beloved by the monks:

"Dat's da art."

Rejoined by the mystery monk, we enter the dimly lit interior of the church, proceeding cautiously up the right side aisle, past a shrine to Mary, behind the choir stalls. In the near-darkness, the baldequin suspended over the altar looks like a UFO. The mystery monks stops us, then scouts ahead. "From here on in," he whispers upon his return, "no talking."

Crossing the sanctuary, we go through a door and up two flights of stairs, then mount a spiral staircase that ascends three more flights, past hundreds of gleaming metal pipes. Some are skinny, like pipes on a wind chime; some are the diameter of pails. They are the pipes for the church's Holtkamp organ. We reach the top of the steps and enter a concrete catwalk, approximately seventy feet over the center aisle. The walls of the catwalk rise only to midthigh. A misstep will send the careless trespasser plunging to the floor, where the novices charged with the clean-up will remark resentfully, "It is tragic, I suppose, although he certainly had no business being up there."

False steps are very much on the mind of John Parente, who has joined us for this adventure and who has clearly begun to regret it. As we scale the third of three waist-high concrete walls, he says, "Now I know how Shelley Winters felt in *The Poseidon Adventure*." Finally, we reach the ladder, which creaks as the mystery monk climbs it. At the top is a metal hatchway, which, when pushed open, exposes the stars. We climb out onto the roof of the Abbey Church. The night is exceptionally clear.

"Let a man consider that God is always looking at him from heaven," clucks Benedict of Nursia in his *Rule*, "that his actions are constantly being reported to God by the Angels."

Basically, we're busted. The Angels have ratted us out. While Benedict would not be pleased with our trespassing, he would approve of the silence that fell over us as we took in the view. Looking toward the monastery, we can spy on monks puttering around in their cells. Beyond the tennis courts are the apartments of the Ecumenical Institute, where Dr. Bob baby-sits in our absence. Lying on my back, I look up at the sparkling firmament. Red lights on the radio towers of surrounding towns wink at the periphery of my vision. I feel gravel in my scalp, but don't care. I am conducting my own personal "Beautiful Night Drill."

The five bells in the banner were made in Holland. The largest weighs more than four tons, the smallest just under two. These bells, unlike their effete cousins in that poem by Poe, do not "tintinnabulate." They rearrange one's chromosomes. They are big and loud—one fails to realize *how* big and loud until they toll the hours from a distance of thirty feet.

"No matter how many times I see the bell banner," says the mystery monk, once the ringing—and the ringing in our ears—has subsided, "I'm enthralled by it." John Parente keeps his peace: I happen to know he is not fond of the bell banner, finding it top-heavy, squat, not pleasing to the eye, "something one might find in front of an airport," he has said.

Spotlit from below, starlit from above, the bell banner escapes its own heaviness tonight, just as Thomas of Aquinas transcends his girth in the sculpture in his side-chapel. In this moment I myself feel a pleasant dizziness, the opposite of vertigo; a sense of floating above the deadline-driven life I've left behind.

Back in the apartment, while John and Dr. Bob engage in an intense discussion of Buddhism, the mystery monk reads to my children a seasonally appropriate bedtime story called "Which Witch is Which?"

Before leaving for Minnesota, I worried that the monks would be slow to laugh, unwelcoming, stodgy. It all seems so long ago.

The children, it has been decided, will trick-or-treat in Mendota Heights, a tony old suburb south of St. Paul. Our base of operations will be the home of Barb Schleck, who is Laura's aunt. Barb greets us in a Randy Moss Vikings jersey. She will not, unfortunately, be able to trick-or-treat with us: her Vikes are playing the Broncos on ESPN's Sunday night game.

Barb is one of those people I find secretly intimidating; she knows more about football than I do, and it's not even her job. Laura's mother, Josephine, had one sibling, a brother named Billy. Barb is the widow of Billy, who attended St. Thomas Academy—the alma mater of half a dozen Johnnies—and the University of St. Thomas. He died in 1976, at the age of forty-three.

While we prepare to venture out trick-or-treating, Devin eyeballs a pair of crossed foils that are mounted on Barb's living room wall. He is dressed up as *Star Wars* archvillain Darth Maul, and has a hankering, I can tell, to trade in his cheap-ass plastic light saber for some cold steel.

The foils belonged to Florian Josef Schleck—Josephine's father, Barb's father-in-law, Laura's grandfather. After graduating first in his class from St. Thomas Military Academy in 1925, then graduating *summa cum laude* from the College of St. Thomas, Florian worked two years for the *St. Paul Pioneer Press*. In 1930 he returned to his alma mater to teach philosophy and German. He also coached tennis and fencing. In a sort of welcome-back article in the November 6, 1936, *Aquin,* the Tommy paper, we learn that Florian was nicknamed "Doc," and that he took lunch every day with six of the school's "most outstanding language students" at the German Table, where "only German is spoken."

Another, shorter clip in the *Aquin*, this one from May 27, 1939, reports that "Mr. Florian Schleck, assistant professor of German in the college, died suddenly Tuesday night of a heart ailment. . . . He is survived by his wife, and son, William, and his parents. He was 31 years old."

The writer of that obituary lacked the time or inclination to find out the name of Florian's wife: it was Gladys Radcliff Madigan Schleck (forever known to her grandchildren as Glad Rad Mad). At the time of Florian's death, Gladys was pregnant with their second child, whom she named Josephine, in memory of the father she never met.

Both *Aquin* articles use the same photograph. Bespectacled Florian manages to look the part of serious academician even as a sly smile pulls the corners of his mouth. He looks like a professor you wouldn't mind running into in a tavern. Florian would have adored his eldest granddaughter, who shared his love of writing and languages. (Laura was an English-Russian double major at Colgate.) One of his colleagues at St. Thomas, it turned out, was a professor of chemistry and physics named Robert Hilgers, who would later move to Fairmont, in the southern part of the state. The two men knew each other only vaguely, and could not have known that one's son would marry the other's daughter.

And Laura wonders why everyone in this state looks like her cousin.

While Laura and I are reconnecting with each other, she is reconnecting with her past. She grew up a couple of miles away, at 642 Ivy Falls Road, in a nice-sized house with great climbing trees and a vast backyard that her father would flood, come winter, creating an ice rink. There is a sweetness and innocence to her reminiscences about the place. When her parents split up, it was as if her years in Minnesota were erased from her life. From the time she was sixteen until this fall, she never returned, never saw, and seldom spoke to her Minnesota relatives and friends. "It's like I was cut off from my past," she says.

She is now reclaiming some of that history. A couple of weeks ago, Laura got in touch with her girlhood friend, Mary Heinz (*née* Jackals), an effervescent blond who could have passed for a Hilgers sister. Laura had not seen Mary in twenty years, but decided to take the plunge and give her a call. It was risky: although these two were best friends as girls, there was the chance that Mary might have no interest in a reunion.

Right. They fell into conversation as if it had been two weeks, rather than two decades, since they'd last spoken. Next thing you knew, Mary was pulling into our driveway in a brown minivan, with her daughters Michelle and Alyssa in the back. They hugged and talked about the things they'd added since last seeing each other: careers, husbands, children, hair colorists. While the children played, their mothers leafed through two old photo albums Mary brought. Inside were black-and-white photos of Laura's family, pre-fracture. Mary was one of the people who knew Laura before the divorce. "She holds a piece of my history," Laura told me. "She knew me when."

In one of the scrapbooks are three postcards Laura had sent after moving away. "I can't believe you *kept* those," said Laura, whose eyes, I noticed, had begun to tear up. I cleared my throat and found some excuse to leave the room.

Trick-or-treating on the tree-lined streets of her old neighborhood, with her two children—it served as a stroll through a parallel dimension, "a glimpse of how my life might have been," she says.

It is enlightening for me, as well. As we crisscross Laura's old neighborhood, the Vikings game is on in every single household we visit. We are able to share with the kids this proud American tradition of begging sweets from strangers even as we stay abreast of a stirring comeback. Having trailed, 12–0, the Vikings beat the defending Super Bowl champions, 23–20. Typical exchange:

KIDS: *Trick or treat!*

LAURA: *Oooh—Almond Joys! Kids, whaddya say?*

KIDS (halfheartedly, already halfway to the sidewalk): *Thank you.*

ME: *Hey, what's the score?*

HOMEOWNER: *Vikes just took the lead. George hit Carter on a thirty-seven-yard scoring pass. We're going for two.*

"We" failed on that two-point conversion, we learned at the following house, but prevailed in the end. While Barb watched her beloved Vikings storm back, the kids loaded up on candy and Laura soaked up her old stomping ground. A grand Halloween all around.

No one who saw us would have suspected that we were carpetbaggers, reaping our chocolate harvest in a neighborhood not our own. BLOOM WHERE YOU ARE PLANTED, was the legend on the crocheted wall-hanging my mother put up in the kitchens of the dozen different homes in which our family lived. Laura and I are determined to stay in the Bay Area, allowing our children to sink deep roots in a community, as we were never able to do. (How do we reconcile that desire with our decision to drop anchor for four months in Minnesota? With some nifty rationalizations, that's how: *Daddy had to write a book.* Why did Daddy have to write a book? *Well, lots of Daddy's friends had written books, and Daddy felt like he needed to keep up . . .*)

The point I set out to make was that, while the leaves are withering, we are blossoming—hitting our stride like the Johnny defense. Willa is flourishing in kindergarten. "She is a joy to teach," her teacher, Mrs. Haeg, told us in our first-ever parent-teacher conference. Willa is among Kennedy's kindergarten elite, Mrs. Haeg added, at recognizing letters and words—"She's ready to start 'blending'"—and socializing. She is angelically behaved, except on those rare occasions when she and Zachary team up to make mischief. Every so often, we are told, those two must be separated. Of course, it's a boy. This is where it's all headed.

Devin has reached an uneasy truce with Swanson's. He'll go, he'll even take a nap, but only if he has Teddy, his loyal, stuffed bear. Once a week, one of us forgets to bring the goddam bear, and is forced to drive home, find Teddy, drive *back* to Swanson's, drive back to campus, *then* sit down to write.

Despite her frequent complaints about the dearth of organic produce and gluten-free products, Laura is as happy as she will ever be in Stearns County. She has become fast friends with Timo and Paul, our monk buddies, and John Parente, our Ecumenical Institute neighbor. She is at once stimulated by the conversations she has with them—discussions heavy on books, religion, and philosophy—and liberated by not being called upon to talk about what we talk about at home with our yuppie friends: *How's the new nanny working out? Can you believe the real estate market? Have you seen the new Volvo Cross Country?*

Things are going better for us in bed. Bear with me here. It's been ten years since Laura and I graduated from our old double to a queen-size mattress. Here at the Ecumenical Institute, we are back in a double. After a fortnight or so of tossing, turning, and inadvertently kicking and clubbing one another—*"Ow!" "Sorry!"*—we're back in sync, two spoons in a drawer.

Things are better for us out of bed, as well. The dirty little secret of our sabbatical was that it took a month or so to *feel* like one. I had book anxiety, the kids had school anxiety, Laura had the predictably snarled welter of anxieties that come calling whenever she senses the slipping away of control.

I read not long ago in the *New York Times* that scientists were able to determine that rats dream. Based on "the firing of clusters of cells in the hippocampus"—the part of the rat's brain in charge of memory formation and storage—the scientists could tell that the rats were dreaming of the circular maze they were forced to run all day. The way I see it, it took us the first month or so of the sabbatical before we stopped dreaming about the maze. Our routines are established, our lives have slowed down. We finally sense the "sense of place" for which this campus is renowned. The longer we are here, Laura says, the more she sees of the guy she fell in love with (me). She notices that I've been putting the newspaper down to listen to her; says I've become less cynical, not as prone to sarcasm. I don't know how to respond to that, other than to thank her, possibly proving her point.

13

CARLETON

For a change of pace, we drove to St. Joe and checked out the Sunday mass in the convent church at St. Ben's. It is vaulted, airy, light, a nice break from Breuer's concrete. The sisters' liturgy, likewise, is sprightly and joyous, something that cannot always be said for the mass at St. John's. A flute-playing nun lends zip to the recessional hymn. As we leave the church, Devin wanders ahead, making the acquaintance of an elderly, smiling nun named Sister Christian, who recently fell down and suffered an abrasion on her forehead. Naturally, she is drawn to my son, who took a shovel to the forehead at preschool and looks as if he were recently interrogated by the LAPD's Rampart Division.

Sister Katherine Kraft, meanwhile, is on bended knee engaging Willa in conversation, no easy task with my shy five-year-old. I introduce myself, and explain why we are here this fall. Sister Katherine notes that my name is derived from Augustine, and we talk for a while about that brilliant saint. "He was a genius," she tells me, "but he fell in with those Manicheans."

After patiently explaining to me who the Manicheans were, Sister Katherine poses a nontheological question: "Why didn't

Gagliardi kick a field goal against Bethel?"

She has not heard the good news. Gagliardi didn't send the field goal unit out against the Royals because he lacked faith in it. That confidence, which had been lost, is found! While the Minnesota Golden Gophers rocked Division I yesterday by upsetting second-ranked Penn State, another miracle occurred at Carleton College, where St. John's kicked not one, but a pair of field goals, causing at least one longtime Johnny fan to swoon in disbelief.

It was a remarkable conclusion to a week that had begun, for me, with a brief journey in the remarkably vile automobile of wide receiver Steve Lynch. After Monday's film session, the senior wide-out offered me a lift down to Flynntown in his '85 Corolla, a cancerous red rattletrap with flames painted on the sides and a genuine rodent's nest in the glove compartment. The mouse has long since been evicted, but Lynch leaves the nest as a conversation piece. Good thinking, I tell him. If a girl is on the fence about whether or not she wants to do you, the nest pretty much closes the deal for you.

I'm looking forward to spending a little extra time with Steve this week, and not just because of the fact that under his Young Republican exterior and Eddie Haskell grin lurks one of the more delightfully twisted and intellectually versatile Johnnies. Carleton is the penultimate regular season opponent: Lynch, as it happens, spent his freshman year on that Northfield, Minnesota, campus before concluding that he had made a mistake, that he had no desire to endure four years of defecating silently in coed bathrooms and having his head handed to him on the football field.

He has to stop by the football offices on his way home. I wait in his illegally parked, bacteria-infested vehicle with his housemates, Soma and Joel Torborg, the president and vice president of the 30-Yard-Line Club, a chummy cabal of seldom-used players who congregate during games at the 30-yard line nearest the bell banner. Members are required to wear their helmets until the Johnnies score, at which time helmets are to be removed. (Headgear goes back on upon the ensuing St. John's touchdown, and so on, and so on, until the scrub is actually summoned away from the 30 to enter the game.) Torborg periodically ranges from the 30-yard line on recruiting missions. A few weeks ago, I saw him in action around midfield, telling a cluster of freshmen in pristine uniforms, "If you get in the game, so much the better. But if you don't, slide on down to the 30-yard line."

The speeches of student senate candidates were recently interrupted by "pressed hams" against the windows of Brother Willie's Pub. One of the sets of buttocks was reportedly scrawny; the other, much wider and ghostly white, even by Minnesota standards—descriptions that correspond exactly with the asses of this pair of asses. My point in mentioning this is that Torborg and Soma are disinclined to wait patiently for Lynch, or anyone. They seek to amuse themselves.

A source of fun arrives when a member of campus security drives up, steps out of his Life Safety vehicle and approaches the flagpole, across from which we are (illegally) parked. I believe it is the first time I've seen one of these campus security shock troops step out of his car. For all I knew, they were hired from a special pool of legless rent-a-cops. After lowering Old Glory, the security man doesn't waste time folding it into a tidy triangle. Thinking himself unobserved, he wads it up and wedges it under his arm.

"Is that why my grandfather fought in World War II," shouts Soma, "so you could bunch up the flag like your own soiled bedsheets?"

"God damn you to hell," adds Torborg, for good measure.

Embarrassed and perhaps a bit frightened—he can't tell where these angry, patriotic voices are coming from—the security man scurries to his vehicle and drives away. Five minutes go by, still no Lynch. Torborg takes the wheel and drives across the lawn, stopping when the Toyota is five feet from the glass doors of the Palaestra. Lynch is in the corridor, kibitzing with some coaches. Torborg leans on the horn and flashes the brights. "What the hell are you doing?" shouts Soma. "What are they going to do?" says Joel, who's gotten precious few snaps this season. "Not play me?"

★ ★ ★

Lynch was the bomb at White Bear Lake High, where he threw no bombs, but ran a true wishbone offense and starred in track. When Carleton offered to cover most of his $30,000 tuition and costs, he asked where to sign. He excelled as a freshman wideout, but had trouble finding much of a social circle outside the football team. "Halfway through my freshman year, I was just really depressed all the time," he told me.

"When I was an undergrad," I recalled, adopting an avuncular tone, "drugs and alcohol were our key allies in the war against depression. Of course, that was before Nancy Reagan and 'Just Say No.'"

Lynch refuses to run Carleton down. "It's a great school," he says. "Very progressive. I lived in a coed dorm, with coed bathrooms. That was eye-opening."

I prompt him: So, you'd be in your favorite stall, reading the paper, thinking deep thoughts, dropping the kids off at the pool, and a girl could just *walk into the bathroom*? That ain't right, bro.

It was the converse, Lynch tells me, that bothered him more. "Walking in on *them*," he says. "That's what I never quite got used to. You forget girls do that."

He had vivid memories of walking into Clemens Stadium as an opponent, seeing eight thousand people packed under the Swayed Pines, hearing in the tolling of the bells an ominous knell indeed. "I remember thinking, 'Now *this* is an incredible place to play.' At Carleton we drew fifty fans, forty-eight of whom are parents, and one of whom is Superfan, a great big fat guy."

He decided to transfer. Coming out of a meeting his first night on campus, Lynch ran into Johnny cornerback Will Gibson, against whom he'd run track. Gibson invited him to come over to his room and hang out with some of the guys. Walking over to Gibson's dorm, Lynch could not help but feel ebullient about the fresh start he was making. He'd undergone a serious football upgrade, and was already beginning to enjoy the company of people with whom he had more in common. While not on a par with Carleton's, the intellectual climate at his new school was still quite robust.

Or so Lynch had been told. When he walked into Gibson's room, he found the cornerback and Soma busily setting up "fifty to sixty *Star Wars* action figures in army formation," recalls Lynch. "They were preparing to reenact the movie's climactic battle scene. Will knows all the characters by heart. He's kept all the original packaging, so he can have all the information on each figure at his fingertips. Then they start shooting at each other—Soma's whining, 'That? That didn't kill me—I'm an Imperial Storm Trooper! I'm armored!'—and I'm thinking, 'Holy shit, what have I gotten myself into?'"

Lynch was somehow able to adjust to his new environs, and is in his second season as a starter for the Johnnies.

"Steve would have been fine if he'd stuck it out another year," says Bob Sullivan, the Carleton head coach now in his twenty-first season with the Knights. "And he'd be all-conference. We'd get him twelve catches a game, not one or two." To Lynch, the best-blocking wideout in the MIAC, it's not even a contest. He'd rather win twelve games a year than average a dozen catches a game for a team on the wrong end of serious, serial ass-kickings.

Asked how they are doing, all these coaches from the MIAC's lower-echelon teams begin to sound the same. Sullivan in particular sounds as if he should surrender his belt and shoelaces. He is 0-21 against Gagliardi, and his fortunes don't look to change this Saturday. "They always play their best against us," he laments, "and we play our worst against them."

His Knights are 2-6 and banged up. Eight starters are out, including his quarterback. "Right now we're piecing it together with tape and string," he tells me. "I don't know if we can even make a game of it. I told the guys just to play for themselves, not even think about whom we're up against. Let's just go out there and try to look like a football team, cause we sure didn't against Augsburg last week."

Like Northwestern in the Big 10, Carleton was tough for a while. Seven years ago the Knights won the conference title. They've backslid of late, while one-time weak sisters Bethel and Augsburg have come up in the world. Three numbers ensure that Carleton will always struggle to compete:

29: median ACT
1280: average SAT
$30,000: cost per year to attend

Sullivan was a 130-pound freshman from Marshall, Minnesota, who was forbidden to play by his college coach. "You're gonna get killed out there," John Gagliardi told him. "You're here everyday, so you might as well coach." So he spent three years breaking down film for Gagliardi, and in the autumn of 1957 and 1958, coached the Johnny freshmen. Gags got him his first coaching job, at Hill High School in St. Paul. In 1979, Sullivan landed the head job at Carleton, then a member of the old Midwest Conference. Four years later, when the Knights joined the MIAC, Gags welcomed his former pupil to the league by doing what he'd done to every other coach in the conference: running up the score on him.

As another MIAC coach points out, "John says, 'I don't call the plays,' but he is the coach, right? He could tell his kids not to throw the ball in the fourth quarter when they're up fifty. He could tell them not to call time outs when they're up by fifty with a minute to play, so they can throw again. And that sort of thing has happened."

"I just shrug it off," says Sullivan. It is impossible to tell, over the phone, whether or not he is actually gritting his teeth. "I know John and I know how he operates. He and I can still have civil exchanges, but he's got some enemies out there. Part of the reason for that, of course, is that he's got more wins than anybody else."

The Johnnies haven't blown anyone out of the tub since Augsburg, more than a month ago. The main reason for that? He is on the table in the training room on Wednesday afternoon, rehabbing. Linnemann is on his back, working his ankle against resistance provided by assistant trainer Amy Behrendt.

I tell Amy what she already knows: they don't pay her enough to touch the bare feet of someone like Linnemann. "She doesn't mind," says Tom. "She's a jersey chaser." He and Amy are friends.

Calmly, wordlessly, she digs her thumb into a tender part of his mending shin, eliciting a sustained howl.

Linnemann is healing ahead of schedule. He wants to come back this season. His cast came off after a month; lately he's been jogging slowly around the practice field. Last week he returned the camouflage golf cart. By never missing a practice, riding the bus, hanging out on the sideline during games—doing everything, I suppose, but playing and puking—he's kept a high profile. Not high enough for him, apparently. At films on Monday, he'd walked in five minutes late and flat-out taken over. Until that moment, Corey had been running the show.

On the screen, there was Kirschner, coughing up the ball. The Ole sideline went nuts. "That's incentive right there not to turn the ball over," said Tom, "so we don't have to sit there watching those assholes jump around."

On Corey's long interception to Ben in the second half, the pick that triggered the blizzard of index cards, Tom froze the film with Sieben twenty yards off the line of scrimmage. "He's open *here*," said Tom. Implicit in the observation: Corey was late getting rid of the ball.

With a cornerback crowding Sieben, Linnemann said, "He's awful close, and I know that shitburger safety won't make it over in time to help out." (That he remained in the Johnnies' thoughts two days after the game would have pleased Carlson.) "Don't be afraid to audible, Corey."

Tom admits he wanted to come in and shake things up; that it's been killing him to watch the offense struggle to make first downs. He is shooting to return for the first round of the playoffs. On the field after the St. Olaf game, Tom stood chatting with Oles defensive coordinator Darrell Kluck, who practically baited him. "Tommy, I *want* you to come back next year, so we'll have one more shot at you," he said. "Come back, Tommy, cause next year we'll have more speed to blitz you."

Kluck should be careful what he wishes for. Linnemann has been floating some trial balloons about returning for a fifth season. While rare at St. John's, such a move would not be unprecedented. Early in his sophomore season, Tom suffered a season-ending high-ankle sprain. He's got a redshirt year in the bag if he wants it. Not everyone would like to see him back next year. Certainly, it would not be good news for junior Pat France, or sophomores Brian Whinnery and Zach McBroom—all of whom could be starting at quite a few D-III schools, and all of whom would like to have Linnemann out of the way, so they can get a chance here. A purist contingent of monks, led by Wilfred, is vehemently opposed, as are some students and faculty.

Those against a Linnemann return argue that five-year players are the province of less divisions and conferences less pure—schools that have lost sight of the true purpose of college athletics. "It's just not St. John's," says Wilfred. "Tom should forget about this fifth-year nonsense."

There is really only one opinion that matters on the subject of a fifth year for Linnemann, and it isn't Wilfred's. Gagliardi turned seventy-three on Monday. He is not at the end of his career, but from where he stands, he can see it. If he is to win a fourth national title, he knows it is more likely to happen with Linnemann calling the signals. Yes, that's a tough break for the trio of talented quarterbacks behind Tom. They lack experience, but can't *get* experience until Linnemann is out of the picture. "It does seem unfair," says Bretherton, the offensive line coach. "But, you know what? This isn't intramurals."

Gagliardi has been seventy-three for four days by the time I get around to wishing him happy birthday. He doesn't smile. The expression crossing his face most closely approximated, I would say, a wince. "What can I say?" he replies. "I'm getting older."

Pointing to an autographed picture of the pope that hangs from a wall over the sofa on which the winningest coach in college football takes an occasional nap, I wonder which of them is older. "He's younger than I am, I think," says Gags, "and he's not doing so hot. Poor guy hasn't been the same since he got shot."

John Paul is actually six years older than Gagliardi, and rallied remarkably after the 1981 attempt on his life by Mehmet Ali Agca. Gagliardi, too, has come back from a physical setback—far less traumatic—that some thought might end his career. In the midnineties, a player rolled up his leg on the sideline, fracturing it. Released from the hospital on a Tuesday morning, Gagliardi was at that afternoon's practice in a golf cart. Just because he's progressive and unorthodox doesn't mean he isn't stubborn and tough as mule gristle.

Like the pope, Gagliardi is a septuagenarian with a few enemies, a lot of friends, and no inclination to hang it up. He's afraid to retire, then find out—after a long weekend cooped up in his lake house, tripping over his grandchildren's Pokeballs—that he's made a hideous mistake. He wonders about the Lou Holtzes and Mike Ditkas and Dick Vermeils of the world, guys who left coaching, but came back to it. "You gotta figure these guys were making a pretty good living away from football," says Gags. "What drove them to come back?"

The pull of the profession is strong. "It's a powerful lesson," he says. "There are times I think, 'Why the hell am I doing this?' But Bowden's still doing it, Paterno's still doing it. Shula'd still be doing it if they hadn't dragged him away. Eddie Robinson the same. I've got some company out there."

The most-photographed traffic sign in all the MIAC—CARLETON COLLEGE, ST. OLAF COLLEGE, EXIT 69—is our clue that the bus ride is nearly at end. Stately Laird Stadium, home of the Knights, seats seven thousand five hundred, and stands on home football Saturdays as a scarcely occupied monument to Carleton's ancient, unrealized ambition to gain admission to the Big 10. Beneath the stands, inside an oval, banked running track, the Johnnies suit up. I'm not getting a real tense vibe from them today. Sokoly, the Wisconsinite, is diagramming a play at the blackboard, imitating Vince Lombardi: "We'll get the seal here, the seal here, and we'll run that play"—he practically breaks the chalk—*"In the alley!"*

Not fifteen feet away, like a Theater of the Absurd extra, a carpenter planes an edge on a wooden locker, oblivious to us. Welcome to the MIAC. The Knights are dressing under the same bleachers, one hundred feet away. As they file onto the field, their cleats clattering on the concrete, their war whoops sound self-conscious and ridiculous.

As is the Johnny custom, Gagliardi calls off the names of the starters, each of whom steps forward to shake his hand. Back in August, Andy Landkammer had gotten Leroy to stop talking about his golf game long enough to confide in the salty old equipment manager, "I'm thinking of hanging it up. With the running backs we have here, I'll never get on the field." Leroy told him to stick it out, be patient, he'd get his chance. "Starting at running back," says Gags, "Krych and Landkammer." A boisterous cheer goes up.

Lando was right. He may never get on the field. Because it is Parents' Day at Carleton, the Knights seniors and their parents are introduced before the game. Lest their feelings be injured, the trainers and managers and *their* parents are introduced, as well: *"Manager John Lee with his parents, Joe and Kelly Lee . . ."*

Brother Mark, within whom Benedictinism and curmudgeonliness wage constant war, asks loudly and within earshot of today's honorees, "Is all this necessary?"

When Corey overthrows a receiver early on, the Carleton public-address announcer says, "Stanger throws it into Goodhue County." That line might have gotten a big laugh from the home crowd if the Johnny fans didn't outnumber Knight supporters ten to one. My feeling is, only *we* can dump on Corey for missing open receivers. Then Stanger uncorks his obligatory, early-game interception, and I think, What the hell, go ahead and rip him.

The story of the first half is the story of the last month: the offense remains erratic; a very good defense keeps getting better. With a minute left in the second quarter, the Johnnies score their second touchdown to go up 14–0. Instead of running out the clock, Knights quarterback Jesse Anderson comes out throwing . . . to Beau, who's been on the warpath since he was introduced in pregame, much to the amusement of his teammates, as "Bean LaBore." Bean's freebie sets up a short touchdown run by Stanger, and just like that the Knights are done.

Krych breaks three tackles and goes seventy-one yards for a touchdown to start the second half. With the score 28–nil, I decide to sit on the grass with Laura and the kids, who've made the drive from

Collegeville. The scab on Devin's forehead, we hope, draws attention away from his self-administered haircut. Despite the efforts of a barber at the Crossroads Mall, he still looks as if someone took hedge-clippers to his hair. Our friend Jim Platten gets a load of him and asks us, "Did you ever vacation at Three Mile Island?"

Platten is a delightfully manic Johnny fan and alum. His obsessiveness manifests itself, interestingly, in the compulsive need to attend Johnny (and Benny) athletic events. The few Johnny fans whose acquaintance he has not made know him as simply "the shorts guy." Unlike Gagliardi, he is superstitious. No matter how bitter the weather, Platten insists on wearing shorts to every football game.

He comes by his allegiance to St. John's honestly. Platten was adopted and grew up in St. Paul. He was a bright boy who thought he might be cut out for the priesthood. He did exceptionally well on the seminary entrance exams. Yet while his friends received in the mail their acceptances to various local seminaries, Platten got nothing. Finally, his mother made inquiries. She was informed by the bishop that a sixteenth-century rule forbade illegitimate sons from entering the priesthood.

It is stories like these that buttress my theory that the Roman Catholic Church, like Major League Baseball, succeeds in spite of the nincompoops who run it. Throughout his youth, Platten's parents went out of their way to assure him that, adopted or not, he was loved, that he was normal—a notion undercut by the very church he sought to serve. It was a cruel blow.

"Long story short," says Platten, "my mother gets on the phone with Abbot Baldwin. He says he's got no problem with the adoption issue. He gets in his car *that day*, drives to St. Paul, administers the entrance exam at my kitchen table, grades it, and accepts me on the spot.

"I was down and out, and these guys took me in," says Platten—who, for the record, decided not to enter the priesthood, and is now married with a high school-aged daughter—"and for that I will be forever grateful." For that he will be forever trouserless.

At Johnny football games, at least.

When Joe Rotondi kicks a twenty-seven-yard field goal to put

St. John's up 38–zip, Platten gets on his cell phone. "You won't believe this," he tells the Johnny alum at the other end. "I know, I know," the other guy says, "the Gophers beat Penn State."

"No, no, no," says Platten, "this is far more remarkable. I'm at the St. John's game and *we just kicked a field goal.*"

On the Tuesday after the loss to Bethel, Jimmy had been watching Rotondi, the backup kicker and a charter member of the 30-Yard-Line Club, boot extra points. He got good distance and height, but took too many steps. "If you want to kick here," said Jimmy, "you've got to shorten your steps."

Rotondi did . . . without sacrificing distance. He kicked a fifty-yarder in practice. He kicked another one. The Johnnies were on to something. Now, with thirty-seven seconds left in the game, Joe-Ro hits from forty to make it 41–6, doubling the Johnnies' field goal output from last season. Platten teeters, then falls to the grass, incredulous. In the bedlam on the sideline, Grady McGovern, the holder, complains to Rotondi, "You keep running off the field. Stay out there so we can celebrate!"

On the field after the game, I seek out Carleton's Andy Quist, a terrific athlete who played quarterback and cornerback today for the Knights. We're discussing the charms of MIAC when we are interrupted by the father of a Carleton offensive lineman. "That's a classless team," says the dad. "Kicking a field goal with hardly any time left—that's classless."

Sorry about those late field goals, sir. The Johnnies—I feel qualified to speak on their behalf—were simply trying to work out the bugs in their kicking game before the playoffs begin, before the inability to hit a chip-shot field goal could bring the season to a close.

Oh, and by the way, as long as you're standing sentinel against classlessness, ask your defensive end, No. 10, why he found it necessary to land an uppercut to the family jewels of Chad O'Hara in the second quarter. "That guy has no idea how lucky he is," O'Hara told me on the sideline.

Because you were about to kick his ass? I say.

"No, because I was *this* close to puking in his face," says Chadwick. "I mean, that was the worst pain I've ever been in."

Offense is pain for the Johnnies. Defense is fun. The Johnny defenders are loose, confident, eleven guys taking turns making big plays. No player embodies this swagger more than Grady, a terrific natural athlete who spent more time on the field smiling than anyone in the conference, and possibly the country, this season.

When Grady chats with opponents, he is not talking trash. He's making conversation. It's as if competing with the other guys isn't enough—Grady wants to get to know them. In a playoff game last season, he broke up a pass and landed in a tangle with the intended receiver. "Nice try, man," said Grady. When the other fellow returned the compliment, Grady noticed he was missing his front teeth.

"Did I do that?" he asked, horrified

"No, I lost those a while ago," came the reply. While walking to the far sideline with the guy, listening to the story of how the fellow lost his teeth, Grady nearly missed the start of the next play.

Today is a kind of homecoming for Grady, a Northfield native who grew up six blocks from the Carleton campus. In the first half, Grady keeps up a running dialogue with a Knight who is an old high school teammate, then makes an acrobatic interception on Carleton's sideline. It's Grady's day.

After the game, the entire team is invited over to his house for potluck dinner. Most of the Johnny moms have brought a covered dish. Shame on Laura and me for bringing nothing except two famished children, who pile their paper plates high with hot dogs, lasagna, and cupcakes. There is Gagliardi, alone at the dining room table, picking at his food. The parents are reluctant to sit and eat with him; they're afraid it will look as if they're sucking up to him.

In moments of reflection on the sideline, John's pose seldom varies: left arm rests on belly; elbow of right arm perches on left wrist; chin rests on the mini-ottoman formed by right thumb and forefinger. (This attitude has been immortalized, in fact, in the Gagliardi Trophy, given annually to the best player in Division III.) I've noticed that, as the season has gotten older, Gagliardi's belly—the foundation of this scaffolding—seems to have shrunk. Peg recently confirmed this. "He loses about thirty pounds a season," she says. "After he sees the game films, he doesn't feel like eating."

We Hilgers-Murphys join twenty or so ball players and their parents on the McGoverns's handsome deck. Quintessential North Star State moment: as the sun sets, dragging the temperature under forty degrees, Minnesotans in shirtsleeves sit on the deck consuming cheesy potatoes and exotic Jell-O salads while remarking on how unseasonably warm it is.

Grady finds me and says, "You want a tour of the house?"

"Of course I do, Grady," I say. "It's why I've traveled to the heartland—to see your rumpus room."

I regret that wisecrack. The McGoverns were kind to invite us, and Grady, I realize, is about to take a risk, to reveal himself to me. Taking me downstairs, he shows me several framed paintings. I recall that he is an art minor and, as college football players go, an accomplished painter. What Dora Maar was to Picasso, Deion Sanders is to Grady: a subject to be lovingly rendered, over and over. Grady shows me several paintings of Sanders, the best of which is a framed portrait of Prime Time in his old Florida State helmet—the contraction NOLES appearing above the facemask. "I copied that from an old *SI* cover," he tells me. Of course Grady would idolize Sanders. At Northfield High, someone told me, Grady wore a necklace with dollar-sign dangling, and answered to the nickname G-Money. He plays baseball, he plays cornerback. He is the Prime Time of the MIAC.

The time has come for us to leave the party. Having skipped their naps and consumed a half-dozen cupcakes between them, my children commence melting down earlier than usual. After thanking Grady's mother, Ann, then wrestling my sucrose-crazed son into his car seat, I lean against the driver's side door and look back at a party in full swing.

The Johnnies and their parents are silhouetted against the garage light, laughing and gossiping; talking hunting, talking football. From the outside looking in, it occurs to me (again) that I have insinuated myself into the times of their lives. By welcoming me and my wife and our children into their scrapbook moments, the Johnny coaches and players and their families have given us our own trove of terrific memories. We will not realize it until we return to our normal lives—until we step back on the treadmill—but this time together for our family has been priceless. The willingness of the Johnnies to scoot over and make room for us, to share their glory days with strangers, is as great a gift.

Maybe they were flattered by the attention. Maybe they sensed my desperation to get back to what is real about sports. Whatever their reasons for accepting me, I was, and am, grateful. I am thankful for every sublime moment I spent in Minnesota, whether it was inhaling Ann McGovern's seven-layer salad (layer number seven: bacon bits), or introducing myself to Josh Hart's good-looking mother and saying, "You must be Josh's sister"; whether it was pub-crawling with Linnemann in Melrose, dropping quarters into the Jurassic-era jukebox at Earl's Bar, or driving with Brother Mark to Little Falls, Minnesota, where I stood for the first time in two decades with my hand over my heart and recited the pledge of allegiance, before delivering a wooden speech to the local Lions Club. I took none of those moments for granted. I am grateful for all of them.

14

GUSTAVUS ADOLPHUS

The showdown is nigh. The Johnnies will face Gustavus Adolphus in the Hubert H. Humphrey Metrodome on Friday night. A win will give the Johnnies the MIAC championship to themselves, and send them to the NCAA Division III playoffs. A loss means they share the title and turn in their equipment. The victory over Carleton ensured St. John's at least a share of the title, and offered Gagliardi a small modicum of relief.

Between the probation and the loss of key players, it has been a season of unusual tribulation for the old man. "Watching him at practice," says a former player, "I didn't see the guy I used to know. He's a bit more distant. He seems tired."

Securing that slice of the championship seemed to energize Gagliardi, a sunny interval that was eclipsed after four days by a call from the *St. Cloud Times*. On Wednesday, November 10, *Times* sports editor Dave DeLand received an anonymous letter criticizing the paper for "covering up" the fact that the Johnnies had spent most of the season on probation.

DeLand handed the letter to Johnny football beat writer

Heather Burns, who got on the phone with Michael Hemmesch, the university's communications officer. Her question—was it true the NCAA had placed the Johnnies on probation?—gave Hemmesch some wiggle room. To his credit he did not use it, answering truthfully and in good faith: while the team was not under *NCAA* probation, it had been sanctioned by the MIAC.

After practice on Wednesday, DeLand and Burns met in Gagliardi's office with the head coach, Hemmesch and Gar Kellom, the vice president of student development. The Johnny contingent asked that the *Times* hold the story until Monday. No can do, said DeLand. You couldn't blame him. The *Times* was already destined to get some egg on its face, trumpeting "news" of sanctions that were levied nearly two months earlier. Holding the story over the weekend, the paper would run the risk of getting scooped on news that unfolded weeks earlier in its own backyard.

Gagliardi's Sicilian blood came to a boil. If the *Times* insists on creating this distraction the day before the team's most important game of the season, then he is finished talking to the paper.

Later that night, he says to Peg, "This is going to look bad for me."

He was right. The *Times* plays the story for all it's worth, and then some. A front-page, above-the-fold headline blares: JOHNNIES FACE 3-YEAR MIAC PROBATION TERM. (A front-page story about a $21,000 embezzlement case at St. Cloud State gets much smaller play.) You have to jump to page four to find out what malfeasance the Johnnies actually perpetrated. Based on the placement of the story and size of the headline, it comes as a surprise to learn that St. John's hadn't thrown the Bethel game, or shaved points against St. Olaf.

While Hover makes pancakes for his Chubby's housemates, LaBore reads the morning paper aloud, emphasizing the phrases that annoy him. Preoccupied with an upcoming test in a class in which he is struggling—it is called Investments, and it sure *sounded* like a gut—Kirschner couldn't care less. Everyone else wonders what the big deal is. "I thought we dealt with this two months ago," says Hover, not yet realizing it has taken this many weeks for the crack investigative arm of the *Times* to root out the story.

Up in the campus ministry, Father Tim is venting, dismissing the *Times* as a "Podunk paper trying to make a name for itself." He is still steamed about a recent series of articles the paper ran detailing the ways in which college students are disrupting the lives of the citizens of St. Joe. On his way out of church one morning shortly after those stories appeared, Timo was stopped by a member of the town council, who asked for his opinion. "I think that if your people stopped trying to make money hand-over-fist by renting the students slum apartments," he said, "and if your people could resist the temptation to sell them liquor, then maybe their conduct would improve."

Having failed to elicit the expected response, the good burgher withdrew in haste.

In the football office, Peg is putting out brushfires, taking calls from concerned alumni. John is in his office with the door shut.

By midafternoon, his black mood has passed. He's allowed himself to be cheered up by a wave of supportive calls and e-mails. For the next few weeks the *Times* will be inundated with critical mail from Johnny loyalists. Reaction on sports-talk radio has run heavily in favor of St. John's.

Sitting at his desk, he picks up a framed, black-and-white photograph that is nearly forty years old. It is a picture of a girl and her little brother at the concession stand at a Johnny football game. Gina Gagliardi is six years old in the picture; Johnny is four. She can barely see over the counter. "It's not very busy," says Gags, studying the photo. "That means the game must be going on. We're down on the field dying a thousand deaths, and Nancy and John are just thinking about getting a box of popcorn. Sometimes when I get too worked up, this reminds me of what's important."

On the eve of the contest that would determine the success or failure of their season, the Johnnies are looser than I've ever seen them. Grady and Brooks Deibele, a sophomore from Sleepy Eye (*Little House on the Prairie* readers will recognize it as the town to which the Laura Ingalls Wilder family repaired for supplies), are rapping a song by Master P. "Oh yeah, we're all just devastated by the bombshell," in the *Times*, Chad O'Hara says with a smile. "Can't you see all the heads hanging in shame?"

Gags is flat-out fired up as he gives his day-before-the-game speech. "All this crap," he says, summing up the probation and the reporting on it in the local fishwrap, "there's nothing new about it. All something like this does is motivate me, and I hope it motivates you."

A playoff berth will be at stake tomorrow, he tells them, needlessly. A loss could result in a five-way tie, with all the tiebreakers stacked against the Johnnies. "Maybe I got a little complacent after we wrapped up a share of the title last week," he says. "Maybe I needed something to rattle my cage. Well, now we have it. We've knocked down all the challengers before, let's do it again. Let's keep that damned train moving down the tracks, got that cowcatcher out there, gonna run over whatever's in our way!"

The Johnnies break the circle with a defiant shout, even though, as Gagliardi concedes to me during the walk to his car, "probably not too many of 'em know what a cowcatcher is."

It is, of course, the inclined frame on the front of a locomotive, designed to clear obstacles—and stray livestock—from the track. Cow analogies in a football context put me in mind of offensive linemen, those most bovine of athletes, and of one offensive lineman in particular. On a Green Bay Packers team with such pear-shaped performers as Frank Winters, Earl Dotson, and Gilbert Brown, it was Bruce Wilkerson who earned the nickname Bad Body.

I met Bad Body in January of 1997. He was an unsung hero on the Packers squad that won Super Bowl XXXI in New Orleans. Cut by the Jacksonville Jaguars in the off-season, he was signed by the Pack a day later and plugged into the starting lineup late in the season. Trick knees and extra lbs. weren't his only problems. Wilkerson stuttered.

I learned this from running back Dorsey Levens, who mentioned it while ticking off things about one another the Packers enjoyed making fun of.

"Obviously," I interrupted, "you don't tease a man over a speech impediment."

"Oh, we *kill* him," Levens assured me.

Wilkerson's teammates raved about his economy of movement, his veteran's wiliness. Bad Body's resourcefulness, it turned out, was not limited to his footwork. When a certain running play was called, the play-side tackle was responsible for getting a pre-snap read of the defense, and making a line call. One of those calls requires the tackle to shout, "Cow!"

In a game earlier in the season, left guard Aaron Taylor told me, Wilkerson sought to make the cow call, but got stuck on the hard "c." After struggling valiantly—"C-c-c-c-c"—he finally bellowed, *"Moooo!"* Everyone knew just what he meant, Taylor recalled. That wasn't the problem. The problem was that half the offense was laughing too hard to run the play.

I catch a ride to the Metrodome with a bus full of monks in mufti—Johnny-red tee shirts, golf sweaters, baseball caps, not a black cowl among them—and Sister Dolores, who sits just behind me. Dolores remarks that the weather must finally be turning: she looked out her window the other day and Devin was actually wearing clothes. When the conversation turns to Johnny football, some of the Benedictines wonder aloud why Stanger can't seem to find his short and intermediate receivers, why he's always looking for the long ball. They'll be singing a different tune on the ride home.

When we cruise past a large new church going up in Monticello, the brothers on the right side of the bus cross over to peer out the left-side windows, as if we are in a commercial airliner going over the Grand Canyon. Upon disembarking at the Metrodome, each monk is handed a Butterfinger. Strolling into the stadium with a half-dozen of the brothers, I was pleased to be asked by one of them what I knew of the Gusties. They were bigger but we were quicker, I reported—a decided advantage on the Dome's artificial turf. The Gusties, I continued, embraced a Division II-type conservatism: play-action passes tied to a power running game, not much blitzing on defense. I was prepared to continue with my analysis when I noticed that all but one of the monks had deserted me upon spying a lavatory. "Gotta hit the head," said the last brother, taking his leave of me.

To be filed under "Phrases that take us by surprise when they cross the lips of a monk": *Gotta hit the head.*

A cold front from earlier in the week has passed. With the weather unseasonably glorious, it seems a crime against nature to play in *any* domed stadium, let alone this abomination of concrete, steel, and Astroturf. But the MIAC requires its teams to play this weekend in the Hump Dome, even though the charms of Division III tend to be obscured by such a charmless venue. Even a healthy turnout by St. John's standards—this game will draw a highly respectable 6,200-plus—will always seem meager and mildly embarrassing when unoccupied seats outnumber seats with fannies in them, nine to one. Gagliardi turned sour when I broached the subject with him yesterday, and remains in a dark mood thirty minutes before kickoff. After shaking his players' hands during "calisthenics," he says, forebodingly, "I don't know. This could be it."

These Eeyore moments from the legend are nothing new to his staff. "He's miserable," Jerry explains, "so now he's going to make you miserable so he doesn't have to be the only one."

While the Gusties go through their traditional cals, Stanger asks the Johnnies for "Two Mary Catherine Gallagher-Superstar lunges"—it's a *Saturday Night Live* reference: ask one of your kids—"wavelike fashion, left to right." The calisthenic is at once sublimely silly and immensely pleasing to the eye. Corey is off to a good start.

The previous Monday, he'd volunteered at the campus blood drive in the Great Hall, site of the original abbey church. With a Red Cross sticker on his chest, Corey fetched orange juice and cookies for those who'd just donated. Following him around while he fussed over the donors—"How are you feeling? Any dizziness? Is there anything else I can get for you?"—I was struck once again by his kindness. With a twinge of shame, I realized that I had come to appreciate him a little later in my visit than I should have.

There's a lot of that going around. Corey has taken so many sacks and presided over such an erratic offense that, despite his 6-1 record coming into this game, there is, among spoiled Johnny fans—some of whom reside in the monastery—an undercurrent of dissatisfaction with him. Corey couldn't care less about that, but his mother could. On more than one occasion, the criticism has driven Mary Jo from the bleachers.

The coaches talk up his calmness, his mistake-free play and his effectiveness as a runner. The guy is essentially a second fullback. His interceptions, they point out, tend to be well down the field, where they don't hurt you. Hearing the criticism and the qualified praise, it is easy to forget that Stanger was an absolute stud in high school; that two months ago he came in cold against St. Thomas and saved the Johnnies' season.

One is about to be reminded.

All right! This is what the monks have been looking for! Corey zips a decisive pass to Sieben on the right sideline. The throw is crisp, confidence-building. The play loses a yard. At the end of a quarter, the Johnnies are down, 3–0.

But they are driving. The offensive line is firing off the ball, taking the play to their more ponderous opponents. Krych is scary good tonight, running harder than he has all season, tearing off seven- and nine-yard chunks. On third-and-eight at the Gusties 15-yard line, Corey drops back to pass, buys time, sees daylight, and gallops into the end zone.

Still early in the second quarter, St. John's has driven back down to the Gusties 4-yard line, where the Johnnies face a fourth-and-one. Forsell, the junior wideout, jogs to the huddle with a pass play.

"Jimmy wants to see a 2314 out of the backfield."

"It's fourth-and-one!" says Corey.

Sieben scolds his teammates. "How about showing some confidence in the play?" He's the primary receiver. He sees his touchdown slipping away.

Sieben is overruled by O'Hara, who is dominating the guy across from him, and feeling pretty good about himself. "Sneak it," he says.

Stanger calls his own number and picks up the first. On the *next* play he fires a touchdown pass to Sieben. Everyone's happy but the maroon-clad members of the Gustavus alumni group occupying the luxury suites overlooking the end zone the Johnnies keep running into.

Watching tape two days earlier, Jimmy had said, "I think we can post the heck out of these guys." On first down from the Johnnies 29, Stanger calls "Pro Right, Cowboy" a post pattern to Lynch, who explodes out of his cut and is wide open in the middle of the field. Corey overthrows him by thirty feet.

No matter. Back at the line of scrimmage, left tackle Spencer Sokoly had been flagged for holding. Now it's first-and-twenty. Jimmy sends Forsell in with another deep post, this one to Sieben.

"Forsell," says Corey, "you take Sieben's route, 'cause he can't run." Sieben missed some practice this week with a sore ankle.

"I can run a *post*," says Sieben, getting pissy.

The protection is nearly perfect. Corey takes a little hop-step to his right, then cuts loose with a majestic bomb. Ben makes his cut at fifteen yards and hears the cornerback say, "Oh shit." Ben catches the ball at the Gustavus 35; the corner dives for him at the 7 and gets tube-sock fibers under his fingernails. Now it's 21–3.

No one's pulse has descended to its normal resting rate when the Johnnies get the ball back on a Novak interception. Corey has decided, understandably, to keep sending guys deep until the Gusties decide to cover them. On the first play of this new drive, he hits Lynch with a fifty-yard strike down to the 13-yard line, then unleashes a rocket to Sieben in the back of the end zone for the Johnnies' fourth touchdown.

St. John's gets the ball back with eight seconds left in the half. Stanger, in some zone to which he will never return, throws—and completes—his eighth pass of the quarter, a thirty-six-yard flag to Sieben. Ben is knocked out of bounds four yards shy of his fourth touchdown of the quarter. There appear to be at least a couple of seconds on the clock as he goes out of bounds. After huddling, the officials declare the half over, then head for a door beyond the end zone.

★ ★ ★

It was an afternoon in early September when the mother of a former Johnny stopped by practice and put a plate of apple fritters in the back seat of Gagliardi's car. When the weary coach collapsed into the driver's seat with his customary postpractice sigh, he was swarmed by bees that had been drawn to the fritters. Gagliardi then executed, according to witnesses, as sudden a movement as he made in the nineties, escaping the vehicle unstung.

If anything, he moved with more alacrity in pursuit of those zebras, cutting them off before they could escape through the door, then laying into them. I stand as close as I can to the brouhaha, enjoying the sight of a seventy-three-year-old venting some spleen. "There are six of you guys on the field," he gripes, "do you mean to tell me none of you was watching the clock?" Dr. Milaca, the team physician, is also hovering close by—"In case anyone should require CPR," he says archly. Bretherton, who works by day in the university's development office and is the administration's proxy on the field, also stands poised, ready to restrain his septuagenarian boss, perhaps even to clamp a hand over his mouth, should Gags start going ballistic.

Now is the time for the coaches who spent the first half in the pressbox to share their observations. "The dip for the crudités this year has more of a ranch flavor," Trewick reports. "Last year it was more of a dill."

John keeps it short. "Keep executing," he says. "Don't let 'em up off the floor. We want that championship to ourselves, right? Those other teams don't deserve it, do they?"

Everyone responds "No!" except Salvato, who shouts "F—— no!"

The game is over. It is true that the Johnnies began the second half by handing Gustavus a touchdown. (The Gusties score after Barry drops a punt snap, resulting in a blocked kick. He redeems himself with a pair of third-quarter picks.) That is to be expected from the '99 Johnnies, who refuse to do anything easily.

In his fifty-first year in the racket, Gagliardi has done one of the best coaching jobs of his career. Walking off the field at Bethel five weeks earlier, minus his two most important players, the nation's winningest active coach found himself staring at the likelihood of a 6-4 season. But the Johnnies have their swagger back. Suited up and seated behind one end zone are the Bethel Royals, who will face Carleton in the nightcap. "Hey, isn't that nice?" I hear a Johnny say. "They're lining up to take their second-place picture."

In the pressbox, I see a tall, handsome, and harried black man hustling back and forth, collating statistics, answering questions. When I introduce myself to MIAC commissioner Carlyle Carter, he is on his way to the copy machine with a ream of paper. Earlier this afternoon he could be seen in one of the concourses of the Metrodome, hawking programs. "Well, our first game was at two o'clock," he said, "and our students had class." Welcome to the MIAC.

Carlyle is a little down tonight. "Here it is, our championship weekend, we've got St. John's and Gustavus playing for the league title, and the *Pioneer Press* sends its small-college writer to a high school game. We could've had a five-way tie for the title, and their editors send him out to cover a prep game. We have one of the best-kept secrets in the country. We have a quarter-million alums in the Twin Cities area, unfortunately, the media doesn't see that."

Carter gives me his side of the Johnny probation story. It is his opinion that Gagliardi has amassed too much power at St. John's. He keeps going back to that phrase "lack of institutional control."

In the end, Carter's repetition of that phrase left me with a smile on my face. I mean, there we were in the press box of a building often used by the Minnesota Golden Gophers—the same Gophers who'd just conducted a purge of an athletic department disgraced by revelations that a tutor had written some four hundred papers for members of the basketball team; by allegations that the head coach knew it; that the head coach regularly gave cash to his players; and that officials of the department intervened in sexual misconduct and assault investigations of star athletes.

Gags, meanwhile, gets off a verbal scud at an official he thinks is doing a lousy job; the Johnnies accidentally get too many "practice opportunities," and Carter wants to paint this as a lack of institutional control. It could be that venial sins are much magnified in the MIAC. Or it could be that it's a little personal between Carter and Gagliardi. I am conflicted as I leave the press box: mildly concerned for the Johnnies, whose every step Commissioner Carter will be watching; and feeling sorry for Carlyle, who's got a wonderful product he's having trouble selling, and an enemy I wouldn't wish on anyone.

I walk briskly through the guts of the Metrodome. I am in danger of missing the team bus. There is a gleaming coach in the loading area, but I don't recognize any of the football players getting on it. They are the Gusties, headed south for St. Peter, Minnesota. "The Johnny bus? It *just* left," one of them tells me.

I retrace my steps to the press box. Maybe my buddy Mike Hemmesch, the Johnny sports-information director, can give me a ride home. "He *just* left," says Carlyle.

At Hubert's, a nearby pub, I cast a wide net for a lift to Collegeville.

Poor Wally Pattock and his wife, Marge, get stuck with me. Wally is driving a mideighties vintage Buick Park Avenue, a car with its own zip code, a car in need of new shocks. We bottom out several times as he bisects Minneapolis in search of the freeway. At a red light, we pull abreast of a car from which emanates a denture-vibrating bass beat.

"When those kids are forty-five, they're gonna need hearing aids," tut-tuts Arlene Truszinski, who is sitting in back, with me. (Even though I am the hitchhiker, Arlene refuses to let me take the middle, or "hump" seat.) It turns out she works full-time in a nursing home. Her husband, Mike, who is so excited to make my acquaintance that he has nodded off on the other side of her, was a butcher for quite a few years. But the Piggly Wiggly opened up, "and it was tough on the little guys," Marge explains. "He got out of the business in '83."

There is a consensus among the sentient adults in the car that the *St. Cloud Times* headline was out of all proportion to the Johnny transgressions. "They do that a lot at the *Times*," says Marge. "A lot of the people working there are just marking time until they can move up to a bigger paper, so they don't really care about the local people's feelings."

They are kind enough to drop me at the LaPlayette Bar in St. Joe, where I expect to run into some of the Johnnies who are of legal drinking age. But I don't know anyone there. I walk over to Chubby's: empty. The boys stayed in the cities to celebrate. I phone a cab company; the wait will be an hour. I walk to St. Ben's, where I wait for the shuttle to St. John's, a conveyance the students have dubbed the Vomit Comet. Even though I feel like a suspicious figure, a man crowding forty amidst students half my age, the shock troops of campus security are focusing their attention on an inebriated underclassman. The Comet is nearly full, but no one sits next to me. I enter my apartment after midnight.

The bad-dream aspects of my evening—missing the bus, searching in vain for familiar, friendly faces, my difficulties getting home—are overwhelmed by my happiness for John and the Johnnies, who are undisputed league champions and playoff-bound, despite all. I am happiest for two guys.

Based largely on his performance in tonight's game—one-quarter of the contest, really—Corey will be named first-team all-MIAC. For all the grief he takes—I'm talking about grief from Johnny fans and monks—Stanger will end up leading the conference in offense, averaging 235.3 yards per game. Long after he had been passed over for the starting quarterback's job, he would plod his weary way up to the film room. He would study the opponent, just in case. Seven weeks ago, the work paid off. Stanger came off the bench against St. Thomas and saved the Johnnies' season. No matter what happens in the playoffs, Corey will always have tonight. More precisely, he will have the second fifteen minutes of the first half against the Golden Gusties, when everything he touched turned to gold.

While wandering the Metrodome after the game, I'd chanced upon Ben and his parents and girlfriend. They were smiling but subdued. Ben's spectacular game—ten catches for 171 yards and three TDs—was nothing out of the ordinary for this clan. From Omer to Dave to Ben, Siebens have helped St. John's beat Gustavus for sixty-plus years.

Ben's touchdowns tonight displayed all of his gifts. One was a bullet he somehow hung on to, highlighting his superb hands; one was a bomb he ran under, showcasing his knack for accelerating while the ball is in the air. The final one was deflected by a defender; Sieben made a cat-quick adjustment to it. Ben is listed in the program at five-nine, a willful exaggeration of which his namesake, Benedict of Nursia, would disapprove. Sieben is lucky if he's five-eight. Coming out of high school he generated zero interest among Division I coaches. Please believe me when I tell you, there are Big 10 wide receivers who play in this building, on the same rug Sieben owned tonight, who could not carry his jock.

That's right, Benny is another Johnny who eschews the inconvenience of a protective cup. (You'd be surprised at how many football players, college and pro, just can't bring themselves to wear one.) Early in the third quarter, after going out of bounds on the Gusties sideline, Ben had reason to second-guess himself. Somehow—this was almost certainly an accident—a Gustavus fist found its way into his groin. He was groaning on all fours when an official asked him what had happened.

"Some guy just punched me in the nuts!" said Ben.

"I'm sorry," said the official. "I didn't see it."

"No problem. Just give me a second here," said Sieben, who took a few more deep breaths and got back in the game.

Taking a shot on the street where you live, so to speak, then staying in the game—that takes guts. It is the story of the Johnnies' week; indeed, their *season*. Injuries ensured that the '99 Johnnies would be remembered as one of Gagliardi's more flawed outfits. They made up for their shortcomings with determination, grit, and, let's face it, kick-ass defense. These guys could've lost four games. They could have finished the season tonight and they would have had an easy out. *We lost too many key guys. The probation thing was a huge distraction.* But they were made of sterner stuff. Every time they took one below the belt, they came off the turf and got back in the game.

15

WISCONSIN-STEVENS POINT

It is standing room only in Gary's cubicle on Monday afternoon. Jerry is studying a roster, Gary watching a video, linebackers coach Chris (Cubby) Govern hacking at the computer like an NSA operative, plundering D3Football.com. for stats and dope on Wisconsin-Stevens Point.

Cheese Reprise: Having begun their season with a victory over a Wisconsin school, St. John's has earned a number two seed in the West Region of D-III's postseason tournament. The Johnnies will host Wisconsin-Stevens Point at noon on Saturday.

Here's what we know about the Pointers: they were ranked in the top fifteen in Division III all year, and shared their conference title with LaCrosse. Their nonconference wins are top-shelf—they beat Northern State and Bemidji State, both D-II schools; and Drake, an I-AA school. Very impressive. In the tape of their most recent win, over Bemidji, the coaches are seen wearing shorts, even though they don't really have the legs for it.

The big thing about the self-styled Angry Dogs is that they are . . . big things. Even by the Brobdingnagian standards of the WIAC, these guys are colossal, cartoon-large, with an offensive line averaging 292 pounds. Phil Trier, the preppy, twiggy defensive tackle, walks in just as Jerry starts reading off the names, heights, and weights of the Pointers' hogs: "Right tackle, Paul Steffeck, six feet four inches, 313."

"Wow," says Trier.

"He's a pup next to the guy blocking you," says Haugen. "Mike Lange, six-eight, 365."

"Get out! Three-sixty-five?"

"Actually, 318," says Jerry. "See, you feel better already! Instead of outweighing you by 180 pounds, he's only got you by 140." Trier says he weighs 200, but no one believes him.

"My advice to you," I tell him, "is to feign an injury early in the game. Because this guy will fold, spindle, and mutilate you. He will eat your face." I ask Trier if he is his family's sole male heir. Gary is the voice of reasoned calm: "Guy weighs 320 pounds and he's at Stevens Point, there's a reason for it. If he could really move, he'd be blocking for Ron Dayne"—the Wisconsin back who will win this year's Heisman Trophy.

Up front on defense, the Johnnies average maybe 220 pounds. "We'll do some shading and some blazes and some stunting," says Jerry.

"We'll shoot gaps, take away their size advantage," says Gary.

"They're laughing at us right now," says Jerry. "That's what we want."

Kirschner and LaBore are working in the Fitness Center, honing their skills. Leafing through a magazine, Nate says to a picture of a model, "I like you, Tommy Girl." Beau just shakes his head. When a curvaceous Benny returns from the water fountain, he is ready with a line: "Hey, we were wondering what color nail polish that was. Is that some kind of silver?"

"I mixed two colors," she says. "It's silver and green."

"You mixed," says Beau. "Sounds like you've got a lot of time on your hands." Nate asks the young woman if she ever found the ring she lost at Chubby's party. She did find it, she tells us over her shoulder, walking away, in her underwear drawer.

"You guys," I say when she is out of earshot, "could not score with twins in a vat of Mazola."

Beau and I take a walk up to Sexton Commons, where a lot of students kill time between classes. Walking past the football field, we see three members of the grounds crew. Painstakingly, lovingly, they are painting fresh, white diagonal stripes in the end zone. They'll move up the field over the next few days, whitening and brightening hash marks and yard lines. The new latex leaps out against the green of the turf. It is the bright white of fresh hope—an offense awakened from a six-week slumber.

"It never fails," Beau tells me. "When the refs are measuring for a first down early in the game, they always mention how beautiful this field is. I tell 'em, 'Hey, you think these monks are screwing around?' You know, give 'em a little friendly shit just to get on their good side."

We walk down on the field to chat with the groundskeepers, who don't seem to mind the interruption. The guy in charge is Rich Froehle. Name sound familiar? This good man, creased and weatherbeaten, is an ex-Johnny who played in the Camellia Bowl. "I still remember tackling Otis Taylor," he tells me. I nod, smiling and thinking, "Yeah, right."

Months later, watching an old tape of the game, I would see the fullback, a No. 41, blocking like a madman, repeatedly springing Beckman and Spinner; making a clutch interception to kill a Panther rally late in the first half. Who the hell is 41? I wondered, looking it up in a yellowed old program. Forty-one is Rich Froehle, the groundskeeper I disbelieved.

Like the Sextons and Siebens and numerous other families, the Froehles are a clan in whose veins course Johnny-red blood. Rich's father, Chuck, starred for the Johnnies in the twenties, and died of a heart attack while watching Rich play against Gustavus in 1965. Rich's son Luke was a stud for Gags a few years back. Beau makes it a point to tell Rich what a fine player Luke was. He compliments him on the quality of the field, the condition of the turf, the geometric precision of the hashes and yard lines. The

Hamline sidelines, by contrast, appear to have been slapped down by Ted Kennedy and Robert Downey Jr. a half-hour after last call.

Concerned, perhaps, that he has said too many nice things, Beau makes a final observation. "Lot of deer shit," he says, pointing with his sneaker at a cluster of offending turds.

"Don't worry," says Froehle. "There'll be a detail."

Later, over coffee and to my great shame, I made a mean-spirited wisecrack about Froehle—something about how skillfully he'd parlayed his St. John's degree into a job as a groundskeeper. "Wow," said Beau, looking at me as if he'd fundamentally misjudged me. "That's really mean." My clothes began expanding, and I could no longer see over the table. I was like the humbled monk in Chapter 7 of the *Rule*, proclaiming, "But I am a worm and no man."

It was completely uncalled for, I agree. I was going for a cheap laugh, and it wasn't funny. But Beau has only begun his defense of the groundskeeper. "You should see his house. It's beautiful. Out in the country. It's like one of the monastic gardens."

Beau has made his point. I'm looking down my nose at a guy who lives in a palace, when in a few weeks I'll fly home to a gingerbread house in California that cost three hundred-plus grand and won't survive the next Big Shake. Who's the idiot?

The outlaw Johnnies have paid their debt to the MIAC. Coaches are once again allowed to preside over film sessions. Jimmy has the remote, the laser pointer, and a list of gripes dating back seven weeks. I write down about every fifth one:

"Spencer, look at that—this guy's got you on your heels. We need a better effort."

"Vonderharr, stay up."

"Pantzke, what are you doing here? We spent a lot of time trying to figure you out. You didn't have a very good game."

"Chad, that's lousy."

"Look at this move, Sieben." Ben was playing with a bum

wheel, but Jimmy is Ming the Merciless today. "Christ, I could cover you. That's not St. John's, that's high school."

The first quarter ends.

"Guys," says Jimmy, "the national championship game is in five weeks, and we'll be watching it on TV if we can't do a better job than that."

Chad's feelings are not hurt by Jimmy's critique, as Chad is not present. The coaches feel fortunate when they can get him to show up forty-five minutes before kickoff, so Monday film sessions would be a bit of a reach. A few nights later, Linnemann and I decide the time has come to spend some quality time with O'Hara on his turf. This entails a trip to Granite City Lanes, where Chad bowls in a league. "Keeps me out of trouble," he says. "If I weren't here," he says, "I'd probably be sitting home drinking a case of beer."

He is, instead, pulling on a Mountain Dew, a soft drink that comprises, as far as I can tell, 50 percent of his diet, the other half consisting of pizza slices cadged from Power Housemates. Tom lives with Chad and has never seen him eat a vegetable.

On the back of his bowling shirt are the words SUMMIT EXCAVATION, the *m*'s of "Summit" bisected by the silhouette of a range of mountains—presumably hillocks of earth amassed by the backhoes, front-loaders, and bulldozers of Summit excavators.

It is a dream of Chad's mother that he graduate from St. John's. It is a dream of Chad's, on the other hand, to enter the excavating profession. "Digging dirt all day, it's every kid's fantasy," he says. "Plus, you're outside, you're getting fresh air."

And the adventure! While working at a site in Willmar a few summers back, Chad was dumping a load from his Bobcat when he felt his minidozer pitching forward, into the hole. An alert uncle, who'd been keeping an eye on the college boy, lowered the bucket of his backhoe onto the roof of the Bobcat—which heroic feat the uncle seldom misses an opportunity to work into the conversation whenever he sees Chad. I foresee soiled coveralls and callused hands in Chad's future. And bowling nights.

Chad gets up to bowl and is transformed from a gangly post-teen to a graceful, rare bird, his cocked arm coming forward with pendulum's precision, the cradled ball kissing the lane, spinning and biting and leaving him with a split that looks like a hockey player's grin. He fails to pick up the spare.

Chad's teammate Jerry has shoulder-length hair and a proud beer gut. My suspicion is that Jerry is one of those guys who, although genetically predisposed to leanness, triumphs over his chromosomes. Jerry's beer gut is more than an arresting protuberance. It is a piece of performance art.

A few years back, Jerry was the passenger in a car that was involved in a serious crash. Since then, he's vowed to ride a bike everywhere—an ambitious, if impractical goal in central Minnesota. He could not be dissuaded from this lifestyle choice even after riding through a plate-glass window at the post office one night—he intended to cut the corner, not realizing there was plate glass in the way.

It was in a bar fight, rather than either of these vehicular mishaps, that Jerry acquired his nickname, One-Nut Jer. He was kicked in the groin and lost a testicle. "That was a tough time for him," says Chad. "It was around then that he got divorced from his wife. She looked exactly—I mean *exactly*—like Momma in *Throw Momma from the Train*."

Befitting one of the athletes comprising the Summit squad, Jerry is not without self-discipline. If he is working the graveyard shift at the nearby Frigidaire plant, he informs the waitress who refreshes the bowlers, "Can't drink tonight, gotta work. Just bring me beers."

When the bowlers are finished, we repair to the bar. Chad talks about the old days, when his grandparents owned this place. "It was different in here in those days," he says. "It was much . . . darker. Me and my friends were supposed to clean the place, but we'd turn on the machines and bowl till seven in the morning. If we got hungry, we raided the candy machines."

Chad's cousin Brandon walks in. He's a nice enough guy, and kind of handsome—for someone missing part of his nose. An uncle's dog did a number on him when he was a kid. There at the other end of the bar is Chad's aunt, a husky woman. "Looks like she wouldn't take any guff," I say. "Got that right," says Chad. "She's a prison guard in Shakopee." After the Gustavus game, Chad crashed at her place in Burnsville. Without warning, like Inspector Clouseau's valet, she ambushed him, repeatedly slugging him with a giant body pillow. "I finally had enough, grabbed a pillow and hit her twice in the head," he recalls. "She went down like a redwood."

Someone asks Chad when we're ever going to see his play, the Cherry O'Harey. The Cherry O'Harey is a hook-and-ladder to Chad. After catching a short pass, the wide receiver laterals to the pulling O'Hara, who calls to mind a collapsing tenement as he turns the corner and heads upfield. If Chad ever scores on that play, he has vowed to earn *at least* a fifteen-yard penalty for the celebration he will stage.

"John always tells us, 'When you score, act like you've been there before,'" he says. "Well, shit, I've never been there before and I'll never be back, so I'm gonna celebrate. I'm gonna spike the ball so hard the air will come out of it. Then I'll get a piece of cardboard and start break dancing on my head.

"I have deceptive speed, hidden speed. You put that ball in my hands, I'm gonna find that extra gear," he says, as if it is in the power of the people at the bar to call his number. "But they won't give it to me."

Linnemann is back in uniform, limping around the practice field, raising hell. He can't plant properly. The balls he is throwing are wobbling and sailing on him. He is so happy to be back in pads that he pretends not to notice. He has taken it upon himself to clean up the second-team's act, whip its sorry ass into shape. Guards Jim Mulrooney and Ted Griffin have been flip-flopping in the huddle, a slovenliness Tom will not tolerate.

"You guys gotta decide who's the salad fork and who's the dinner fork, then stick with it," he says.

"What does that make me?" Says Dirlam, the center.

"The plate."

"I don't wanna be the plate."

"You're a freshman, you're the plate. Deal with it."

★ ★ ★

Calisthenics have been scrapped. Now that we're into Daylight Savings, every minute of practice is spent running plays. At 4:45 the sun is already under Sexton Commons, staining the western horizon blood-orange. The gibbous moon over the Big Screen coordinates nicely with the silver maples and birches. That high band of pressure that kept the jet stream off our backs has been breached: only the hardiest souls are still in shorts. Most of the team has opted for the standard-issue gray sweat pants with the convenient elastic waistband, which allows unoccupied Johnnies to stand around with their hands down their pants, warming one set of extremities while adjusting another.

Over on the defensive field, the scout offense is doing its damnedest to simulate the Pointers' size. To give the defense an idea of what a pulling, 300-pound guard looks like, 220-pound Bryan Bohlman jogs to the line of scrimmage with 170-pound receiver Brooks Deibele on his back. The ball is snapped, and DeiBohlman pulls and actually gets a tiny piece of Pahula. It is the loudest laughter I've heard on the practice field this year. Tremendous size doesn't intimidate this team. "You can be big," says Jerry, "but you'd better be quick."

I cut out of Wednesday's practice early. Willa has accumulated thirty-five stars on her chore chart, thus earning a dinner at the Timber Lodge, the restaurant with the slogan: Small Portions Are for Californians. (After three months in this place, we feel entitled to rejoin: And Big, Wide Asses and Multiple Angioplasties Are for Minnesotans.)

Willa requested the Lodge. She likes the small, gratis boxes of crayons they hand out, and the kid's menu with the maze and hidden-word games. She gobbles shrimp, gulps lemonade, kicks off her boots, stands up in our booth, turning around to watch the television behind us. Extreme skateboarders are catching sick air on ESPN2.

"Whoa! Whoooaaaa—he's *out of control*!" Willa shouts. Three businessmen at the bar turn to look at her, then me. I wonder if a five-year-old has ever been tossed from the Timber Lodge.

I am delighted to be here. On a normal autumn Wednesday I'd be reading my fifth sports section on some cross-country flight. It would be the day's last, non-red-eye flight to my destination city. I would book the flight knowing I would not arrive in Buffalo or Boston or Indy or Pittsburgh or Dallas or Tampa Bay until the wee hours of the next morning. But I take that late flight because, having arrived home Monday evening, I can't bring myself to leave on Wednesday morning.

Late in the season, I start cutting corners, just to get an extra day at home. I start taking red-eyes, the business traveler's equivalent of slaking one's thirst with seawater. I know I'll pay for it on the other end, but do it anyway, feeling I have no choice.

Instead, Willa and I return home and join Laura and Devin on the couch. We read Harry Potter, then say prayers.

The whole prayer thing was Laura's idea. We started doing it a year or so ago. Sitting on the couch, we go down the line, thanking God for something. It took me a while to get into the true spirit of the exercise. Having been ordered to pray for most of the first half of my life, I'd done as little of it as possible in the second, and never noticed a difference. I'd always been nagged, during prayer, by the suspicion that there was no one on the other end, listening. I recognized my own attitude toward God in a 1994 *Harper's* story, which read:

"Things make much more sense if you assume the world was created not by an all-good and all-powerful being, but by one that is 100 percent malevolent but only 90 percent effective."

I remember reading that to Laura, hugely amused. She smiled for up to two-tenths of a second. We had been together eight years, and, while I was only beginning to pick up on it at the time, Laura had ceased to be amused by my briny agnosticism.

A few things happened, and I started coming around. We became parents. It's tough to watch your children come into the world and continue to doubt the existence of *some* unseen, benevolent puppetmaster.

We had an intense, cathartic fight in France in the spring of

1998. We'd had a blast for a week in Provence, and had just begun a week in Paris. We came out of a movie theater—we'd just seen *Deconstructing Harry*—when, from out of the blue, Laura lit into me. Basically, she was fed up by my continual cynicism; it no longer amused her. It worried her. It was symptomatic of stunted emotional development, a spiritual autism.

"So," I said, "I'm guessing you *didn't* like the movie." She was not to be charmed or placated. Sulking, I walked until two in the morning. We barely spoke the next day, going our separate ways—me to the Louvre, she to the Musée D'Orsay. On one level I fumed, knowing that I hadn't done anything to provoke her. On a deeper level, I knew she was right. That night I gave her a volume of poetry by Ted Hughes and a note saying I would try to do better.

Since then, to make a short story long, I have opened my mind, if not to traditional prayer, then at least to contemplation and meditation. Some of my monk friends suggest that it's all of a piece. When it comes time for our family to offer thanks to God, I reach down for something for which I really am grateful. I no longer try to sabotage the proceedings.

That is not to say Laura and I are always able to restrain our laughter at some of the prayers our children offer up. After a day in which he spied, from his car-seat vantage, a giant vehicle he recognized from one of his many truck books, Devin said, "Thank you God, for seeing a combine harvester." On a day that had featured a visit to a department store, he thanked the Almighty "for moving stairs and elevators."

After prayers, we brush the children's teeth, then herd them toward their rooms. Within three hours, usually, they are fast asleep. Once they have given up the ghost, run the race, fought the good fight, I like to stand over their beds, listening to their breathing, drinking in the sight of their sweet faces in repose.

How strange that such a simple thing, the sight and sound of my children gone grudgingly to slumber, is the thing, when I am traveling, I miss the most.

Maybe you have children. Maybe it doesn't seem strange to you at all.

* * *

The apartment next to Chubby's is called Driftwood, and it is no prize, either. It houses Pete Corkrean, Alex Wesley, and Josh Hart. On Thursday night these defensive linemen defended themselves before the town council. They had been cited for hosting a loud party. Wesley is a terrific game-day player who is known for his surliness toward the scout teamers who help him prepare. Soma intends no disrespect when he says, "I guess you could call Alex the dick of the defense."

So it is surprising and a bit disillusioning to see this Grinch address his elders in truckling, pleading tones. Beseeching the council for clemency, Wesley spoke earnestly of the scores of people he had turned away at the door. To hear him tell it, the saturnalia was a book-group discussion that took an unfortunate turn. Anticipating swift, partial justice, Corkrean prepared for the kangaroo court a tee shirt that said, IF ASSHOLES COULD FLY, THIS PLACE WOULD BE AN AIRPORT.

The beauty of this proceeding was that it was televised on local cable-access channel. When the Driftwood miscreants returned from their meeting with the village elders, they found a sign on their door, courtesy of Linnemann:

ONE BEER: $2.50

FINE FOR A LOUD PARTY: $450

SEEING YOUR FRIENDS APOLOGIZE TO THE MAN ON TV: PRICELESS.

As the Pointers trickled out of the dressing room Saturday morning, across the running track and onto the field, they were greeted by a curiously congenial Beau LaBore.

"Hi, how ya doin'?" he asked them. "Nice weather, huh?"

"How was your bus ride? Uneventful, I trust?"

"Welcome to Collegeville!"

They grunted sullen rejoinders and looked at each other. What was up with this clown? Later, riding a Life Cycle to warm up his tweaked hamstring, Beau explained himself. "These guys are like every other team from Wisconsin. They get off the bus and walk in here with their chests out, *talkin' real low,* no expressions on their faces, like we're supposed to be intimidated. It pisses me off. So I stand outside, and as they come walking by, I give 'em a big smile and say hi to 'em. It drives 'em crazy to say hi back."

The Pointers try a reverse on the kickoff. Hover foils it. Hover's name, by the way, rhymes with "clover." Betraying a few early-game butterflies, Timo pronounces it like the verb, to hover.

Jerzak makes the next tackle. This is a hopeful portent—the smallest guy on the field dropping one of the visiting brutes in his tracks. The Johnny offense pratfalls, but Phil Barry, the punter and secret weapon, buries the visitors on their 5. A few plays later the Pointers punt it back, with St. John's netting a cool thirty yards in the exchange. One pass to Kirschner and three Moore runs later, the Johnnies lead 6–0.

"A lot of bleeders today," a trainer observes. Week-old scabs from Metrodome turf burns are coming off. Pointer defensive tackle Keith Berens, who is built like the fast-food Big Boy, blows out a knee early. The Johnny immobilizer reaches not quite halfway around his sycamore-like thigh. The Johnnies have no flat-bed cart, and trundle him off the field—to sustained applause—in a golf cart that Leroy Henkemeyer the equipment manager swears has never run the same since.

After leading his team to a field goal, Pointers quarterback Dave Berghuis is moving the offense again in the second quarter. With just under a minute on the clock, he decides to pick on Beau. As Linnemann says, "Bad Idea Jeans."

Watching LaBore intercept the ball and pull away from the intended receiver, one is reminded that Beau was a stud running back for the South St. Paul Packers. Running interference for him, Jerzak is bowled over. As Grady leaps into Beau's arms after the sixty-six-yard return for a touchdown, LaBore sidesteps him like a matador. (He will swear afterward it was an accident.) Grady's spectacular dry dive will be the highlight of Monday's films.

The score is 16–3 in the second half when Berghuis is replaced by senior Ryan Aulenbacher, who promptly completes a bomb down to the Johnnies' 9-yard line. Two plays later, Aulenbacher takes a three-step drop and looks. He's got a receiver slanting inside.

Hiding in the weeds, reading Aulenbacher as if he were the

marquee at Radio City Music Hall, is LaBore. Beau steps in front of the pass and kicks off Act II of the Beau Show, tipping the ball to himself, tucking it under his right arm and taking off down the sideline for his second touchdown of the day. This one goes ninety-two yards, and puts LaBore in the NCAA record book for most interception-return yardage in a D-III playoff game. As he curls into the end zone, once again the beneficiary of a Jerzak block, LaBore turns to accept the rowdy congratulations of his teammates. This time Grady is careful to stay on his feet.

Arriving at the sideline, Beau is mugged by Moore, who shouts, joyously, repeatedly, rhetorically, "Are you serious?" It is a transcendent moment and a snapshot of the season, the wounded offense thanking the defense for bailing it out and keeping it alive. Rotondi misses the extra point, but some brainiac Pointer plows into the holder. On his second try, Rotondi gets it right, putting the Johnnies up 23–3.

Now you see some of the Pointers start to sulk. When he thinks he is being held, Pahula complains to an official. From the Stevens-Point sideline comes a voice, saying, "Oh, suck it up, 58, you pussy."

"I looked to see which one of their players it was," says Novak, "but it was one of their assistant coaches."

A stir goes through the crowd with four minutes left in the game. Barry's third interception in two games has given the Johnnies possession on the Pointers' 39-yard line. Jogging onto the field, lugging the eight screws and plate that doctors drilled into him two months ago, is Linnemann. He calls four running plays, getting the team down to the 4-yard line. What is shaping up to be a sweet sidebar to the game story sours on second down. Tommy calls a pass play, and is picked off in the end zone by a Pointer linebacker, who sprints past the Johnny bench before being overtaken at the far 21-yard line by a hustling Lynch.

One of Gary's jobs is to stand between John and Jerry, to be an ambassador, a shuttle diplomat. As the Pointers push the ball toward the end zone—they will score a touchdown with twenty-five seconds left in the game—Gagliardi starts crowding Jerry, as is his wont.

"What are we in?" he asks his defensive coordinator. "How are we going to stop 'em?"

"Well," snaps Haugen, "you can start by not throwing the goddam ball on the goddam goal line."

"I know, I know," says John, backing off.

Linnemann's goal line play-calling provokes some grumbling. "The run was working, our line was dominating, but [Tom] wanted to be the guy who came off the bench and threw a touchdown pass," said one defensive starter. "The thing that saved him," said LaBore, "was that he got up off the ground and tried to make the tackle. That was cool." In a spectacle at once ballsy and pathetic, Linnemann scrambled to his feet—he'd been knocked flat—and gave chase, running like a man with a prosthesis. It became painfully clear, as Tommy hobbled across the field, that he was still not himself—that he was not about to ride in, to the accompaniment of cavalry bugles, and lead the Johnnies to glory. Six thousand onlookers in the Natural Bowl realized in a single play what Gagliardi had known for weeks: this team will go as far as Corey Stanger can take it.

Spencer and Lange, the six-eight, 318-pounder, find each other after the game and share a titanic embrace: they played together in high school in Mayville, Wisconsin. Then Lange calls the Pointers offensive line together. The monsters circle up, their arms around each other. "For me and Wally it's over," says Lange, "but you guys better kick some ass next year. I'm so proud of you guys, you don't even know . . . " His voice breaks.

When the scrum breaks up I congratulate him on a great season and ask him how it went out there. "They were very quick," he says. "We expected them to be fast, but they were faster than what we thought. We had hoped to get ahead of them, then get our big bodies on them and wear them down. But it didn't work out that way."

The behemoth who has devoted his life to football stands under a sunless sky on a strange field, slowly awakening to the fact that he's got no more football to play.

"I'm so glad to have been on this team, win or lose," he says.

"We were such a family this year. I knew it could end at any time. I just didn't think it was gonna be so hard." His voice breaks again.

The cynic must be wary at such moments, lest his cynicism be damaged beyond repair.

I liked Lange. I don't know what his career plans are, but they can always use another good guy in the WWF.

16

CENTRAL

The steepest price the team paid for its crimes against the MIAC was to be deprived of Gagliardi's Monday afternoon monologues. It's nice to have him back. "All right, okay," he says after shuffling onto the stage, "we'll try to skip around a little here."

Try to skip around? He'd have to try not to. The first item on his agenda requires him to take a hard line, which is a reach for John. Thanksgiving is in four days. Most of the students will be off campus by Tuesday afternoon. The football players aren't going anywhere. The team will practice at one o'clock Wednesday, ten o'clock on Thanksgiving morning, and three o'clock Friday.

"If anybody misses practice without an excuse," warns Gags, trying to sound like Vince Lombardi, "they're done. If you don't want to practice, that's fine, but you're done playing football at St. John's." Having drawn that line in the sand, he proceeds to erase it. "If you're a long way from home, and you wanna go home, and we can spare you, well, okay."

The Central Dutch will bus 375 miles due north from Pella, Iowa, for Saturday's second-round matchup in Collegeville. They are polar opposites of the Pointers—undersized, quick, opportunistic. St. John's and Central are two of sixteen teams still standing. In its infinite wisdom, the NCAA has added this season a fifth round to its Division III football tournament, meaning that the two teams who make it to the Stagg Bowl may have played five games on top of their regular season schedule. (One team per region received a first-round bye.) That this extra half-season tramples on the spirit of D-III did not occur, or did not matter, to the sages of Indianapolis, home of the NCAA.

"I've got a good news announcement," says Gagliardi, skipping around, as promised. "Phil Barry's been invited to punt in the Aztec Bowl in Mexico City, all expenses paid." The Aztec Bowl pits a team of U.S. all stars against a Mexican team. "I'm just reading the fine print here," says Gags, squinting at the official letter of invitation. He begins reading aloud. "This form must be filled out and returned no later than 5 P.M. November twenty-second." Looking up, he asks, "What day is today?"

Thirty or forty guys answer: "The twenty-second."

Barry sprints down the aisle and snatches the form from Gags. He has a little less than an hour to fill out the form and fax it to Aztec Bowl headquarters. (He makes the deadline and will average a whopping 44.5 yards on five punts in that game.)

Snow is in the forecast, and that's okay. We've had a mild, gorgeous fall. As surprising as the balmy weather are the locals who seem to begrudge us Californians its warmth, who cannot mask their disappointment that we have not been required to suffer. When Laura and I explain that we have lived in the east, gone to college in upstate New York and frequently visit the Sierra Nevada mountains in winter, they smile and nod indulgently, confident that we only *think* we know what we're in for. Because they know what we do not: that temperate California climes have thinned our blood; that the pervasive decadence of the Golden State has stunted our capacity for *bearing up*. The severity of a Minnesota winter will catch us unprepared. Of that much, they are certain.

Even saintly Father Tim could not resist a brief lecture, after hearing Laura complain of the cold one recent evening. "Minnesota cold means you walk outside and wonder, briefly, whether or not you will *survive*," he scolded. "This is not cold."

Laura shops at an upscale grocery store in St. Cloud called Byerly's, where patrons are discouraged from carting their purchases into the parking lot. Shoppers must pull up to a designated spot, where employees trained in the loading and arranging of groceries put them in the car for you. Byerly's management means well, but this system is a pain in the ass. In the Byerly's stockman lottery, Laura keeps drawing a grating old busybody with a goiter. He saw our car's California plates and it was all over.

Spying the short pants on Devin one afternoon, he warned Laura the kids weren't dressed warmly enough. (Fine, Gramps, why don't you try getting long pants on him—he'll kick your bridge down your throat.) After giving Laura earnest advice on the type of oil to put in the car, he concluded that, on account of its "California engine," the car probably wouldn't start anyway.

"But it's a Swedish car," said Laura. "I'm told it gets cold in Sweden."

"But they assemble them in Detroit," he says, making it up as he goes along. "If they know the car is going to California, they make it for California conditions."

Laura pointed out that the car's previous owners lived in New Jersey.

"New Jersey?" he says, reluctantly conceding defeat. "Then you might be okay."

Tuesday, November 23: At last, snow. But not much of it—just flurries with no accumulation. Amy Behrendt, the Johnny athletic trainer who is kind enough to baby-sit for us some mornings, tells me that Willa and Devin sat outside on sleds, trying to scoot themselves down the hill, crying with frustration. For months they'd been promised they could go sledding "when it snowed." Well, it was snowing, dammit, so they were going sledding!

Amy explained to them that the grass had to be actually *covered* with snow. They didn't take the news well. Early the next morning, with the frost still heavy on the grass, the kids and I bundled up and went outside. I would take the rope attached to their sleds and, with a running start, buggy-whip them down the embankment. It worked surprisingly well, the children topping out at speeds of sixteen to eighteen mph. It was on about her fifth run that Willa's sled caught an edge. Watching her catapult down the hill, I was reminded of Joe Mannix tumbling out of the moving car in a memorable episode of that classic crime show. Willa squirted a few tears before I was able to convince her—this is a key to successful parenting—that she was more scared than hurt.

Central head coach Rich Kacmarynski may be a pup in his profession—he just turned thirty—but he knows a few tricks. The tape the Dutch sent to the Johnnies is fuzzy and out of focus. The poor quality of the video makes it tough for the Johnny coaches to discern jersey numbers, but cannot disguise the fact that Central's defense is gnarly. They blitz, dog, and shoot gaps. They slant and stunt. They do more twisting than Chubby Checker. While the Johnnies were stuffing the Pointers, Central was thumping Wisconsin-LaCrosse. St. Norbert of De Pere, Wisconsin, meanwhile, was taking the pipe against Augustana, completing an 0-for-3 opening round for Wisconsin schools. The conclusion is inescapable: too much cheese.

"This will be by far the most confusing game for us," says Spencer, speaking for the offensive line. He is one of a dozen guys watching Central video on Tuesday afternoon.

"They're in two-lock here," says offensive assistant Dean Taylor. "Good time for a draw."

"Nose slants a lot," says Jimmy. "We gotta double down, or he'll slant into the play."

Outside, it has stopped snowing. The guys are fairly certain Gagliardi will move practice indoors, anyway.

"The ground is wet," says Salvato. "Wet is big. Wet means slippery."

He is right. They practice in the fieldhouse, where it is clear which unit is struggling and which is peaking. On the defensive side of the field, there is wisecracking and laughter. Novak is flying around in orange, see-through mesh tights over his jock. (He was a pumpkin for Halloween.) Over on offense, the line is struggling with its assignments. Body language is tense. Gagliardi is cranky.

"Jeezus Criminy, pay attention," he says to a confused hog. "If that guy sneaks in, you block down. That's all it is—bronze blocking. Royal is bronze blocking."

And what could be simpler than that?

His mood is lighter in the locker room after practice. He asks Joe Linhoff, the kicker, where Linhoff is headed for Thanksgiving.

"To my girlfriend's," says Joe.

"Your girlfriend's?" says Gags, in mock alarm. "When did this happen?" Until recently, Linhoff was a member of the campus ministry: Gagliardi had him pegged as a future monk. "Christ, I thought you were going to the seminary," he says. "I thought you were gonna be the abbot in twenty years, and then you could give me a raise."

We are delighted to have been invited to the Petersons' for Thanksgiving Dinner. My sister Lorin began dating Rod Peterson in 1991. We suspected, at first, that she was merely enamoured of his chiseled, youthful body—he is seven years her junior—and his 1974, goldenrod, convertible Cadillac Eldorado, featuring a 501 cubic-inch engine, telescoping steering wheel, and the Twilight Sentinel, which sensed the approach of an oncoming vehicle and automatically dimmed the high beams. Best damned party car I've ever ridden in.

But the relationship had legs, and in the summer of 1996, Rod hired a small plane to pull a sign over our beach house: LOR, WILL YOU MARRY ME? They were joined in holy matrimony the following summer at St. Mark's Cathedral in Minneapolis. Rod's parents, Dr. Rod and Nancy, have kindly invited us to their twelve-acre spread in the Minneapolis suburb of Shorewood. I still remember my last glimpse of the estate. I was leaving a postreception party. Lorin had never looked more radiant—not even on the day of her first marriage—than at that moment, standing in the doorway, waving goodbye. As we drove around the circular driveway, Mark leaned out of the car window and belched prodigiously. Tossing a crumpled beer can onto the lawn, he gave a thumbs up to his newlywed sister, who was flanked by her latest in-laws. "I swear to God, Lor," shouted Mark as we drove past, "your weddings get better every time."

Poor Nancy Peterson must set four extra places at her table today because her eldest son married a woman from a brood whose members accept your invitation to Thanksgiving dinner before it is all the way out of your mouth. Nancy greets us in the driveway in her apron. Dr. Rod, an orthopedic surgeon, takes Devin by the hand, down to the spacious playroom. Inside a wooden trunk, they find wonderfully preserved toy trucks from the doctor's Nebraska boyhood. While Devin would later allow himself to be lured outside, to tour the barn and ride in the tractor, it was to these antique toys he returned throughout what might have been the finest day of his young life. Willa buddied up with her old friend Emma Whicher, with whom she served as a flower girl at the wedding my brother Mark found so enjoyable. Laura spent so much time discussing with Nancy their shared passions—yoga, poetry, Russian literature—that everyone accused her of sucking up to the hostess.

It was a splendid Thanksgiving, a Thanksgiving replete with spirited, educated conversation and excellent wine, a Thanksgiving *just* a trifle more upscale than the feasts to which I had become accustomed in the Murphy household. This was less a reflection on my parents—particularly my saintly and patrician mother, Patricia—than the offspring to whom they sought, in vain, to teach manners and apply polish. Nowhere in the Peterson household, for instance, was there any sign of a Beef Jar.

The story of the Beef Jar is not pretty or uplifting, but it is a testament to what I had to overcome, sharing a household with three brothers ranging in height from six-five to six-seven; and in weight from 250 to 300 pounds. Chris, Matt, and Mark could generally be counted on to roll out of bed by noon on Thanksgiving Day, in time for the pregame show of the first NFL game. It was our mother's special turkey day custom to put out walnuts and figs, so those watching the game had something to nosh on. Lunch for each of my brothers would have been sandwiches comprised of a pound or two of cold cuts, washed down with the first of the day's beers. I am not talking about imported beer. I am talking about beer that could be had for ten dollars a case, or less. Think Schlitz, think Blatz, think Stegmaiers. Think Genesee Cream Ale.

Before dinner was served, a cheese tray might be placed in front of the torpid princelings, who as they lolled on sofas and La-Z-Boys looked as if they themselves were ready to be tethered and walked down Central Park West in the Macy's parade. The salt on the crackers accompanying the cheese would, of course, arouse in them a thirst that could only be slaked with another brew or two.

After choking down four thousand or so calories at dinner, the boys would migrate back to the den, where the TV, as I recall, was never off. On the same ruggedly handsome table on which the figs, walnuts, and cheese were placed, there also resided a piece of glazed pottery, a vase with a narrow neck and a round, broad bottom. It was an attractive piece of stoneware, although afterward I could never think of it as anything but evil.

I believe Chris was the first of my brothers to conscript that vase into service as a receptacle for his methane emissions; the first to produce that muffled staccato tooting—such a mirthful, innocent sound!—signaling that his malefic vapors had been trapped. After laughing uproariously, Matt and Mark would flatter Chris by imitating him. One of these mutant Three Stooges had the bright idea to cap the vessel, and a coaster was placed over the vase that became known as the Beef Jar.

What do you do with a jug full of farts? These geniuses provided the answer: sit around watching the tube, pounding a postprandial beer or four while trying desperately not to nod off. Because the first one to fall asleep got the Beef Jar under his nose. With the coaster removed, the jar was surprisingly effective as an unholy wakeup call; smelling salts from hell. The bastards got me once, and I'll never forget the acrid, sulfurous insult to my olfactory system.

So don't come around me with your stories of captured flatulence. I don't think it's the least bit funny, and I don't think the Petersons would either.

★ ★ ★

As I lay down to sleep that night, following a wonderful Thanksgiving, I could not stop smiling. No, I wasn't thinking about the Beef Jar, or even about the stellar hospitality of the Petersons. My thoughts kept returning to a play from that morning's Johnny practice, which had been underway for twenty minutes when Joe Steingraeber came jogging down the gravel road toward the field. Steiny, a reserve wideout, had told his scout-team buddies that he was cleared to go home to Wisconsin for the holiday, so they were confused to see him approaching the huddle . . . until they realized that it was an imposter wearing Steingraeber's equipment.

Are you familiar with the scout team? These are the guys who aren't first- or second-string. They spend most of practice running the plays of the upcoming opponents, giving the starters a "good look." In donning Steingraeber's equipment and joining the scouts, I was returning to my roots. For two undistinguished years as a wide receiver at Colgate, I was sustained not only by the occasional jayvee-game reception, but by the anger one could induce in the defensive coordinator, one Seymour (Red) Kelin, by showing up his first-stringers.

Joel Torborg, another scout team wideout, had the temerity to fall down laughing when he saw me. I took a couple snaps on running plays; it felt good to prowl the secondary, roughing up defensive backs. "Hey, Cubby," I finally said to linebackers coach Cubby Govern, "I didn't suit up just to push Grady around. Gimme the damn ball."

Riffling through his stack of Central Dutch plays, he found one calling for the wide receiver to run a twelve-yard square-out. I clapped as we broke the huddle, split out eighteen yards to the right and settled into my old three-point stance. It all came back to me. I pushed inside and then broke sharply toward the sideline—to the extent that these thirty-eight-year-old wheels do anything sharply. Knowing he would never hear the end of it if he were to be beaten deep by a sportswriter, cornerback Will Gibson was giving me a nice cushion. Quarterback Zach McBroom's pass hit me in the heart. I couldn't have dropped it if I tried.

The offense was going through its motions when, a field away, a roar went up. "I looked over," Linnemann told me later, "and I thought, 'So Steingraeber made a catch. What's the big deal?'"

Gagliardi sent the team away with an oration echoing Prince Hal's speech to the troops on the eve of the Battle of Agincourt. "A lot of guys abandoned ship," he said, taking a sad look around. Gags was right—why, there couldn't have been more than 120 players on the field. It was downright lonely out here. "You guys that made it, we appreciate you being here." *We few, we happy few, we band of brothers.* "As for the ones that aren't here, it's their loss.

"Do you think the Lions and Cowboys are complaining about playing today? We're one of sixteen teams still standing. It shouldn't be a nuisance, an inconvenience, to be out here. It's a goddam privilege."

Now my left knee is throbbing slightly—I guess I planted too hard making that cut. My hamstrings and groin have tightened. There is a twinge in my left shoulder. (Having sought YAC—yards after the catch—I lost my footing, executing a face-plant at Gibson's feet and landing awkwardly on the shoulder.) I treasure every ache. My ears are still ringing with the cheers of my scout brothers. I agree with Gags: it was a goddam privilege.

Friday finds me watching the Texas–Texas A&M game in the Mendota Heights den of Barb Schleck. As the Aggies pull ahead in the second half, I see one of their players perform the throat-slashing gesture on himself.

He's kidding, right? Eight days earlier, tons of logs from the traditional Aggie bonfire collapsed on and killed twelve people on the College Station campus. Flags around the Lone Star State are at half-mast. Forty busloads of Aggies made the 105-mile trip to Austin for a candlelight memorial. An Air Force flyover preceded the game. Students at both schools spent the week talking about mutual respect and common ground, and now this idiot is pantomiming an act of murder.

The NFL, at least, had the sense to ban the gesture earlier in the week. While this proved to be sound public relations, it failed to solve the league's more pervasive problem: many of its players are thugs. Early on the morning of November 16, Cherica Adams was shot four times while driving through a residential neighborhood in Charlotte, North Carolina. Adams was the pregnant girlfriend of Carolina Panther Rae Carruth. Shortly after the shooting, her son was delivered in emergency surgery, ten weeks short of full term. Adams died on December 14, the day before Carruth was arrested in western Tennessee. Police found him hiding in the trunk of a car.

Pro or quasi pro, the Aggie player running his finger across his throat symbolizes all I am escaping this autumn.

The Johnnies already have two Our Fathers under their belts when I catch up with them on Saturday. As they bunch at the fieldhouse door before jogging onto the field to play Central, I sense extreme anxiety.

"All right, you guys, nobody's gonna stop us," says Kirschner.

"F—— no," someone agrees.

This prediction turns out to be slightly off the mark. The Johnnies gain sixteen yards in the first half, at which juncture Stanger will have twice as many interceptions (two) as completions (one). He is sacked eight times on the afternoon for sixty-five yards in losses. The only thing keeping me from reserving a U-Haul at halftime is the fact that the Johnnies only trail 3–0. Their defense has been equally stout.

Gags goes through his halftime ritual, sitting cross-legged in the folding chair, shuffling through recipe cards. Arrayed before him in various attitudes of futility are his offensive starters. Kirschner is worrying an acne blemish along his jawline; Krych picks grass and dirt out of the hair on his calves; Salvato seems to be studying the rafters above the chalkboard. Corey, leaning back on his helmet, is a welter of abrasions, grass, and paint stains. I want to tell him to hang in there, that it will all be over soon.

Midway through the third quarter, Barry intercepts a tipped ball, returning it to Central's 24-yard line. Hugely inspired, the offense . . . loses just one yard on its next three plays. That's good! At least Stanger wasn't sacked out of field-goal range, as happened earlier in the half. Rotondi's forty-two-yarder toward the bell banner is long and true. The game is new.

Central answers with its longest drive of the day, down to the Johnny 9-yard line. A Tim Pahula sack—one of his five on the day—ensures that the visitors must settle for a field goal. The Dutch lead, 6–3.

On the pass play that took Central down to the nine, it had been Novak—the preseason all-American who this week was named the MIAC's most valuable player—who was caught out of position. He'd played a hunch, gotten burned, then had to stand there and take it while LaBore scolded him. On the following series, Novak was hypervigilant about dropping into his zone. That's how he found himself in position to make the interception that set up the game-winning touchdown. Novak returns that pick to the Dutch 19-yard line. Three Moore rushes get the Johnnies to the five.

More on Moore. In addition to the torn ligaments and sprained ankle in his left leg, Moore tore ligaments in his right thumb against Gustavus. Without the services of half his body's connective tissue, behind a line having a poor day, against the toughest defense the Johnnies have seen this season, Moore will carry twenty-eight times for seventy-nine yards. He will crack 1,000 yards for the season, despite missing all or parts of five games. I will leave Collegeville in awe of him.

From the 5-yard line, Stanger rolls right, and is pressured immediately. As he is clobbered, he throws to a spot in the corner of the end zone in which Sieben suddenly materializes. Touchdown. Rotondi's extra point is huge: the Johnnies hang on to win, 10–9.

The shadows cast by the Swayed Pines cover all but the northeast corner of the field, where Sieben caught his touchdown pass, and where Central's senior fullback Josh Brandt, a very tough kid, kneels sobbing. Who can blame him? This was anyone's game. The Dutch outgained the Johnnies, 236 yards to 147, which doesn't change the fact that they will be turning in their equipment on Monday. The Johnnies, particularly those on offense, are muted in victory.

I think back to the Tuesday after the Bethel loss, when injuries and ineptitude threatened to gut a promising season. Jerry challenged the defense to play smarter, to play to its potential. "Great defense can carry us," he said, and he was right. It has carried the Johnnies to the national quarterfinals.

"You're lucky you won today," Mike Grant is telling Gagliardi a half-hour after the game, "with all those drops." He is referring to four near-interceptions that Johnny defenders failed to hang on to.

Grant is sprawled on the sofa Gagliardi uses for naps. This former Johnny, who played for and coached with Gags before turning the program around at Eden Prairie High, has been highly visible on the sideline at Johnny games this season, fueling speculation that, when (and if) Gagliardi ever vacates his job, Grant wouldn't mind interviewing for it.

Gags is at his desk with what appears to be a poultice, or possibly a Hacky Sack, on his head. Closer inspection reveals that it is one of those disposable handwarmers that his daughter, Nancy, gives him before cold-weather games. (So chilly was it at kickoff that even Jim Platten, the Shorts Guy, wore trousers today. Only one lunatic spectator in six-plus thousand insisted on wearing short pants to the game. Devin Murphy, take a bow.)

There aren't a lot of guys who could come in and make themselves at home on Gagliardi's couch like this, but Grant is one of them. Gagliardi respects winning coaches, and his protégé is 81-8 in eight seasons at Eden Prairie High, having won the state title in 1996 and 1997. They chat about the Eagles' recent loss in the 5-A quarterfinals of the state tournament. Mike tells John it takes him ten minutes to get over each loss.

"Bull*crap*," says Gagliardi, who goes on to make the equally preposterous claim that he has learned to put tough losses behind him. "Like LaCrosse," he says, referring to the come-from-ahead playoff defeat in Wisconsin three years ago. "I've never seen that film."

"John, you lie," says Grant, who recalls Gagliardi waving him into his office one afternoon. Gags wanted Grant—and anyone else who happened to be walking past his doorway—to bear witness to a brutal call that had gone against the Johnnies in that game.

"Well, that was just one play," says Gagliardi, grinning. He wonders aloud how he has done it for all these years. He thinks of Bud Grant. "Your dad was what, fifty-seven when he retired?"

"Yeah, but he's got a hobby," says Mike, who tells of how, just yesterday, the Minnesotan known as Old Stone Face, now seventy-two, had walked through a swamp and dropped a massive buck from three hundred yards. Since Gagliardi has no hobby, Mike is implying, he cannot retire.

Just because John does not hunt deer does not mean he does not confront them. The next day I will see him on the game field, shooing away a deer family, taking sudden steps toward them, gesticulating, scolding. Grudgingly, they trot into the woods behind the visitors' stands, only to return when he leaves.

Gagliardi's one-man war on the deer is a source of vast amusement to his staff. "John," Gary Fasching has asked him, "what if they decide to charge you?"

What indeed? Who would replace the legend? The players' choice would be Gary, a great guy and a sharp coach who won two state championships at St. Cloud Cathedral. A lot of Johnny alums want Grant. A couple of days after the Central win, I drove to the Minneapolis suburb of Eden Prairie to spend some time with him. I found myself wandering through the most massive high school I've ever been in. After twice asking directions, I located the classroom in which Grant was teaching his economics class.

"C'mon in," he says. "Take a seat."

"Ninety percent of the wealth in this country is controlled by less than 5 percent of the people," he is telling the children of some very affluent Minnesotans. "And those 5 percent, they have us conned into thinking that we're haves, rather than have-nots. We got nothin'!"

Addressing me, he says, "I told these guys I used to be a liberal democrat—I went to St. John's. Then I came here to Eden Prairie, and I realized, if you don't know anybody that's in poverty, who cares? If you don't know anybody in Africa, then who cares?" Now he is addressing the class again: "And what does that apathy do for you?"

No takers.

"It frees you up! It gives you peace! I used to worry about people. I used to care. But when you don't care about anybody else, you're free! Have a good day everyone. We'll finish this up tomorrow."

Of course he is not advocating the apathy he appears, on the surface, to be advocating. But these are the children of privilege. "Some of them actually tell me, 'Hey, it's survival of the fittest,'" Grant tells me. "I ask them, 'Do you honestly think that someone born as a crack baby in Chicago has the same chance that you have to succeed?'"

Grant has some range, intellectually. He has his masters of arts and education, plus forty-five credits. When his call for compassion falls on deaf ears, he tries the end-around. By taking their argument to its logical conclusion—it's not my problem!—then running it past his students, he hopes to jar them out of their indifference.

Grant himself grew up in middle-class Bloomington, not far from Metropolitan Stadium, where the steamy breath arising from the facemasks of the Vikings came to symbolize the team's dominance of the National Football Conference in the seventies. The fact that Bud Grant's Vikings were 0-4 in Super Bowls still detracts from the astonishing fact that his teams *made it* to that many title games.

During the Vikings' heyday, Mike recalls, "I remember going out Christmas shopping for my mom, once a year, Dad and all the kids. I remember that I would straggle behind to avoid the finger-pointing, all the people whispering, 'There's Bud Grant.'"

Mike, now forty-two, describes himself as "a good high school player, not a great high school player, the kind of guy John has made a living on down through the years." The Gophers asked him to walk on. Several Division II colleges offered partial scholarships.

He and Bud took a visit to St. John's, not expecting much to come of it. "I was pretty close to going to the University of North Dakota," he says. "I remember driving to St. John's and thinking, 'Every time I go to Grand Forks I'm gonna drive right by this place.'"

According to legend handed down by Gagliardi, it was a succulent meat loaf sandwich, served in the refectory, that sealed the decision for Grant, who started three years at tight end for the Johnnies. He played on three conference-championship teams and the last Johnny squad to win the national title. After blowing a 28–0, third quarter lead in the '76 Amos Alonzo Stagg Bowl, the Johnnies eked out a 31–28 win over Towson (Maryland) State.

After graduating, Grant worked two seasons as an assistant for Gagliardi, whom he describes as "as smart an individual as I've ever met." It is an impressive tribute to Gags that the son of an NFL Hall of Fame coach cites his college coach, rather than his father, as his primary football influence. "John is a brilliant tactical coach. Brilliant," says Mike. "Other coaches have bought into this idea that it's the St. John's mystique, or the fact that John gets all the best players. They don't realize they're getting outcoached."

To the extent that he can, Grant uses Gagliardi's philosophy on his players. "We spend more time on individual work," he says. "Younger kids have to be taught. Early in the year we have a little bit of live contact. A lot of high school kids don't understand yet the tempo at which the game has to be played. So sometimes we go full speed ten minutes a day for four days at the beginning of the year. After that, it's very similar to St. John's practices."

Grant will not cut anyone, and regularly has three hundred or so players out for the team. As in Collegeville, calisthenics are a gag-filled shambles. He is more likely to quote Monty Python than Winston Churchill. "Sometimes coaches create a culture where kids cheapshot and use intimidation and swear," Grant told a reporter from the *Star Tribune* in 1997. "I don't know if any of that gets you a first down. We try to create a culture where everyone is relaxed, kids are free to make mistakes without worrying that they're going to get chewed out.

"I wear this old blue windbreaker John gave me," he told me. "It's got battery acid stains on it. Before the game, I go to shake hands with all these other coaches who look so sharp in their nice jackets. I'll pull my shirt out, so it's hanging out a little bit. I know they must be thinking, 'God he looks so bad I *know* we'll beat 'em.'

"People don't understand what John has known most of his career: there are minor details to championship teams. And John knows what they are. Eighty percent of coaches practice things that have nothing to do with winning a game. That's why they lose.

"In economics we talk about opportunity costs and efficiency. John is the most *efficient* coach I've ever known. I have twenty coaches here, and when they come to me with an idea or a suggestion, I ask what John would ask: 'Is it gonna get us a first down?'"

I stopped him: You've got *twenty* coaches? "We got three freshman levels, 9a, 9b, 9c," he says. "We've got a double jayvee schedule. I was interviewing for a college job once and was asked, 'Coming from high school, do you think you'd be ready to handle a college program?' I had to try hard not to laugh.

"We average six thousand fans per game here," he says. "Our program raises over $100,000 for the district. We fund-raise another $30,000 for our program. I've got this going on, and I teach a full schedule. Would I be ready to manage a college program? I can't imagine only having a hundred players to worry about. That would be a luxury."

The next class is filtering into this room, so we wander into the hall. I broach the topic I have driven eighty miles to discuss: would Grant be interested in coaching at the college level?

"Sometimes I get philosophical and think, 'What would I do with more money?'" he says. "I've got a car, my wife has a car. Nicer toys, a bigger house, I guess. You go that D-I route, you get fired, maybe you get a job in Washington. You're fired and maybe you get a job in Arizona. I think coaching is as much management of people as it is about *x*'s and *o*'s, and I'm confident I could coach on that level. But I don't know if it makes sense to me."

What about the St. John's job? "There's something about St. John's—something about the *pace* of the place," he says. "It would probably be healthier for me to be at a pace like that. My wife would enjoy it, it would be a great place for my kids. But I'm happy here, too."

Grant knows the issue is moot, since Gagliardi has shown no signs of wanting to step down. "My only hope for John is that when he's done, he's done on his own terms. I hope it's his own decision, not a health issue. I hope he feels good about how he's set up the program for the future. He deserves that for everything he's given."

Grant says hello to a giant in the corridor: it is junior tight end Mark LeVoir. He is six-seven, 290. Miami, Michigan, and Florida State all covet him. In a few months, he will sign with Notre Dame. Beware the Eden Prairie Eagles in 2000. "Our right tackle's 300 pounds," he says. "Our right guard's 260, our left tackle's 285. We'll be huge. Come to think of it, we'll be bigger than St. John's."

I am more impressed by the fact that, with Grant in charge, they'll be having as much fun.

17

PACIFIC LUTHERAN

The phone rings in Antoinetta Gagliardi's house every Saturday that St. John's plays a football game. Before she can pick it up, according to family lore, she must put her rosary down. To soothe her nerves and succor the Johnnies, the 98-year-old knocks out a few hundred Hail Marys while the team is on the field.

If the Johnnies win, it is John who places the good news call to his mother's home in Trinidad, Colorado. When they don't, Peg's is the voice Antoinetta hears. Peg agrees that the system is not really fair to her. She's okay with that. "She adores John," Peg tells me. "She asks me, 'Didn't I make you a good husband?'" Every month Peg sends Antoinetta fresh flowers. Every month, John gets a call from his mother, thanking him for them.

Antoinetta still speaks with a heavy Italian accent, and doesn't do so well on the phone with strangers, Peg tells me. I'd planned to visit Antoinetta in Trinidad, maybe stop in and see her on my way home, shout a few questions at her hearing aid, then hit the road. But that plan is on hold. Her health has taken a turn for the worse. A month ago she needed a blood transfusion. "She isn't eating now," says Peg. "She says 'Johnny, I'm not hungry and they keep pushing me.' John says, 'Well, if you're not hungry, don't eat.'"

A note on the bulletin board in the monastery asks the monks to pray for Antoinetta.

The Benedictines aren't paying Gagliardi a fortune, but he has lived in the same house for nearly fifty years. The price was right for his kids' college educations. And there is this other perquisite that, while harder to assay, must be worth something: when in need, he can petition a monastery full of holy men to pray for and with him.

Since the win over Central, I've been beset by a series of Admiral Stockdale moments. *What are we doing here?* How is a team with a three-and-out offense in the national quarterfinals? The Johnnies' upcoming opponent, Pacific Lutheran, barely crept into the playoffs as the seventh and final seed in the Western region. Not that the Lutes care where they're seeded, or, for that matter, where they're playing. Last week they traveled to Waverly, Iowa, and put the wood to top-seeded Wartburg, 49–14.

Pacific Lutheran is located in Parkland, Washington, in the shadow of Mt. Rainier. The Lutes are coached by Gagliardi's West-Coast doppelganger, the delightful Frosty Westering, whose grandson, Chad Johnson, quarterbacks the team. The word is, Chad has some serious game. "I'm gonna look through the damn rule book," says Gagliardi. "There's gotta be something in there against that."

Westering won three NAIA Division II titles at PLU before the school switched to the NCAA in 1998. His Lutes are a hoot, a fun-filled addition to Division III. Frosty's offensive coordinator is his son, Scott, who presides over a carnival of motion, misdirection, and exotic formations. Last year the Lutes threw sixteen screen passes in the first half against St. John's—four in the first series—none out of the same formation.

The Lutes are simply the classiest team St. John's has faced. When a Lute gets knocked on his butt, he congratulates the opponent. When he knocks you on your butt, he extends a hand to help you up. When a Wartburg player went down with an injury on the field, a bunch of Lutes dropped to one knee and said a quick prayer for him.

"I love those guys," says Grady, "and I'm glad they're coming back here. I just wish they weren't so good." The esteem is reciprocal. Says Anthony Hicks, the Lutes' brute of a fullback, "I tell recruits that if you want to have fun playing college football, you either come here or go to St. John's of Minnesota. I love that place."

Last year the Johnnies played their best game of the season to earn a 33–20 win over PLU in the first round of the playoffs. The day before the game, Frosty and a few of his players dropped by the football office. Gags wasn't in, so Linnemann and O'Hara gave the visitors a brief walking tour. They went up to the bookstore and bought some Johnny bread. Chad told the story of how, when he was a kid, he and his buddies would play football in the parking lot after Johnny games with a loaf that was always mashed and inedible before it got home. While touring the campus, the group ran into Gagliardi. Led by Frosty, they gave him the Lute salute:

Frosty: "Hey, John!"
Lutes: "Hey, John!"
Frosty: "Go, John!"
All: "Attaway, John!"

A couple weeks later Linnemann got a tee-shirt and a note from Frosty, thanking him for his time, wishing him luck. "They were such great guys," he says. "Obviously you hate to lose, but losing to them would be different from losing to some Wisconsin school." Leroy recalls the Lutes' visit with amazement. "They left the locker room as neat as a pin," he says. "No tape balls, no paper cups, no dirt clods from their cleats. It was like they were never here. Nice guys. Too bad we had to beat 'em."

Linnemann is recalling the Lutes' visit as his pulse descends to normal. He's just pounded out three miles on a treadmill in the fitness center. While rehabbing his leg, he's working out more than he ever did as . . . a star athlete. Tom was up in Gags's office earlier today, assuring the coach that his bad leg won't snap off, midshin, if he is tackled. "I can move," he said. "If you need me, I can play."

Tom badly wants another crack at the Lutes. "Their corners play off," he says, "there are a lot of hot reads"—a lot of zipping the ball to Sieben immediately after taking the snap. Corey's arm may be stronger, but Linnemann is more proficient at making those quick reads. "I'm made to attack this defense," he says wistfully. "It's like Cliffy's dream board." I look blankly at him. "You know—the *Cheers* episode when Cliff goes on *Jeopardy!* and the categories are 'Beer,' 'Useless Facts,' 'The U.S. Postal Service,' and 'Living with Your Mother.' Norm's in the audience, and he goes, 'This is Cliffy's dream board!'"

"You seem quiet today," he tells me. I explain to my friend that I have already begun the process of psychologically disengaging myself from this place. Laura and the kids fly out in four days, on the eve of the game. (Laura wants Willa to have a couple of weeks in her California kindergarten before Christmas.) I will stick around as long as the season lasts, plus a week or so, then pull the U-Haul home, solo. With its offensive shortcomings, the team cannot keep winning forever. And so I have begun the endgame; have begun girding myself for disappointment.

"Tell John to put me in," says Linnemann. "I'll write you a happy freakin' ending."

That night Laura and I have reservations at Anton's, a fancy restaurant in Waite Park, a suburb of St. Cloud. The "roof" of each booth is designed to evoke a Conestoga wagon. The lighting is dim, the ambiance in our "wagon" is romantic, but Laura is displeased that her mashed potatoes are served with gravy; she is wheat intolerant, and gravy is thickened with flour. "At least they remembered not to put croutons on my salad," she mutters. This is a woman counting the days.

In three days I will drive the gang to the airport. Four months have flown by. Laura is hosed: she'll have the kids by herself for at least a week and a half. Her misgivings about this are offset, in part, by her happiness to be going home. (What does she miss about the place? When I asked, she started ticking items off on her fingers: "Weather. My own bed. My own house. The food. The coffee.")

Willa, on the other hand, is not at all anxious to go. She is coming off the signal triumph of the semester: she conquered stage fright, singing and dancing with gusto at Kennedy Elementary's concert last night. As we watched her, our hearts cracked with joy.

The good will was not necessarily mutual. Afterward, when we sought to tell her how proud we were, she hissed, "Why didn't you put me in my Thanksgiving dress?" The other girls in her class all wore fancy dresses. "Bad Mommy," said Laura, chastising herself. After a minute of huffiness, Willa allowed herself to be soothed by our generous praise. After school today, she dissolved in tears when she realized that she alone, among her classmates, would never finish her "nursery rhyme pop-up book."

The kids cried a lot in Minnesota, but never for long. They were resilient. They adapted. When the mildest November in memory prevented them from sledding, they improvised, pushing Devin's mattress halfway off its boxspring, then "sledding" down the "hill." During these hijincks, a screw protruding from the frame of the bed gouged a trench in the drywall. But hey, that's why you leave a damage deposit! (Sister Dolores dunned us for the hole in the sheetrock, but turned a blind eye to the crayon on the wall.)

Over our salads—which are, she notes, overly reliant on iceberg lettuce—Laura tries to get me to admit that I will be pleased to be rid of family for a week or so: to watch the WWF two evenings a week, maybe enjoy a few nights out with the boys. You have me wrong, I say. First of all, the Chubby's residents with whom I normally watch wrestling are on academic Red Alert, scrambling to complete work they've been blowing off since Halloween. Second of all, I'm going to miss my posse. We've been together virtually every day for four months—more time than we share in a typical year. I've gotten used to it. I'm spoiled.

The following night we are invited to a prayer service/party at the home of John Parente. It is not like any party my brothers might be interested in. *I've been all over this place—where the hell's the keg?* Nor is it like the social functions we attend back home—no health club–honed moms in black cocktail dresses kvetching about the inadequacies of the nanny; no bond traders sharing their opinions on how the 49ers screwed up their salary cap. For this and other reasons, it is exhilarating. We join a dozen or so other guests: some theology grad students whom John has befriended, a few of the Institute's other resident scholars, the odd nun. Upon our arrival, we are encouraged to make "symbols" with construction paper and crayons. I make a paper airplane, Devin confiscates it. "Let's quiet," John instructs us after a quarter hour of scissoring, gluing, and coloring—he means be quiet, but don't stop there; to calm and focus our minds—"and touch our brokenness and blessedness and be receptive to the stirrings of God in our heart."

Devin takes this to mean that he should get naked. He then joins the rest of us as we parade and dance in a line around the apartment. Next, John has us form two circles, a smaller one within a larger one. The members of each circle walk in opposite directions, bowing to one another. John asks us to "linger in the bow"—looking meaningfully into the eyes of the bowee. If I can hug other men without self-consciousness, as he has helped me learn to do, I can certainly linger in a simple bow.

Devin the Gregarious participates in the dance and hand-holding, Willa the Prickly remains at the table, working on her art.

Back home, Laura asks me how I liked the party. It's strange, I say. You drive to the upper Midwest to write a football book, next thing you know some Buddha-looking guy is telling you to get in touch with your brokenness and blessedness. And you make a good faith effort to do that—to acknowledge your flaws, accept them; then dwell on the good things in your life.

It was stimulating. It wasn't the sort of thing I envisioned myself doing when I took the sabbatical—*Willa, can you finish coloring in the windows on my airplane? It's time for Daddy to join the dancers*—but it is the sort of thing that has made the sabbatical interesting. Not much about our sojourn went according to plan, and that wasn't a bad thing. Gagliardi proved more enigmatic—tougher to reach, and pin down—than the grinning football saint with whom I spent two days in '92. His program isn't all sweetness and light. When practice isn't going well, he can ride your butt as well as any of several better-known ogres: Holtz, Spurrier, Schembechler. Not every Johnny, either, walks around with a perpetual smile on his face.

When you have 159 guys out for the team and do not play a freshman or junior varsity schedule, you're going to have pissed off, disappointed people. Years ago, Gagliardi put an end to his post-practice stroll through the locker room on Friday. That's when the "travel list" went up—the names of the guys who would suit up for away games. It got to be such a downer for the coach to see the disappointment on the faces of the players left behind that he started going straight up to his office, or home. "It's a business of breaking hearts," says Gags.

To be quite honest, I'd come into this thinking of the Benedictines as black-cowled set pieces for this book. For some of the same reasons nuns are automatically funny—witness the success of the wind-up toy "Nunzilla"—I looked forward to mining the monks for humor, at their expense. Instead, they came alive, befriended us, educated us, fed us, saved us from social exile. I don't know how many of the football players I'll stay in touch with, but Father Tim and Brother Paul are our friends for life.

To be just as candid, I came into this season looking down my nose at Division III. Approaching this level of football from D-I, or the NFL, it's almost impossible not to. But every day I watched the Johnnies I was struck anew by the caliber of athlete Gagliardi has induced to play for him. I said it up front, it bears repeating: My boys could play.

The primary reason for this time off from work was to shore up my marriage. It was a noble goal; I made sure to put it high in the book proposal I sent to my agent. He's a sportswriter, I hoped people would think, but he's got some SNAG in him (you know—Sensitive New Age Guy).

Driving 2,000 miles with your kids in the backseat is no way to summon one's inner SNAG, or to inject previously undiscovered joy into a marriage. The whole "shoring up" thing would really begin upon our arrival, I told myself. Then we did arrive, and my main concern became taking enough notes to fill a three hundred-page book. Laura and I learned that achieving uncharted intimacy with one's spouse is best attempted when one is not simultaneously undertaking a massive writing project. Many was the night that I would help put the children to bed, then walk up the hill to my office, there to compose awful sentences and paragraphs that never made it into this final draft. After a month in Minnesota, Laura said, "You worked six days a week when you were working, and you're working six days a week on sabbatical."

At least we slept together every night. That was something new and different. After a while—after the leaves had begun turning, but before they all fell off—I calmed down a little, as did Laura. In spite of ourselves, almost, we became closer. I got a better grasp on her frustrations, and a newfound respect for what she goes through in my absence. She tells me that hanging around with monks and artists softened me in a good way; opened my mind, smoothed some of the burrs on my personality. Since we've been here, she's seeing more of the guy she fell in love with.

In the end, this place had its way with us.

The phone rings at 10:40 P.M. on the eve of Laura's departure. Beau is on the line. He wants to talk about . . . schoolwork.

Beau had been out of sorts at the Fitness Center this morning. He had fought a term paper to a stalemate. "The intro is fine," he told me. "The intro is the shit. And I like the ending. It's the middle that I'm having problems with." We batted around a few ideas, but nothing came of it. "This isn't like me," he said. "Usually I dominate papers."

Now he is calling with good news. By substituting one phrase for another he has solved the conundrum, found his way out of the woods. He reads me the new passage. "Very strong," I say. "Short declarative sentences, inexorably sweeping the reader to your conclusion."

"It builds," he agrees.

The awfulness of his timing notwithstanding—trust me, it was awful—Beau's call is endearing and refreshing. A couple of weeks ago there was a bloodbath at the "U"—Dienhart and another high-ranking athletic department official were forced to resign—resulting from a scandal brought to light by the ex-tutor who told the *Pioneer Press* that she'd written hundreds of papers for Gophers hoops players.

If Beau wants to call because he's fired up about a breakthrough he made on a paper, well, that's the kind of call I am here to take.

Frosty is in the house. The Lutes are staying at the St. Cloud Holiday Inn, and have bused over to see the campus on this Friday afternoon. Frosty finds Gags in his office. They decide to walk over to the Refectory for lunch. After they have gone through the cafeteria line and returned with their trays, Frosty tells a joke about the pope:

In the twilight of his life, Colonel Sanders wanted to make a donation to the Vatican. He will give $1 million, provided the words in the Our Father be altered to say, "Give us this day our daily chicken."

"No go," says His Holiness.

"Make it ten mill," says the colonel a year later. "Can't do it," says the pontiff.

"A hundred million and that's my final offer," says the colonel a year later. The pope gets on the phone with the cardinals and says, "What's the status of our contract with Wonder Bread, anyway?"

John laughs—politely but not uproariously. He's got a picture signed by the pope in his office. The joke reminds Gags to ask Frosty if he needs any Johnny bread. His colleague responds, perhaps a bit too quickly, "No, no, don't need any more. We've got four, five loaves already." *Please, we'll do whatever you want, just don't make us take any more of your bread!*

Here they sit, the Churchill and Roosevelt of D-III, eating Jell-O and talking about their health plans. My favorite meal in Minnesota? No contest. It was lunch with this pair of unlikely revolutionaries, a couple of seniors with two real hips—both of Frosty's are artificial—24 grandchildren, 638 wins, and six national championships between them.

Before the Lutes head west, Frosty will dig up a copy of his book for me. It's called *Make the Big Time Where You Are.* It is a short and slightly claustrophobic read, recounting a weekend-long conversation between two men whose main physical activity is building, then adding logs to, a crackling fire.

Of course, by leveling even this mild criticism, I become guilty of the close-mindedness Frosty warns against in his book. The further I read, the less attention I paid to the book's conventional shortcomings. Because the further I read, the more I realized that this book—or passages from it, at least—should be required reading for anyone in the country who would presume to coach young people. Like Gagliardi, Frosty is one of the good guys, someone who is in his profession for the right reasons. For example, he's heavily into "put-ups"—the opposite of put-downs. It's a simple thing, really, but not enough people do it well: patting people on the back, telling them, "Hey, good job."

God bless Frosty Westering, for in his book he also inveighs against the mindset he describes as "No. 1 or No One." By that he means the attitude, far too prevalent in this country (during Olympic years in particular) that if you don't finish first, you are nothing; you might as well not have competed, and by the way, please cease and desist in using your Old Spice deodorant stick, for you are a QUISLING LOSER not worthy of masking the STENCH OF YOUR FAILURE with our product.

"The goal is not the end of the road," Frosty writes. "The goal is the road." Exactly! As so many of us realize too late, the joy is in the journey.

The drive to the airport, our last Minnesota meal together (Burger King in the terminal), even the goodbyes themselves—Willa turning to wave one final time even as she entered the jetway—none of it was depressing, per se. Laura and I were distracted by logistics of parking the car, transporting the luggage, securing boarding passes. They were excited to go home. The solo drive back up I-94, the entrance into the empty husk of our apartment—now my apartment—*that* was depressing. I try to reflect on how quiet it is, how productive I will be, freed from shrill demands for stories, toys, milk. Under the silence is loneliness. If it will make me miss Devin less, says John Parente, he would be happy to walk around the grounds of the Institute in the nude. I take a rain check. Part of me hopes to see the Johnnies play for another two weeks after tomorrow; to book a flight to Virginia for the Stagg Bowl. And part of me feels that the boys've had a nice run, that they can feel free to check out anytime now.

The Lutes take the field the next morning under slate skies and between a human promenade comprised of a surprising number of parents and supporters. The amplified yet soothing voice of Father Tim bids all Johnnies to "Please join me in extending a warm welcome to all Pacific Lutheran alumni, fans, and family who have joined us today."

The ensuing, muffled ovation of gloved hands sounds like rain on the roof. To my ears it is the sound of class. The mutual respect between these schools makes my heart soar; it is still soaring when Linhoff's kickoff is fielded by a Lute, and Brother Mark, standing to my left, bays at the top of his voice, "KILL HIM!"

And the Johnnies are. Killing them. Chad Johnson—Frosty's grandson, the southpaw quarterback—is having the worst quarter of his career. Beau picks him off on the Lutes' first series and gets facemasked on the return. St. John's takes over on Pacific Lutheran's 21-yard line and comes away with a field goal.

Not long after, Johnson hits Phil Trier in the hands with a pass: Trier, the cat-quick defensive tackle, is so surprised he drops the ball. No matter. After the Lutes call a timeout to look for their composure, Johnson is intercepted by Grady. Johnson looked like Steve Young on tape, but he's playing like Stevie Nicks. I see his teammates rubbing his arm on the sideline, encouraging him, trying to help him find his mojo. The Johnnies convert Grady's pick into six points.

With the halftime score 9–6 in his favor, Gagliardi settles into his folding chair, accepts a can of Sprite from Brother Mark, and initiates with his offensive starters the back-and-forth that is equal measures Socratic Method and Throwing Shit Against the Wall to See What Sticks:

Gags: "That sixty-two opened up nice down there."
Corey: "Two-three-one-four's gonna work on the outside guy."
Jimmy: "Look for the backs, cause those 'backers are either blitzing or dropping way the hell off."

Now the gumband is off the recipe cards. While John angles for a Big Play, I am doing some sleuthing. I want to know if the Lutes are as pure as they seem. Stun me with examples of their hypocrisy, I say to various Johnnies. Tell me they're out there talking shit. "After I ran for a first down," Corey reports, "one of their linebackers helped me up and asked me, 'Aren't you getting tired?'"

Zach McBroom, backup quarterback and longsnapper, informs me that when he approached the line of scrimmage for the Johnnies' third punt, the noseguard said, "Excuse me, but do you guys put those names on your helmets yourselves?"

Climbing into the longsnapper's head just before he must perform his unnatural task. Benign, yet devious. I like it.

"We gotta come up with a big play," Gags is telling the troops before they jog back onto the field. "Big plays are made by"—he stumbles here, searching for the cliché that goes, roughly: Big-time players make big-time plays in big games. To his credit, he can't come up with it. He starts over—"Big games are made by"—he falls silent again, as the players exchange quizzical looks—"great . . . players." At last the old coach cuts his losses and calls for another Our Father.

"Fourth one today," whispers Linnemann. He must be counting the one from this morning's mass. "You know what I'd like?" he says. "I'd like it if just once he said, 'Let's line up and do the Hava Nagila.'"

The score is still 9–6 at the end of the third quarter, when it is announced over the public address system that a black Mercedes is illegally parked in front of the stadium. "Probably a Lutheran's," cracked one of the monks with whom I was sitting. "Tow it," said another, and we all had a good laugh.

As if in Divine rebuke to this unBenedictine sentiment, the bottom promptly fell out for the home team. The Johnnies had just gotten a first down at the Lute 18-yard line. The offense was clicking. A touchdown would pretty much have guaranteed St. John's a trip to the national semifinals.

"All the way! All the way! All the way!" shouted Father Cyprian Seitz, a feisty octogenarian who said nothing fewer than three times. The call was a sweep to halfback Aaron Krych, who was stripped of the ball by a blitzing Lute linebacker. The ball was scooped up by a 270-pound defensive tackle who went chuffing up the far sideline, a kidnapper cradling the Johnnies' season in his arms.

I remember the dumbfounded silence of the monks as this catastrophe unspooled, and I remember how it was broken, a ruddy-faced brother to my right drawing these syllables out slowly, incredulously: "Ho . . . lee . . . shit."

The Lutes punch it in three plays later, taking their first lead of the game. The Johnnies go three-and-out. On 3rd-and-eighteen the Lutes call a draw to Hicks, the monster fullback from Tumwater, Washington, home of (I'm sure I don't have to tell you) Olympia Beer. Hicks, a transfer to PLU by way of the University of Washington, is not touched until Gibson rides him down sixty-four yards upfield. Four plays later, Hicks is in the end zone.

The Johnnies punt again, and never do get the ball back. To eat clock, the Lutes feed the Johnnies a steady diet of Hicks. "Rip it out, Red," comes the shout from the St. John's sideline, as if that hadn't occurred to the guys on defense, as if the dee hasn't been carrying the team for the last two months.

At midfield after the game, Gagliardi lets Frosty do the talking: "You shut us down completely in the first half. Early on you just killed us. We couldn't run our sweep at all. Boy, are your linebackers good."

I strike up conversation with Isaac Williams, the Lutes' starting right tackle. Having barely squeaked into the playoffs with a low seed, Pacific Lutheran had just finished its third straight playoff game on the road. Was the travel starting to wear on the Lutes?

"It's tough, flying somewhere every week," says Williams. "But to be honest, I wouldn't have wanted to be anywhere but here today." He looks around at the emptying bleachers of Clemens Stadium. His gaze takes in the century-old Swayed Pines lording over the stadium and sheltering it from westerly winds. Looming over the south end zone is the bell banner. On the field, around us, are my boys, bearing up okay in defeat. They aren't the Whos down in Whoville, hands linked and singing despite the theft of Christmas, but the guys who've been crying are pretty much over it, and I'm starting to see some smiles.

Not far away, Johnny linebacker Brandon Novak stands with his family on the field. No one is saying anything. His jaw is set, his gladiator's mug streaked with tears. He allows himself roughly ninety seconds of emotion, then twists the spigot off.

I ask Isaac what he likes about this place.

"You know coming in you're going to have fun," he says. "You know you're not going to get cheap-shotted. You're going to play a clean game in front of classy fans against a coach who's legend. This has to be the coolest place in the world to play football."

Seven years earlier, I'd been thinking pretty much the same thing.

The PLU crowd has commandeered the same corner of the fieldhouse where the Johnny offense scratches its head at halftime. After every game, the team and its fans and family assemble for what they call "Afterglow." It is a "sharing time," I am told by Isaac, "a form of fellowship."

Frosty stands within the circle, the yellow helium balloons he has been handed nicely accessorizing his bright-yellow windbreaker pants. He is busy meting out "put-ups"—props to the coaches, the captains, to the player's mother who brought a box of apples all the way from Wenatchee; and to the bus driver.

"Harry here is our bus driver," he says. "He takes us all over the place."

Well, yes, Frosty, that would be his job. No matter. Harry is about to get himself a Lute Salute:

"Hey, Harry!"

"Hey, Harry!"

"Go, Harry!"

"Attaway, Harry!"

And one of the captains stands and announces, "I know it's not important to him, but today was Frosty's 275th win."

"Hey, Frosty!"

Etc.

Gagliardi is circulating in a subdued dressing room, meanwhile, shaking hands, moving from player to player. I hear him say, "Good job, great season, good job. . . . What the hell happened on that draw?"

Later, Frosty visits Gags in his office, taking a seat on his couch. "Boy, did you shut our sweep down," says Frosty. "Normally, you tie a series of plays to that, but we couldn't."

"That five is a player," says Jimmy. "Boy, he tackles."

"Jonathan Carlson. He's from Gig Harbor," says Frosty. "Right across the Sound."

The small talk lasts a few minutes, then Frosty is on his feet, saying, "I want you to know how much we respect you guys."

"Frosty," says John, "you outcoached me completely."

"Oh, stop it," says Frosty, bear-hugging him. Despite not being the embracing type, Gags is a willing participant in this one. His smile is a weak beacon barely cutting the fog of his disappointment.

Then Frosty is down the hall and gone. Two weeks later, in the national championship game, the Lutes will be severe underdogs to the Professors of Rowan College, who stunned D-III by snapping Mount Union's fifty-four-game winning streak in the eastern semifinal. Rowan had eight Division I transfers on its roster, Pacific Lutheran just one. The seventh-seeded Lutes had traveled 15,000 miles in the postseason alone. Sure, the joy was in the journey, and all that, but this was ridiculous! Surely Frosty & Co. would crash to earth in the title game. One Rowan player, a transfer from the

University of Maryland, told reporters that by knocking off Mount Union, Rowan had already won the championship. Pacific Lutheran, he said, would be "just another team to beat up on."

He was right. The game was not close. The Lutes jumped all over Rowan. The final score was 42–13.

Back in Gagliardi's office, Mike Grant has dropped by with his son, Ryan, a fourth-grader. Mike seeks to cheer John up, keep his mind off the loss. He talks about his own team's recent, narrow loss in the state's 5A semifinals. "They did everything right against us," says Mike. "They even got a fake punt on us."

"Even Mom saw that one coming," says Ryan.

Ignoring that, Mike tells Gags about a fishing trip he took to the Ozarks last summer. "A lot of people are retiring down there," he says.

"How are the mosquitoes?" says Gags.

"That's just it," says Mike. "There's not much standing water, so there are very few mosquitoes."

John looks at the ceiling, as if he is taking it under advisement. He will play in a weekly poker game with Carlyle Carter before he invests in property in the Ozarks. Both men know this, just as they know that to cease making small talk is to leave a vacuum into which the anguish of the season-ending loss will come rushing.

"They deserve it," Gagliardi finally says. "They pulled it out. And we lost another one in the fourth quarter."

"Hey!" says Mike, "you gotta remember the ones we won in the fourth quarter." He brings up a long-ago last-second pass to halfback Jim Roeder that allowed the Johnnies to kick the field goal that won the '76 Stagg Bowl. "Remember? Back at the hotel, we all jumped in the pool. People thought we were insane."

Now Gags is up, heading out into the corridor to confront the offseason. Taking his usual shortcut to the parking lot, he walks through The Cavern, where the Johnnies watch film. Lute plays are drawn up on the marker board; it is clear that the visitors spent a cozy halftime here.

"Who the hell let 'em in?" grouses Gagliardi. The visitors are supposed to be confined to the visitors' locker room, dammit. Yes, it is far more cramped, and that's precisely the point. They're the visitors. That's why they call it the home-field advantage. His shirt is still wrinkled from Frosty's embrace, and Gags is begrudging his friend a comfortable halftime. "You should see the places we end up in," he grumbles.

Settling into his car he heaves a nuclear sigh, a sigh that is a seine, dragging up every bitter playoff loss he's ever endured. Is it possible there was a measure of relief in the sigh, as well? Gagliardi milked eleven wins out of a team with serious problems, turning in one of his better coaching jobs at the age of seventy-three. He's got twenty-two wins in two years and a better team coming back next season. A load is lifted, the La-Z-Boy awaits.

Gags will have one night to mourn the season. The days that follow are given over to mourning more profound. Around 12:40 A.M., Minnesota time, Antoinetta drew her last breath. John and Peg got the news on Sunday morning. Befitting the owner of such a worn Rosary, Antoinetta went peacefully, having so frequently sought the prayers of the Virgin Mary, "now and at the hour of our death."

Amen.

18

LAST CALL

The lake is frozen, the Johnnies are done. At dusk I return to Clemens Stadium for one final stroll up and down the St. John's sideline, my beat for the last twelve weeks. Here, in solitude unavailable to me this afternoon, I will let go of the season. Here, I will bid bittersweet adieu to the Natural Bowl, my favorite sports venue of all time. Here, I will search for the Starbucks commuter mug I left under the bench during the game. The goddam things go for about seventeen dollars, and this is the second one I've lost this season.

I never do find the mug. Later that night I drive into St. Joe, where my boys are blunting their disappointment. While they drown their sorrows, while John sleeps, Antoinetta goes to her reward. John will soon fly to Colorado to bury her. When he returns, it will be my turn to leave. We have moved into the post-postseason, the season of wakes and goodbyes.

Half of St. Ben's is in the kitchen at Chubby's when I show up. The air is heavy with cigarette smoke and perfume. After the game, Beau was surprised on the field by his girlfriend Nikki Dold, an ex-

Benny who is, if I may speak frankly, spectacular. Nikki had flown up from Atlanta to see him. Crushed in defeat though they may be, I get the sense that these guys will somehow make it through the night.

The gathering at the Power House, two doors down, is more subdued. Linnemann is on one of the scary sofas, holding hands with Becky. With less than a minute left in the game, he and Sieben took a walk to the end of the bench. I ask Tom what they talked about.

"I said, 'Hey Frog, remember that touchdown I threw you in fourth grade?'" Tom tells me. "How many touchdown passes you think I've thrown you over the years?"

Ben didn't know. He was choked up, having trouble speaking. Tom tells the story again, of how he didn't understand football when he met Sieben in preschool. "Ben said, 'Pick up the ball and throw it to me.' And that's what I thought football was—throwing the ball to Ben. It was always Ben and some other receiver," says Tom, confirming what every other pass-catcher on the team has long suspected. "I guess I'll have to learn football again."

Becky pats his hand. "This is hard for you, isn't it?" she says.

I run into Sieben later that night at a St. Joe's bar named Sal's. He tells me he's thinking about going to a combine in Chicago, where Arena Football League scouts will be holding clipboards and deciding futures. "Do you think I have a chance?" he says. I know you do, I tell him. You should go for it. He ends up bagging the combine. I think talking about it for a couple weeks eased his transition from football player to ex-football player.

No sign of Chad. He is with his girlfriend. "Par for the course," says Tom. "The guy didn't get any nooky for twenty-two years, and now he's making up for lost time."

I would like to see Chad. I want to know how it feels to have fallen two wins short of the goal he, Linnemann, and Sieben set for themselves in a hotel room in Aberdeen, South Dakota four years earlier. *Let's go to St. John's and win a national championship.* Tommy is a bit morose tonight, veering occasionally into bathos. At least he still has a chance at a ring. The guy who spent part of the season in a golf cart, the guy with half a toolbox in his leg, the guy for whom the dream seemed dead as disco is now the only guy who still stands a chance of living it.

I am packing boxes the next morning when I look out a window and see the sun glinting off the swingset and seesaw with which my children had a love-hate relationship. Memories tug me sharply back to August and September, when Devin and Willa wore out the grass under those swings. The seesaw, they had little use for. Its fulcrum—the pipe on which it rests—is far too high. The kids would get on, then find themselves six feet in the air, hanging on for dear life. They did, however, enjoy being spun on the old wooden carousel. "Faster, faster!" I recall them shouting, and I obliged them, even though the apparatus had not been oiled since Johnny Blood coached here. "Faster!" they cried, and I obliged them, because children *want* to believe that their father is limitlessly mighty.

"Faster!" they cried, and I obliged them, until I felt something tear in my right latissimus dorsi, the muscle which, ideally, fans out from one's back like the fin of a stingray, but which, in the waning years of one's fourth decade, fans hardly at all, but rather, drops unimpressively toward one's love handle.

Wincing, I stopped spinning them, provoking a torrent of complaints. "Daddy is hurt," I told them. "Daddy is in pain. Swing on the swings. Talk amongst yourselves."

Now I miss them ferociously. The whole point of this trip was to spend more time together, and here I am in an empty apartment, nursing a hangover I wouldn't have if Laura had been around last night. I am ready to leave Collegeville, but I want to thank Gagliardi to his face, to say a proper goodbye. I will wait until he returns from his mother's funeral.

The absence of the savages and their mother has allowed me time for contemplation. I have made an important decision. I have decided to enter the monastery. Actually, Timo invited me to spend a couple of days and nights, attending prayer services, eating with the Benedictines, becoming even more attuned to their daily rhythms. When I phoned Laura with the good news, her reaction disappointed me. Maybe the kids were driving her to distraction. Maybe it was subconscious resentment on her part, since, as a woman, she could never be tendered such an invitation. Regardless, some of her comments seemed to betray a failure to appreciate the richness of my opportunity. "Whatever you do," she said, before ringing off, "don't jerk off in the monastery."

I am assigned the cell of a monk named Rene, who is abroad for the semester. "Cell," of course, connotes a small and Spartan living space, but Rene's room is not so opulent or comfortably appointed. It was roughly the length and width of a Pullman sleeper, with a sink, a closet, and, under the desk, a discreetly placed bedpan. In the absence of Laura, my guiding light, I'd been spending a lot of time watching the James Bond marathon on TBS. I half expected to open Rene's closet and be attacked by Jaws, the giant, steel-toothed assassin with whom .007 does battle on a train in *The Spy Who Loved Me*.

At dinnertime, Timo escorts me to the refectory, where we avail ourselves of the well-stocked salad bar. In a nearby fridge are milk and various juices, including the nectar of the prune, available to elderly monks for whom the monastery's strict horarium is an insufficient source of regularity.

Abbot Timothy is at the next table. I have heard wonderful things about him, and now I see him using the blade end of a butter knife to coax the ketchup out of a Heinz bottle. It is part of his greatness that he knows instinctively that it is both time-inefficient and unbecoming the dignity of his office for him to continuously, and futilely, whack the bottom of the ketchup bottle with the heel of his palm.

At that evening's prayer service I am always behind, finally finding the verse or psalm just as the monks have finished reading it. An Asian man to my left knows just where everything is: I take mean-spirited pleasure in the difficulty he has pronouncing the letter *l*.

I have brought my computer to the monastery, and work well into the night on a story for the upcoming *SI* swimsuit issue. That morning's gospel had inveighed against "stain and defilement," and here I am, a guest in a holy place, contributing to a publication that will excite in millions the sin of lust. When I do turn in, I sleep poorly. I awake feverish and with my throat on fire. The nurses in the monastery's infirmary test me for strep throat. The test comes back positive. The Divine message seems clear: Don't come in *My house* and compose smut for your little stroke magazine.

I attend the noon prayer service, then pack. Nineteen hours after entering the monastery I take my leave of it, secure in the knowledge that I would have made one of the worst monks in history.

The phone rings that afternoon and it is Peg Gagliardi. I take the opportunity to thank her for the going-away presents she lavished on my children. She has found out, somehow, that I have strep. She is a mother to four children, a surrogate mother to 150 football players, her mother-in-law has just died, and here she is calling me to see how I am doing, if there is anything I need. Our attitudes toward football aren't the only thing John Gagliardi and I have in common. Both of us married women of whom we are not always worthy. Both of us, to borrow a phrase from the students, are overchicked.

The seniors make a series of speeches three nights later. The squad's bandy-legged alpha male goes first, and his words stay with me the longest. As Novak stood on the stage and faced his teammates, the intensity he'd always shown on the field was now distilled in his gimlet eyes, which misted as he spoke:

"Live it up, underclassmen, because it goes by fast. It goes by fast, but it'll be the best four years of your life. And once you've played your last game, you'll look back and say, 'This is the greatest place on earth to play football.'"

All season, it had seemed to me, Novak was the Johnny most focused on the end of the road—a national championship. *Gotta run the table now.* Listening to him now, I realize how wrong I was. Novak gets it—has always gotten it: the goal is not the end of the road. The goal is the road. Two hours before the Pacific Lutheran game, Novak, Sieben, and a handful of other Johnnies could be seen dancing outside the Metten Court apartments. Someone had cranked up his car stereo, and the boys were grooving to a raunchy song called "Back That Azz Up." From such pregame dance parties to his nude Chippendale locker-room antics to those orange, mesh tights on the practice field to his flying tackle of the LaPlayette's heavily ornamented Christmas tree later that night, Novak was a guy who wrung maximum joy from the journey.

Spencer comes the closest to crying. Phil Barry carries on a defensive tradition. "Jerry," he says, "if you will stand up and signal me a defense, I will make one last call."

Haugen is immediately up and semaphoring. Reading the signals, Phil barks out, "Red-Silver, 90-Plus, Three Cover. *Break.*"

The crowd goes wild.

Grady says he won't remember the games, he'll remember the friends. Soma, who cut such a heroic and athletic figure running scout team plays in his electric-purple tights, concurs with Grady.

"Looking back years from now," Soma says, "I, too, will remember the friendships. I won't remember the statistics or the accolades. Because I had none."

Chad O'Hara is a no-show.

I suspected this might happen. With my departure imminent, I would receive more social invitations than I could respond to, let alone accept.

I suspected this might happen, and was sadly mistaken. I did, however, get at least *one* invite in my final days on campus. Timo and Paul take me out for a farewell dinner on Friday night. Before leaving, we watch Timo's tape of the *South Park* Christmas Special, all of us taking particular pleasure in the sight of a crudely animated Satan singing:

> *Michael Landon's hair looks swell,*
> *It's Christmas time in hell!*

The restaurant Timo has chosen is the 400 Supper Club in, and overlooking, Pleasant Lake. It is "very Centrasota"—Paul's description. It is also hosting a large Christmas party, forcing us to accept a table in the bar area, under the dartboard. To combat the melancholia and dyspepsia that descend on us after the meal, we smoke and drink.

Paul complains that the school will soon outlaw cigarette sales in the bookstore, forcing him to drive to the Avon Texaco for his heaters. "I'm thinking of selling them out of the choir office," he carps.

We are glum because we've become fast friends; it'll be sad to say goodbye. Mortality, moreover, hangs in the air like cigarette smoke. A few days after Antoinetta passed, so did one of the Benedictines, Father Sebastian Schramel, whose death, while deeply mourned, came as no surprise.

A few years back, Paul recalls, he rounded up four of the monastery's older monks, including Sebastian. They boarded a van and headed north for a three-day idyll at the Benedictines' lakeside cabin. Before they left, Paul recalls, a nurse in the infirmary had given him scores of pills, several schedules, and strict instructions to follow them. Paul nodded earnestly, folded the schedules, put them in his pocket, and never looked at them again.

"During the drive up we got into a discussion—okay, a fight—on liturgy," says Paul, "which is a hot-button issue for those of us who spend two hours a day in public prayer." After one stop to purchase bait and allow the oldsters to respond to what Benedict calls "the necessities of nature," the gang arrived at the cabin. While unpacking, Paul produced a bottle each of Scotch and brandy. "Wel-l-l-l," said one of the older priests, "It's after five . . ."

The conversation grew livelier, ranging from priestly vocations to celibacy to the abbot to the very existence of God. "I don't recall having supper that night," recalls Paul. "I think we ate peanuts, Ritz crackers, and salsa."

Breakfast was fatty bacon and heavily buttered toast. The monks fished and sat in the sun, even though, Paul says, "I'd been told to keep them out of the sun." Cocktails began—what were the chances?—"a bit earlier than usual that day."

On the third day, the monks finished the hooch and, in a spasm of guilt, popped many of the pills they had neglected to take. To spark conversation during the drive home, Paul went around the van, asking each of its drugged, hungover passengers to cite something he had learned during their holiday. Sebastian's response has always stayed with him:

"I'd always heard that drugs and alcohol don't mix," said the old priest, "and now I know it's true."

The following night I receive a last minute invite to Edelbrock House, residence of Torborg, Barry, Lynch, Soma, Gibson. They are pitching horseshoes in the moonlight when I arrive. It is part of their celebration of Festivus, a secular holiday borrowed from *Seinfeld*. Around midnight there is a mass migration to St. Joe. I end up wedged into the backseat of a car next to a St. Ben's junior from Billings, Montana, who informs me she was Wonder Woman for Halloween. I find her claim highly plausible.

That was the night my friend Carla got in a catfight; the night the cops chased a Johnny—not a football player—who'd climbed onto the roof of Sal's. This was the night, after last call at the Lafayette, on the way to an after-party, that my compadres and I fell in with a group of Bennies leaving a semiformal party. One of them could not go on. Her new shoes were killing her. I did the decent thing, offering to carry her. We had a nice chat for about five hundred yards, until the build-up of lactic acid in my biceps made further chivalry impossible.

That was the night a Johnny sneaked up on me from behind and put me in a half nelson—he thought I was someone else—forcing me to take him down hard and pin him. After helping break up a fistfight, then conducting a lengthy flirtation with a sloe-eyed Benny named Sherene, I turned to Linnemann and said, "I think it's time for me to go home."

I wasn't talking about the Ecumenical Institute.

Three days later I rise with the dawn and put the bell banner in my rearview mirror. (Actually, I put it in my side-view mirrors, as the rearview mirror reflected only the letters RIESAE GNIVOM SEKAM painted on the U-Haul.) I beeline for the lower left-hand corner of Minnesota, where I-90 slingshots me toward South Dakota and an interminable succession of billboards hawking tourist attractions like the Corn Palace (FROM EAR TO ETERNITY; TO EAR IS HUMAN) and Wall Drugs (FREE ICE WATER). It is only upon exiting Minnesota that I encounter my first serious snow of the winter. Plows are out from Pukwana to Murdo. The front passes through by 4 P.M., which finds me in Kadoka, the self-proclaimed Gateway to the Badlands. To me it looks like the Gateway to More of the Same. By dusk I am crowding Rapid City, where I take Route 16 into the Black Hills, which, as I wend my way through them, are particularly black, night having fallen.

As I crest one of the Black Hills north of Custer, South Dakota, the eastern sky erupts in light. What appears to be one of the Four Horsemen of the Apocalypse turns out to be the spotlit Crazy Horse Memorial, which has been fifty-one years in the making and could be that far from completion. The Oglala chief is riding out of the side of a mountain, pointing in the direction of Custer, just as everyone figures he did on June 25, 1876, when the dashing, doomed Army lieutenant colonel rashly led a force of 225 exhausted soldiers against one of the largest forces of Indian braves ever assembled, with predictable results.

I pull onto the shoulder, turn on the hazard lights and get out to study Crazy Horse at my leisure. The memorial is miles away, yet fills the sky. Its scope is barely comprehensible. They say you could fit Mt. Rushmore in Crazy Horse's armpit. A local in a jeep pulls over, mistaking me for a motorist in distress.

I explain that I am just admiring the memorial.

It's pretty at night, he agrees. He tells me that his father, a blacksmith, custom-designed drilling equipment for the memorial. And his buddy, an ex-Green Beret demolitions expert, helps out with some of the blasting.

That's funny, I say. I was just visiting a guy whose father was a blacksmith. We bid each other good night and get back into our cars.

I flopped that night at a Holiday Inn Express outside Cheyenne, having logged nine hundred-plus miles in a day. Coming down out of the Black Hills, my thoughts were with that other son of a blacksmith, who'd returned from his mother's funeral in suprisingly high spirits. My last day with Gags was my best day with him.

Gagliardi was back in his office Monday morning, selling the program to a promising linebacker from St. Paul's Totino-Grace High, the mention of which reminds Gags of ex-Johnny Roland Buller—another Totino-Grace alum. "Nice thing about Roland," Gags mutters, "he never fumbled."

Gosh, what could he mean by that? Gagliardi has told his players to let go of the season-ending loss, something he will do as soon as he stops fogging a mirror.

The schoolboy gone, Gags admits that he is not yet in recruiting mode. "I'm still trying to figure out how we lost that game," he says.

He graciously accepts my condolences on the loss of his mother. "She had a great life," he says. "Even to the last she knew what she was doing. There was a snowstorm, and she said to my sister from her hospital bed, 'Be careful driving home.' She was a mother to the very end."

The bereavement leaves his voice as he describes the food with which the Gagliardis were deluged. "Cheese trays, pepperonis, salamis—more food than you could ever eat. Lot of flowers, too," he adds, less enthusiastically. "My sisters went crazy over the flowers, but you can't eat flowers. I liked the food."

He invites me out to the family's lake house for lunch. It is another unseasonably fine day; the ice on Big Watab Lake is receding. Inside, the hallways of the house are occluded with great mounds of gifts, wrapped and unwrapped. "Every year Peg tells me it isn't going to be a very big Christmas," says Gagliardi, stepping around a pile of boxes. Peg makes no apologies. The family has all but ignored Thanksgiving for decades. Don't blame her if she goes a little overboard on the holidays she *is* allowed to celebrate.

Over pizza, John recalls that as a boy, "we didn't even know what day Christmas was." He tells the sad story of how, as a little girl just off the boat, Antoinetta hung out a stocking for Christmas, on the advice of her friends. Unfamiliar with the tradition, her parents ignored the stocking, which hung empty Christmas morning. His family never was that big on Christmas, says John.

His thoughts are with her. Earlier, he'd said he was still wondering how his team lost to the Lutes. Now he offers up this theory:

"The old gal just couldn't pray us through any further."

I give Peg a hug in the doorway on my way out. I won't soon see her again. I never do hug John. I made friends for life at this place. The Other John, John Parente, the painter and religious studies teacher, has moved to Oakland. As I type this, Laura is on the phone, making dinner plans with him. Timo's been out here, as have Linnemann and Becky. But the guy I set out to learn the most about did the best job of keeping me at arm's length, of remaining a mystery. On our final day together, he decides it's safe to throw a door open.

Driving me back to campus, he dips his customary ten miles per hour below the speed limit while foraging with his free hand for a cassette. He puts on some gospel music. We talk about the NASDAQ—he is a keen follower of the markets—and my planned route west. He recommends Route 23, through Willmar and Marshal. I am gazing out the window, trying to memorize the sun-splashed landscape on my last day in Minnesota, when I notice something strange about the music.

The vocalist belting out "A Mighty Fortress Is Our God," has a clear and melodic voice, but he can't quite reach the high notes:

Who breaks the cruel oppressor's rod
And wins salvation glorious.

There is a nasality in this voice that I recognize from scores of jokes, pep talks, and ass-chewings. In August, a friend of John's confided in me a deep secret: that in his spare time, Gagliardi tapes himself singing his favorite music. It has rankled ever since that Gags would not share with me this intriguing aspect of himself.

As I look at him I notice he is side-eyeing me. With forced casualness he asks, "Do you like this kind of music?" He doesn't know I know it's him.

"I do, I enjoy it very much. This is you, isn't it?"

"How did you know?" he says, as if I have correctly guessed his name is Rumpelstiltskin. I quickly assure John that, had my source been able to keep a secret, I would have mistaken his voice for that of a trained professional.

He explains that he likes to have all his favorite songs on one tape. "You buy a tape because it has a song you like," he says, "but then you can never find the damn song."

It is pathetic and sad and speaks to my cowardice that I've been around four months and have waited until our final minutes together to ask Gagliardi the burning question. Is he chasing Eddie Robinson? Does he intend to stick around for the four, five, or six additional seasons it will take for him to surpass his friend?

A few months later, he will have a stock answer to that question: Noting that Stagg coached until he was ninety, and Robinson finished with 408 wins, Gags will say, "I figure if I can win three games a year for seventeen years, I'll knock off two birds with one stone."

Driving back to campus on this winter afternoon, he tells me he "isn't chasing any record." He doesn't know how much longer he will coach, he says. He hopes to live to be ninety—a not unreasonable expectation—but will retire well before then. I tell him what people say behind his back—that he'd *better* not retire, since he has no hobbies.

"I've got plenty to keep me busy," he says, grinning like the Sphinx. "People don't know me."

He is right. They don't. He wouldn't have it any other way.

We turn right onto Route 159 in front of a student who *thought* he had a shot at making his two o'clock class. Enjoying the music and the day, and not much in the habit of checking his mirrors, Gagliardi has no clue that he is being tailgated. I cannot help taking pleasure in the agitation of the Johnny in my side-view mirror.

That's right, kid, I'm thinking. You're stuck behind John Gagliardi doing forty in a fifty mph zone. Deal with it. He was here first.

Bretherton, the offensive line coach, knocks on my door that evening. He tells me he has brought "a little something" from John. That's all well and good, I say, but grab the other side of this desk and help me get it onto the U-Haul. The desk loaded, I turn my attention to the gift. It is a poster-sized print of a painting I have admired all season, artist Terrence Fogarty's rendering of a Johnny-Tommy game at the Natural Bowl, entitled *A Day at Collegeville*. In the painting, the sun is out, St. John's is ahead, and all the icons are in place—the Swayed Pines, the bell banner, and Gagliardi, who has written in the lower right-hand corner of the print,

> *Austin,*
> *Thanks for being a part of our team.*
> *—John Gagliardi*

The pleasure was mine, John. It was a goddam privilege.

EPILOGUE

My brother Matt tells the story of coaxing his distressed gray Chevette from Western Pennsylvania to Vail, Colorado, where he worked the door at a subterranean watering hole called The Club. His passengers for that midwinter journey were fellow doorman Lester Fox, he of the extravagant mullet hairstyle, or BIFPIB (Business In Front, Party In Back); and Weiser, an aged and gaseous black lab owned by Matt, whose previous dog was named Bud.

Driving west on I-70, the bouncers decided to pull off the highway near Manhattan, Kansas, for some grub. Left alone in the Chevette, Weiser choked down a one-pound bag of Almond M&Ms. Matt owned that wretched hatchback for another seven years, and never was able to rid it of the stubborn vestiges of the vile and voluminous wind broken by his hound over the remaining seven hundred miles of that journey. "It was about ten degrees out," recalls Matt, "so we had a choice: roll down the windows and freeze, or sit there choking on the chocolate dog farts."

My thoughts turned to that intrepid trio while retracing their path during the fall of 2000, cruising from Kansas City to Manhattan for a Big Twelve rumble between the Oklahoma Sooners and the Wildcats of Kansas State. The home team was coached by the Anti-Gagliardi, the kind of man who would chastise an assistant, while the bus idled at a train crossing, for not calling the railroads ahead of time to find out if the track would be in use. "Most of you understand, my time is spent with football, and that's an eighteen-hour day," he once told reporters. "The rest of the time is spent with family."

I wasn't in the MIAC anymore.

I still had two months of sabbatical when I got home. Most of that time was spent in the stand-alone office behind our house, trying (unsuccessfully) to finish this book in time for a fall-2000 release. That fortunate failure gave me this chance to chronicle the most remarkable St. John's season in twenty-four years. The foundation for it was laid before I left. Even as he hobbled around on crutches, Linnemann had floated the possibility of returning for a final campaign. (He still had another season of eligibility, a severe ankle sprain in his sophomore season having earned him a medical redshirt.) The idea drew hot opposition from some of the students, none of whom ever mustered the courage to register their objections to Linnemann's face. Their sentiments were reflected in a rather cowardly, anonymous editorial in the Record: "Tom L., your glory days are over, park your golf cart and graduate."

There was one opinion that loomed larger than others in Linnemann's decision, and it wasn't that of some gutless editorialist at the school paper. When he walked into Gagliardi's office and asked if it would be okay for him to come back the following season, a brief silence fell over the room. Then the coach spoke. "Do you want me to get down on my knees?"

Linnemann was coming back, but first he had to leave. He and special teams commando Mike Mikkelson decided to do some traveling in January. Next thing I knew I was getting e-mails from Europe:

Austin—
What's up, dude? In Bavaria right now. I'm typing on a German computer so all the letters are different, and there are umlauts all over the place. We're going to the Caracalla baths today—some Roman place they thought cured the body. Looks like it's naked bathhouse time! (I'm going to the mixed area, that's always the most fun.) Prague was incredible and so was Austria, but the beer is starting to catch up . . .

While Linnemann immersed himself in, uhh, *culture,* the Johnnies who stayed behind found ways to entertain themselves, to hear Beau tell it:

Last night was a fun one—Taco Tuesday and liter beers for two bucks. The end of the night found us well, tinkering with some of the living room furniture. It is now firewood . . . After noting that a recent, heavy snowfall had enabled his housemates to snowboard off the roof, he signs off, *"Hope all is well with you and your family. Things are the same without you."*

The word out of training camp was that Gagliardi was a bear. "John has PMS," said Beau. "He's just crankier than hell," Tom agreed. The old man griped about the way the defense held hands in the huddle; it bugged him no end that Richard Hatch was the last man standing in the original *Survivor.* He took it out on his players. The older guys were flattered by Gagliardi's orneriness: if he was riding them harder than most of his other teams, they realized, it was because they were better than most of his other teams. Eight starters returned to a defense that, by the end of the '99 season, was playing better than any in the country. The offense had question marks—wide receiver and offensive line foremost among them—but it was sure to improve with Chris Moore and Linnemann healthy. Even by St. John's standards, the 2000 season had the potential to be special.

I monitored the Johnnies from a distance, while chronicling programs more talented and less charming. Despite the brutal travel schedule I kept during the fall and winter of 2000, my family suffered less than in football seasons past. In addition to giving us a glimpse of what our marriage might be like when removed from its customary chaos, our time in Minnesota gave Laura a renewed appreciation for having a second set of adult hands around. One of the first things she did upon returning to California was hire a babysitter, who also cleans the house once a week.

Was it our imagination? Laura and I concluded, finally, that it was not: our children's behavior actually was *improving*. Willa was joyfully immersed in first grade, making quantum leaps in reading and critical thinking. She suffered periods of intense crankiness, such as when being driven to CCD after school on Tuesday—

"Why do I have to go to CCD? It's stupid!"

"Sweetheart, we just want you to learn about God."

"I already *know* about God!"

—but those storms quickly passed. Perhaps unfairly, we were more startled by the intellectual strides taken by Devin, whose vocabulary improved dramatically, and who in early December made so bold as to recite to us the gifts of the Magi: "Gold, murkincense and fur."

Having outgrown his nudist phase, he entered a Hefnerian Interval, characterized by the desire to wear pajamas at all times. (When he starts dating twins and smoking a pipe, we'll worry.) Laura is writing magazine articles and working on her screenplay, which she had better sell soon, come to think of it, so that we might someday be able to afford the babysitter.

We welcomed my rival, River the standard poodle, into our home. How happy we were! How baseless had been my jealousy! How groundless were our fears that there was no room for a dog in our lives! As he settled into his crate that first night, we were transformed, suddenly, into the Waltons:

DEVIN: Good night, Mommy, good night, Daddy, good night, River!

WILLA: Good night, Mommy and Daddy, good night River!

LAURA: Good night children, good night River!

Etc.

River was a noble animal: three years old, with championship lines. He was fifty-five pounds, head-high to Devin, whose affection for his new pet manifested itself, sometimes, in disturbing ways. Devin loved to pet River, but when a grownup was not watching, the boy's hands tended to wander. It became an adult refrain in our house: "Devin, you *cannot* touch the dog's penis."

"I'll try," was his less-than-reassuring response.

River endured Devin's depredations in baleful silence for a week. Then he would growl, and bark. River had been with us three weeks when he nipped Devin over his right eye. Devin had it coming, is my guess. A sad ultimatum was issued: Son, if you do that again, we have to give River back.

River made the decision easy for us, rising up on his hind legs a week later and biting Devin's face, leaving the terrified four-year-old with three punctures and some scrapes. The combatants had been alone in a hallway. Devin says River's attack was unprovoked. I don't believe him. Not that it matters: Laura had that dog in the car within thirty minutes. River is back with his previous owners. We had a group cry that night, Devin sobbing harder than anyone, saying "I miss River!" while tears rolled over his just-formed scabs. We'll try again with another dog when the boy has more sense.

My old friends got off to a smoother start, opening their season with a nonconference waltz past Wisconsin-Eau Claire, 49–14. Pertinent stats: Linnemann threw for four touchdowns, Moore ran for three, and I had nine messages on my machine at home after that game. All were from Platten, aka the Shorts Guy, providing updates from the game. A sampling:

"Hi, Austin, it's Jim, I'm pulling into the parking lot for the first game of the 2000 campaign."

"First pass attempted by Eau Claire is picked off by our man, number two, Andy Hover. The Johnnies are now driving—it's a beautiful thing."

"Austin, this is Carla, you don't know me, but Jim told me I'd get a kick out of your message."

And so on. Laura and I considered taking legal action against

Platten, or obtaining some kind of restraining order, but in the end, let the matter drop.

The Johnnies expected a sterner test in their next game. Face-painting, hair-dyeing, body-piercing strong safety Jason Carlson was one of nineteen returning starters for St. Olaf. I remembered Ole defensive coordinator Darrell Kluck challenging Linnemann on the field after the '99 game. *I want you to come back . . . next year we'll have more speed to blitz you.*

Really? Gagliardi pulled Linnemann after four series, with the score 21–0. Final score: 42–6. After routing Augsburg, the Johnnies braced for their first tough game of the season. Tommy Week was upon them, and Linnemann grew weary of being asked if he was afraid of re-breaking his leg. "I'm more afraid of eating the food at Sexton Commons," he would reply. Linnemann was instructed to slide, rather than take any direct hits. When he did as he was told early in the game, bailing out to avoid a safety's tackle, the frustrated Tommy said, "You pussy."

"I *know*," said Linnemann, motioning to his coaches. "That's what I told them!"

While the offense sputtered at St. Thomas, the defense was dominant in a 17–0 win. "I like the way the team is coming together," Beau wrote after that game. "When the defense gives up a touchdown, the offense gets it back. When the offense struggled, the defense pitched a shutout. We keep inching toward the perfect game."

St. John's won its next three games by a combined score of 147–23, all the while looking ahead to the contest everyone knew would decide the MIAC championship. The marquee game in all of D-III on October 28 was at Bethel, where the Royals, 7–0 and ranked eighteenth in the nation, hosted the undefeated, sixth-ranked Johnnies.

Linnemann, who had been burning to avenge the 1999 loss to the Royals, hit wideout Blake Elliott for a forty-two-yard, first-quarter touchdown, putting the Johnnies up, 10–0. Playing at home and showing true character, the Royals rallied to take a 27–23 half-time lead. Bethel speedster Nate Klint opened the second half with his *second* kickoff return for a touchdown of the game. Once again,

Royals fans could be seen jumping up and down on their bleachers in a rhythmic fashion that looked, Platten told me, "suspiciously like dancing."

They had reason to celebrate. Linnemann threw five picks as Bethel hung on for a wild upset win: 43–36. After twenty consecutive losses to St. John's, the Royals had beaten them for the second straight season. This year there would be no help for the Johnnies from another MIAC team. Bethel would finish the regular season undefeated, clinching the conference crown and the automatic playoff berth that goes with it. The Johnnies' only hope for reaching the postseason rested on an at-large invitation from the NCAA selection committee. Only three such berths were doled out for the entire division. Things didn't look good.

They weren't looking so hot for me, either, on the evening of Thursday, November 9. I was in West Lafayette, Indiana, reporting a story on "Drew's Crew"—the Purdue receivers on the other end of Boilermaker quarterback Drew Brees's passes. The story wasn't due for another three days—or so I thought. At 5 P.M., I got a message from my editor: "We wondered if you could get the piece to us tomorrow morning."

Hey, no problem. We all know how overrated sleep is. I knocked the story out overnight. Instead of attending Purdue's game against Michigan State that weekend, I was free to go home.

Forgive me, Laura, for I did not go home. All season I'd been jonesing to see another Johnny game, but it hadn't worked out. Every Saturday I was in a press box in South Bend or Pasadena or Norman or Eugene. The Johnnies were down to their final regular season game. Without calling a soul at St. John's I boarded a flight from Indianapolis to Minneapolis.

I drove straight to Chubby's, rapping the door with two knuckles even as I opened it and walked in. There was Moore, his hair 'froed out, his grin unchanged. (Remember Jack Nicholson's sublime turn as the Joker in *Batman*? Remember those dimples? That's Moore.) There was Nate Kirschner, on his way to making a handful of all-America teams. There was Andy Hover, my old WWF tutor. When I crashed in his room, I saw on his desk a framed picture of us.

What was I doing there? Who goes this far out of his way to hang out with a bunch of guys half his age? Examining my motives during the drive from the airport, I kept coming up with the same answer: they are my friends. If these guys were drawn to me, originally, because they were impressed that I wrote for a national magazine, our friendships flourished for different reasons: my genuine interest in their stories and respect for them.

Longing to see the field again, I drove to the campus, ventured under the Swayed Pines and looked down on what should have been an unoccupied pitch. But there was a trespasser! At the far 30-yard line, exposed by the moonlight, was an apparent lunatic—some nut coming out of a linebacker's stance and running after imaginary foes.

I had stumbled upon Beau's night-before-the-game ritual, which begins—I later learned—with him seeking the blessing of Father Don Talafous, then walking to the stadium, where he plucks three blades of grass from one of the end zones, then stands there, visualizing himself making plays. That done, he walks out on the field, always alone, always between 9 and 10 P.M. on the eve of the game, and makes "plays."

"What the hell are you doing here?" he asked me. "What the hell are *you* doing here," I answered. We embraced and explained ourselves. Walking back to the parking lot, Beau gave me his take on the Bethel loss.

"It wasn't the worst thing that could've happened," he said. "When you're winning the way we were winning, you get away from fundamentals, you start taking shortcuts. It's almost impossible not to. Since the loss, we've got our focus back. We've got our edge. You watch. This is a good thing."

"Not if you don't get into the playoffs," I said.

"We'll get in."

They got in. They beat Concordia, 35–14. How fine, how *right* it felt, standing on the sideline in biting cold, walking my old beat, greeting old friends while the Johnnies kicked ass and Platten cast aspersions on the visitors. When a Cobber celebrated after making a hard tackle, Platten remarked to him, "Sure you're excited. The sugar beets are in, you probably already bagged a deer, it's all good, right? Look at the scoreboard, yokel."

The next day the Johnnies were awarded one of the three at-large playoff bids. Their first-round game would be in Menomonie, Wisconsin, against UW-Stout, the champions of the WIAC. At their team breakfast a few hours before kickoff, the Johnnies could be heard laughing heartily at the cover of the game program, which showed the Blue Devils captains, shirtless and flexing. "It's almost like they don't get it," Linnemann told me. "Speed kills. No matter how big and mean you are, big plays will beat you."

And the Blue Devils were big and mean. "Almost every time I came up to the line, they'd be saying stuff like, 'You're f—— dead, number eight. We're gonna kill you'—typical Cheese League jackasses," said Linnemann. "As much as that hurts my feelings, I think I can handle it. I mean, I get worse than that from *our* fans."

The game was played in freezing mud and snow. "They made us look like midgets," wrote Dusty Wagner, a Johnny grad who dropped me occasional e-mails, "and we made them look like, well, a Wisconsin state school: big, kind of slow, four or five personal fouls." The Blue Devils did indeed commit four personal fouls, not including an early facemask that set up the Johnny's first touchdown. Beau had fifteen tackles; Linnemann completed eighteen of thirty-four passes, three for touchdowns, in a 26–19 win. Another playoff win for Gagliardi, another first-round exit for the Cheese League.

Back in Arden Hills, the Bethel Royals were being trounced by our old friends, the Lutes, 41–13. As the MIAC champs turned in their equipment, the Johnnies looked forward to a second-round rematch with the squad *Sports Illustrated* had dubbed in its college football issue "The Nicest Team in America."

It bears mentioning that I pitched and wrote that story, so captivated had I been by Pacific Lutheran's sensational run to the '99 Stagg Bowl. The piece occasioned a bit of grumbling in Collegeville, where the gentlemanly Johnnies believe *they* are the country's nicest team.

To those who had the nerve to complain to me (Father Tim), I pointed out that any squad that features Alex Wesley on its roster is not the nicest team in America. Readers may recall having met Wesley, aka the Grinch, the choleric defensive tackle prone to taking out his frustrations on scout teamers. I bring him up now to give belated credit where it is due. The '00 Johnnies had a fun-filled air attack: Linnemann threw forty-six touchdown passes, a single-season school record. The secondary was superb—thirty picks on the year!—as were LaBore and Pahula, the linebackers. But the strongest, deepest unit on this team was its once-in-a-decade defensive line: Wesley, Josh Hart, Nick Bruns (a transfer from St. Cloud State), Brian Zirbes, who returned from a semester in South Africa sporting dreadlocks he kept all season; and my friend Phil Trier, the 200-pound defensive end who lied about his weight to the end. These guys averaged about six-two, 225 pounds. They were quick, superbly coached, an absolute bitch to block.

"That was the most boring game I've ever played," Beau griped after St. John's spanked Macalester, 48–6. "The goddam defensive line made every tackle."

The Johnnies flew into Seattle on Thanksgiving Day, then bused to Tacoma. In keeping with their Thursday-night tradition, Linnemann and his tight end, Kirschner, left the team hotel and found a bar. "We figured, hey, it's Thursday night," said Tom. "If we don't go to a bar, we might not play well."

November 25 dawned wet and miserable in Puyallup, Washington, home of Carl Sparks Stadium, where the Lutes play their home games. Temps in the low forties, dark skies pissing rain that never did let up all day. Both offenses spun their wheels for most of the first quarter, until the Johnnies went seventy-four yards in two plays to take a 7–0 lead on the last play of the period. In an augury of the zaniness ahead, the Lutes promptly went sixty-three yards for a touchdown on *their* next two plays. "It went like that the whole game," said Tom. "We'd score, they'd score. It was like playing in the backyard."

The teams traded touchdowns again in the third quarter. Early in the fourth, on the fifteenth play of a homely and interminable drive, Linnemann saw Jeremy Forsell, his sure-handed wideout, flash open in the end zone. But Tom was late delivering the ball. His pass was deflected by a PLU safety, the ball arcing lazily eight feet in the air before dropping into the outstretched arms of the kneeling and grateful Forsell. With six minutes left in the game, the Johnny defense held, forcing the Lutes to turn the ball over on downs. With a 21–14 lead, advancing to the national quarterfinals would now be as simple for St. John's as running out the clock.

Of course they screwed it up. Nothing is simple for these guys. Moore fumbled at the end of a twenty-two-yard run. Hustling Lutes cornerback Devin Pierce punched the ball out, and PLU recovered. Taking over on the Johnnies 49-yard line, Lute quarterback Chad Johnson willed his team toward the end zone. In the teeth of fearsome Johnny pass rush that sacked him five times on the afternoon, Frosty's grandson scrambled four times for thirty-two yards. With no timeouts left and the clock ticking under ten seconds, Johnson rolled right and pitched the ball to Shipley Ennis, who dove in from a yard out. The Lutes, who believe they get better as the game goes on, had completed another fourth-quarter comeback on the Johnnies. In the 494th game of his college coaching career, Gagliardi was about to experience his first overtime.

The coin flip to determine who would get the ball first was the damnedest thing. The captains met at midfield and basically started yukking it up. The starting quarterbacks couldn't stop laughing. "Can you believe this?" said Tom. "Isn't it great?" said Chad. Hover, Corkrean, and Zirbes were high-fiving their Lute counterparts. These guys should have been sick to their stomachs with anxiety. Instead, it was a coffee klatsch on turf.

In the NCAA's so-called "Kansas Plan" overtime, each team gets a crack at the other's end zone, starting at the 25-yard line. The Lutes won the toss and opted to give the Johnnies the ball. The boys in white promptly dug themselves a third-and-nine hole, but no matter: Linnemann hit Kirschner for eleven yards and a first down. Moore lost three yards on a sweep left, and you could almost hear Tom say to himself, The hell with it. I'll throw it to Nate until they stop him.

They never did. Linnemann hit his pubcrawling partner on a thirteen-yard completion to the 3-yard line. On first and goal, after consulting the list of plays taped to his left forearm, Tom said, "Blake and Jeremy, line up on one side, Nate, you line up on the other side. Get open, and I'll throw you a touchdown."

Nate got open, Tom threw him a touchdown. Now the Lutes needed a touchdown to hold serve. Recall that their offensive coordinator is Frosty's son, Scott, an amateur pyrotechnician whose game plans reflect his avocation. The Lutes' offense is a fireworks display of exotic formations and legerdemain: it had already enlivened this dreary day with a reverse on a kickoff return, a hook-and-ladder, and a halfback pass.

Live by the sword, die by the sword. On first down at the Johnny 13-yard, the finest quarterback of his division handed the ball to Ennis, whose misbegotten pass toward the end zone was intercepted by Johnny free safety Brad Beyer, who was immediately tackled by a euphoric LaBore as the rest of the Johnnies poured onto the field in celebration.

Into the eye of this red-and-white storm wandered a sole Lute. It was Johnson, whose brilliant college career had just been terminated. He was all smiles, congratulating the victors, thanking them for the game, wishing them luck the rest of the way. The Johnnies lined up to embrace him. Scott Westering clamped a powerful hug on Linnemann, shouting in unconscious imitation of Ned Flanders, "Gosh*darn* that was a good game!" Frosty, meanwhile, waded through the pockets of Johnnies, shaking hands, meting out hugs, his smile a defiant rebuke to the rain and the result on the scoreboard.

Looking down on the scene from above, one saw a kind of red-and-white and black-and-gold protoplasm—every member of both teams standing on the field in the rain, winners consoling losers congratulating winners. The Lutes were so gracious in defeat, said Beau, "I think I went a little 'Lute' myself. Someone could have kicked me in the balls and I still would have had a huge smile on my face. It was crazy. It was unreal. I didn't want to leave the field." That soggy tableau of sportsmanship was the best thing I saw on a football stadium all season.

★ ★ ★

I had to settle for seeing it on videotape. While this drama was unfolding to the north, I was covering Notre Dame's prosaic victory over a bad USC team at the LA Coliseum. To keep track of the Johnny game, I phoned my parents, who were tensely monitoring the MIAC Internet homepage, which was posting updates. Pat and Rex groaned when it went into OT, then cheered the news of the Johnny victory as if they'd bet their nest egg on that outcome.

I told Rex I was determined to be at Kuyper Field in Pella, Iowa, for the Johnnies' quarterfinal game against Central Dutch. You should fly out for it, I said. We'll meet in the middle. It'll be a blast. To his everlasting credit, he called my bluff. He arrived in Pella a couple hours before I did, giving him a chance to scope the town. Central's odd nickname ceases to be a mystery the moment one enters this quaint village, where windmills dot the landscape and a sixty-five-foot "Tulip Toren" lords over the town square. We stayed at the Dutch Mill Inn, and broke bread on Friday night at the Strawtown Inn, where Sarah, our server, appeared at our table in authentic Dutch costume. Out of her earshot, my father noted that the get-up made her look like that woman who comes in third in the music festival won by the Von Trapp Family Singers.

"Are you a student?" he asked.

"No, I have two kids," said Sarah.

How old?

Take cover, Pellans, I thought, my old man is breaking out the bonhomie! By this time tomorrow he'll know half the town. Before we left the restaurant, we were on intimate terms with Sarah, the maître d', and the three couples seated closest to us.

This ability, indeed this compulsive *need* to reach out to strangers, to make connections in a world he finds increasingly alien, is one of my father's most endearing qualities: the opposite of misanthropy. It reflects his bedrock belief—counterintuitive in a Republican, I believe—in the family of man. His ability to form rapid allegiances enables him, moreover, to enjoy virtually any sporting event, even a small-school football game in the frozen center of the continent.

In the hotel room on Saturday morning, I saw him poring over a map of the area, plotting his postgame escape route. When the game ended, after all, he would have a mere four hours to drive the thirty-five miles to Des Moines. "Everybody and his mother will be on Route 163," he said, grimly tapping the problem artery. "Business 163 takes me a little out of my way, but at least I won't get stuck sitting in traffic."

Of course, after we'd done an hour of postgame bonding with the Johnnies, many of the three thousand or so fans in attendance were already gone. Thus was Rex seated at his gate a comfortable two hours and forty-five minutes before his flight left, which, as he will tell you, sure beats the alternative.

The game itself? The story line the newspapers couldn't resist was Linnemann's grit: After limping to the sideline in the first quarter with a sprained left ankle, then having an herbal wrap applied to it—"They released my *chi*," cracked the quotemeister—Tom came back and led the Johnnies to twenty-one unanswered points in a 21–18 win.

The real story was the Johnny dee, which settled down and stonewalled the Dutch attack. I sought Beau out on the field afterward, to tell him as much. He'd tallied his usual dozen tackles, and was now surrounded by family: several of his seven siblings, his mother, Carol, and the legendary hard-ass, his father Tom. Swept up as I was in the euphoria of victory, I strode over to Tom and reintroduced myself. He looked at me as if I'd asked to borrow money.

"Don't worry," Beau told me later. "He's that way with everybody."

Rex renewed acquaintances with Gagliardi after the game. I got a jolt out of having a couple of my favorite septuagenarians together in the same frame. Winging my way home—I'd flown in and out of Kansas City—it occurred to me that I'd spent very little time before or after the game with any of my Johnny buddies. (Linnemann was whisked away for NCAA-mandated drug testing. "If you want me to prove I'm not on steroids," he said, "I'll just take off my shirt.")

I was fine with that. For me, this weekend was a great gift, a chance to share some quality time with the Tyrannosaurus. My father is seventy-two and lives 2,800 miles away. Despite the distance, we are close. It is a peculiarity of our relationship that we seldom feel *quite* as close as when we are alongside one another, facing forward, and monitoring the progress of a football game.

"You've never seen us lose," Gags said to Rex before we hit the road. "How are we going to get you down to Texas?"

How were they going to get Tom LaBore down to Texas? With the win over Central, the Johnnies had made it to the national semifinals, the final four of Division III. Their next opponent would be the Cowboys of Hardin-Simmons University, in Abilene. Most of the Johnny fans that made the 2,400-mile round-trip took charter planes. Tom LaBore had no intention of flying. The man had never flown before. "I can't believe a guy like you is afraid of flying," Beau said to his father.

"I ain't afraid," Tom growled. "I just don't feel like it." He meant every syllable of that. Tom and Carol drove from South St. Paul to Abilene and back.

The Cowboys, ranked number two in the nation, had won the South region with a dramatic, 33–30 win over their despised in-state rivals, the Trinity Tigers. A year earlier, Pacific Lutheran had faced Trinity a week after edging the Johnnies. The Lutes ran the Tigers out of the stadium, sacking Trinity quarterback Mike Burton eleven times in a 49–28 win that wasn't really that close. The memory of that game prompted hopeful murmurings among Johnny followers, who speculated that perhaps the South region was a little weaker than the West.

This was, in fact, the case. After handing the Cowboys an early 7–0 lead, the Johnnies took control of the game, cruising to their easiest win of the postseason. The defense was dominant, as it had been in all but a single game this season, forcing five turnovers. The offensive star was Blake Elliott—Blake 182, as Linnemann dubbed him—the sophomore wideout from Melrose who emerged, over the course of the season, as Tom's designated big-play receiver. For the second of his two touchdown catches against the Cowboys, Elliott somehow stretched out and snared the back half of the ball, recovered his balance and ran it in for a sixty-seven-yard score that put the game out of reach. The Johnnies won going away, 38–14.

For the first time in twenty-four years, St. John's was headed for the Stagg Bowl.

After boarding their charter flights, most of the Johnnies and their supporters—excluding, of course, Tom and Carol LaBore—were back in Minnesota before bedtime. Several (dozen) of the boys unwound at the LaPlayette, where the TV over the bar was tuned to *SportsCenter.* Suddenly, the cry went up: "It's us!"

There, on the tube, were highlights of the Johnnies' win that afternoon, including both of Linnemann's touchdown passes to Blake 182. "The place went nuts," Tom said. "It was like Tijuana on a Friday night. There we were, watching ourselves on *SportsCenter.* How much better than that does it get?"

No better, and possibly much worse, I told him. Awaiting the Johnnies in the Stagg Bowl would be Mount Union, the New York Yankees of Division III, winners of three of the previous four national titles. To reach the finals, the Purple Raiders from Alliance, Ohio, had gutted Widener, 70–30.

"Win four playoff games on the road, play Mount Union," Tom said. "Nice reward."

I spoke to Linnemann from a pay phone in the Minneapolis-St. Paul airport. I was about to get on a Mesabi Airlines turboprop to Aberdeen, South Dakota, to report a feature on Josh Heupel, the Oklahoma quarterback. Heupel's dad, Ken, is the head coach at Northern State, the D-II school that recruited Linnemann, Sieben, and O'Hara five years earlier. It was in a hotel room in Aberdeen that those three agreed to "go to St. John's and win a national championship." Now Linnemann stood poised to achieve that goal.

The Johnnies begin every season thinking national championship. Gagliardi tells them not to, they do it anyway. Why not? St. John's has been to the national semifinals five times since 1989. Still, I could not seem to wrap my arms around the fact that these guys—Tom, Beau, Hover, Moore, Nate, Trier, Hart, Wesley, Jerzak: my *boys*—would be playing on ESPN2 for a national championship. I lacked the vocabulary to tell them how pleased for them and proud of them I was.

I was also a little bit afraid for them. I mean, Widener was a good team—the Pioneers won twelve games this season—and Mount Union hung seventy on them. Raiders coach Larry Kehres came into the game with a career record of 163-17-3—the best winning percentage in NCAA history. The Raiders won the Stagg Bowl in 1993, 1996, 1997, 1998, and were heavy favorites in this one. One needed only visit the Ohio Athletic Conference chat room on the D3.Football.com website to pick up on that. When a St. John's supporter came in and suggested that the Johnny defense might hold Mount Union under twenty points, he was mocked.

"Twenty points?" riposted one poster. "You're not going to hold us under 30!"

In the days before the game, the Johnnies minded their business and kept their eyes on the prize. They followed the lead of LaBore, who told me on the eve of the game what he had been telling classmates, professors, reporters, and teammates all week: "This is just another game. If we do what we do best, things can fall into place for us. I know they can."

No team all season mulched the proud Johnny defense the way the Purple Raiders did on their first possession of the 2000 Amos Alonzo Stagg Bowl. Before the smoke from the pregame fireworks at Salem Stadium had evanesced into the mist, quarterback Gary Smeck had moved his team sixty-two yards for a touchdown, the drive capped by an eight-yard pass to his tight end, Adam Irgang. "Hey," LaBore told his teammates on the sideline, "they did everything right, we did everything wrong. This isn't all bad. We'll get it figured out."

I would say they got it figured out. The Raiders, who came into the Stagg Bowl averaging fifty points a game, were shut out on their next *twelve* possessions. "Everything they did," said LaBore, "we had an answer for."

And that was a good thing, because the Johnny offense, God love it, couldn't get out of its own way, cobbling together all of twelve yards in the first quarter. Again and again, the Johnny dee bailed out Linnemann & Co.

After the season, Gary Fasching sent me a copy of the ESPN2 broadcast of the game. You can tell that tape was from the network: instead of commercials, you hear the voices of announcers Pam Ward and Don McPherson, chatting until they come out of the break.

"That was a great defensive stop for our guys," says Ward after the Johnnies stuff the Raiders on their second possession. She and McPherson have a laugh at her use of that possessive pronoun. "These guys are great, though," says McPherson, who was teased by Linnemann before the game for coming in second in the 1987 Heisman Trophy balloting. "They're so much fun," agrees Ward.

That's what I'm *talking* about.

Late in the second quarter, Linnemann finally gets something going, converting a third down with a clutch pass to Kirschner, then scrambling to make probably his best play of the game. With the pocket collapsing, he spun out of trouble and feathered a sand wedge of a pass over the head of a Raider cornerback and into the simian arms of Krych, who bulled to the 3-yard line. Two plays later Moore was in the end zone. The halftime score was 7–all.

The ESPN crew kept making a fuss over the fact that Mount Union's offensive line outweighed the Johnny dee line by an average of fifty pounds per man. (The differential was greater than that because, as has been pointed out, Trier refuses to tell the truth about his weight.) After four straight series of futility, we heard from sideline reporter Holly Rowe, who was lurking near the Raiders bench. The offensive linemen, she said, were "becoming very tired and very frustrated. There's a lot of negative talk on that bench."

A cavalcade of Johnny heroes snuffed Mount Union possessions in the second half: Wesley and Pahula stuffed the Raiders on third and one. "Wow," says Pam during the commercial. "These guys don't hit in practice, but they're hitting now."

Hover got a pick. Jerzak took a receiver out at the knees at the line of scrimmage, for no gain. When Linnemann's second interception extinguished the Johnnies' only promising drive of the second half, Gibson intercepted Smeck on the very next play, Gibby's second of the day. Smeck had thrown five interceptions all season; the Johnnies picked him off three times.

The light mist turned to rain as the offensive futility stretched into the fourth quarter. Beyer, the hero of the Lutes win, blocked a field goal to preserve the tie. ("We might not make that 5:30 flight," Pam notes.) Tommy promptly threw his third interception of the day. Driving into Johnny territory, the Raiders finally sensed momentum swinging their way. On fourth and one at the St. John's 21-yard line, Mount Union went for it. Cheating up before the snap, LaBore made the most memorable tackle in the finest game of his sterling career, shooting the guard-center gap, repulsing the blocking back in textbook fashion and hogtying the ball carrier. Time out for a measurement . . . No! The Raiders were a foot short. The Johnnies took over on downs.

In the booth during the commercial, Pam says to Don, "You are officially not getting out of town."

In the stands, a hard man, a determined stoic, smiles in spite of himself. Earlier in the week, Carol LaBore had told her husband that he could get to Salem however he liked. *She* was taking the charter. In the end, Beau told me, his old man stood outside the airport, smoked an entire pack of cigarettes, then walked in and got on the plane.

In the Hollywood version of this epilogue, the Johnny offense lopes onto the field with six minutes to play and gets the job done. Gagliardi gets his fourth national title, Linnemann gets his ring and says to Sieben and O'Hara, "Guys, this is yours, too. It's *all* of ours."

What really happened was, the offense laid another egg, and Charlie Carr jogged out for his ninth punt of the day. The Raiders started their final drive at their own 32-yard line. For the first time, the exhausted, battered Johnny defense began to look a little ragged. Over the next four minutes, the Raiders drove to the Johnny three. With five seconds left in the game, Kehres sent out the field-goal unit.

★ ★ ★

As my flight had approached Roanoke, Virginia, earlier that morning, my expectations were modest. I hoped to see a clean game, a competitive game, a game after which both teams could be at peace with the outcome. Failing that, any goddam game would have sufficed. As it was, I saw no game at all. When the pilot of USAir flight 403 got within three hundred feet of the fog-shrouded runway in Roanoke, he said the hell with it, and pulled into a sharp ascent. That was as close as I got to the Stagg Bowl—a flyover in a DC-9. The pilot cheerfully informed us that we were headed for our "backup airport" in Bristol, Tennessee, where no one would be permitted to disembark. Once there, we took on fuel and headed for Pittsburgh. I might have been upset, but for the flight attendant's assurance that USAir wished to apologize "for any inconvenience this may have caused you."

Please. How could you inconvenience someone by holding them hostage in a tube, then flying them to a city hundreds and hundreds of miles from their destination? Don't be ridiculous.

I tried to be Zen during my incarceration, but that proved impossible, due in large part to the hangover from which I was suffering. The *SI* Christmas party had been the previous night in New York City. Normally I blow those off, but this year, Laura decided she wanted to attend. In the back of my mind, I knew it was risky to fly on the day of the game. But once Laura bought a pair of Via Spiga ankle boots and got her hair highlighted, we were *going* to that party.

Pulling the GTE Airfone from the seatback in front of me, I dialed my parents' house, paying ten dollars per minute in order to enjoy my mother's play-by-play of the game:

"Okay, the Johnnies are back to receive a punt. Wait a minute. St. John's is in white. Okay, never mind, *Mount Union* is back to receive the punt."

I got off the plane in Pittsburgh and scoured the terminal for a TV. I found one in a bar, but a bunch of guys straight out of *The Deer Hunter* were watching the Steelers game. They probably don't get ESPN2 here, anyway, I told myself, moving on. I phoned home again, and this time Rex picked up. While his play-by-play was a slight improvement over his wife's, John Madden sure as hell doesn't have anything to worry about.

I called just after Beau's epic stick, the score still tied, 7–7. With mounting anguish, Rex recounted the slapstick of the Johnny offense.

"Okay, third and nine, *Oh Christ*! Whew. Got it." (Linnemann is stripped as he drops back to pass, but recovers his own fumble.)

A final punt, and now it was the Raiders' ball:

"Okay, four minutes to play, here we go. Beg your pardon—goddam chicken commercial."

"Oh shit. Completion to the Johnny 48."

"Now they're showing John on the sideline. He looks like he ate some bad shrimp. Third and seven at the 35—completion to the 21. Ouch."

"Fifty-five seconds to play, fifty-four, fifty-three—aww, hell, Aus, he got another first down."

I did not press Rex for names or numbers. I sat in an unoccupied gate area, cell phone to my ear, as time ran out on my boys.

"Looks like it'll be a twenty-two-yard field goal. How long, Mom? Twenty. God, I hope he misses. Johnnies call a time out. Gonna ice the kid."

The kid was Rodney Chenos, who endured a second timeout called by the Johnnies, then won the game with a splendid kick. My guess is that Pam and Don made their flights.

If I had to hear the news in this fashion—second-hand, on a cell phone, surrounded by people who say "yinz"—there was no one I'd rather have break it to me than the old man, his glaring inadequacies as an announcer notwithstanding. Getting the bad word from Rex did not cushion the blow so much as make it easier for me to respond genuinely. When it's just him and me, there's no need for me to try and disguise the fact that I'm slugged-in-the-gut, kicked-in-the-teeth disappointed, if I am. And I was.

We consoled one another and said goodbye. I stayed where I was for a while, slumped in my seat, gaze downcast. I made a visor with my right hand and hoped I was weeping unobserved.

Fireworks in the background sound like small-arms fire, on the tape, as the Raiders leap and embrace and losers are asked to leave the field. Holly thrusts a microphone in the face of a supremely relieved Larry Kehres, Mount Union's coach, who ignores her question and offers this: "I almost feel like Coach Gagliardi's team deserved to win this game."

What a classy thing to say. I miss Division III.

Wesley, the Grinch, screamed his frustration at Linnemann as they walked off field after the game. Tom brushed it off, and those two patched it up a few days later. Wesley is a hothead, but a good guy. During a slow moment at a prayer breakfast the morning before the game, he had turned to LaBore and whispered, "The *real* national championship starts tomorrow night, and I know we'll win that one." By all accounts, they did.

When I last spoke to Tom, he was sitting on the floor of his unfurnished new apartment in uptown Minneapolis. The game had been over for a month and a half, and he was at peace with the outcome. "The whole season was so much fun," he said. "And I did what I set out to do. Played in a national championship."

He and Becky were on hiatus, although Tom didn't rule out the possibility of getting back with her. He's working with Target as a business analyst in the audio electronics department, and moonlighting as a roving reporter for local radio and television stations at high school and college basketball games.

That last bit of news delighted me. In addition to being a friend, Tom Linnemann is the best quote I ever met. He is a natural with a microphone in his face, a guy who could go far in this business, a guy who could end up on someone's Celebrity Wall, someday.

Beau spent the spring semester student-teaching at Sartell High, just down the road from Collegeville, suffering from his usual lack of self-esteem. "Teaching is great. I am dominating," he wrote in one e-mail, signing off, "Peace—Professor LaBore." When he wasn't updating me on his job, he pestered me for help finding him a position as a graduate-assistant coach at a Division I program. I told him I'd do what I could, after explaining that if I dropped from the sky and into the path of a car driven by a D-I coach, the chances were roughly fifty-fifty that the guy would swerve to miss me.

It saddened me to learn that Beau couldn't find his folks after the title game. I heard from numerous Johnnies that the Stagg Bowl people were a bit fascistic about clearing the players off their precious turf as soon as possible. Parents had to leave for the airport before they had a chance to talk to their sons. Knowing that his mother would be worried, he left on her voice mail a message which, Carol tells me, she never intends to erase: "Sorry we missed you. Don't worry about us, and don't worry about me. I feel good about the way I played. I left it all on the field."

Taking pity on me, USAir bumped me up to first-class for my Pittsburgh-to-San Francisco flight. Reclining in leathery comfort, nipping at a wee dram of the Hair of the Dog, I assayed the reasons for my little outburst in the airport.

I was hungover and exhausted, having gone to bed at 2:30 and risen at 4:40 A.M. I was deeply frustrated, not being able to attend the game. I felt sorry for the Johnnies, who played so courageously, only to fall short, and sorry for myself. With Beau and Tom and the rest of the seniors crossing over, joining me in the Real World, my connection to successive Johnny squads will become more and more tenuous. For a couple seasons, I felt like part of a team. I was crazy in love with football again. It was sweet while it lasted.

It can't last. Word out of Collegeville is that the Johnnies are having another stellar recruiting year. It always helps when the guys you're after can watch you play on TV. Don't be surprised if St. John's is back in the Stagg Bowl in a year or two, with Gagliardi at the wheel. As of this writing, he needs thirty-one wins to catch Robinson. Time to start worrying, Eddie.

A month or so after the season ended, Beau was roaming the campus when he came across Gary Fasching, who was squiring around a pair of recruits. "I'd like you guys to meet Beau LaBore," said the coach. "Beau was a great linebacker for us."

One day you're blowing up running plays on national TV, the next, your former coach is referring to you in the past tense.

"Every year we have to replace irreplaceable players," says Gagliardi, "and every year, somehow, we manage to do it." He flashes that grin and I am reminded, as ever, of a fox.

That is the good news and the bad news awaiting all Johnnies. No matter how good you were, you can and will be replaced. It's like Beau said. Things are the same without you.